THE PROGRAM BOOK

jim McGuinness

FOR RECREATION PROFESSIONALS

Albert Tillman
California State University, Los Angeles
with
Ruth Tillman

MAYFIELD
PUBLISHING
COMPANY

Library of Congress Catalog Card Number: 72-87825
International Standard Book Number: 0-87484-189-5

Manufactured in the United States of America
Mayfield Publishing Company
285 Hamilton Avenue, Palo Alto, California 94301

Drawings by Jim M'Guinness

CONTENTS

v

PREFACE

There was a time when program was king.

Somehow, there has been a subtle dethroning because of the slow withdrawal of caring professionals from the field. The playground and recreation center battlefields have lost their warriors.

Administering budgets, manipulating pressure groups, putting aside space, planning for the future are certainly important. They are necessary functions, but what about program: those magic moments of joyous participation that erupt when the available resources have been stirred together just right. Planning, yes; leadership, yes; but it is program that gives recreation its identity as both a field and a profession.

It's time we stopped playing everyone else's game — psychologist, sociologist, political scientist, finance officer — and applied our best men and efforts to program.

Crown program. Long live the king!

jim Mc'Guinness

Chapter 1

RECREATION-- A WAY OF LIVING

In 1937 L. H. Weir wrote a minor classic book entitled *Europe at Play*. In it he says, "Recreation in an intelligently ordered life needs no excuse or reason for its existence. It was not a problem among so-called primitive people. It became a problem only when society became more highly organized, civilized, and motives of material gain became dominant, leading to an over-emphasis of work. This was not so unfortunate in itself until science and invention placed into the hands of the materialists the tools which took much of the joy and satisfaction out of work. Recreation then became a social problem. It represented an element of life that needed to be recaptured for large masses of the people of the highly civilized countries."

Primitive peoples did not have a problem integrating their survival life styles with play. They organized play and ritualized it to the point that it deserves the more formal identification as recreation. Even in contemporary primitive cultures many activities, even play not directly devoted to survival, are still concerned with survival.

The Eskimo, in the last throes of his original culture, continues to make every behavioral move count. His children play, but the games are as imitations of adult life, a preparation for adult responsibilities. The use of the toy bow and arrow leads to hunting skill. The big Eskimo builds a snowman in the shape of a polar bear, and the little Eskimo learns to identify bears and to shoot his arrow into the vital areas of the snow animal.

The Aruntas, Australia's backland aborigines, have a life that can only be described as continuous ordeal. Water is precious; the only time in his life that an Arunta runs is to pursue a distant shower of rain. His food supply is so minute and his life energy so limited that he invented the boomerang, which returns if he misses his target. His dog is trained to retrieve the game while the Arunta sits in the shade of a rock, moving only to avoid the dehydrating sun.

For such people life is purposeful, a constant challenge, with each person vitally needed for the group to survive. But what of the other extreme, the man of leisure, who has all his wants met? In an era in which affluence has become an important aspect in the lives of large numbers of people, the emergence of the man of leisure gives us a sharp contrast.

Egypt's last king is an extreme example. Farouk set as his life course absolute indulgence; his entire day was spent only in pleasing himself, supported by an unlimited treasury. Farouk himself literally burst and died one night after consuming a dozen quarts of orange soda pop, six dozen oysters, half a gourmet supermarket, and then frolicking with three women. He left the largest collection in the world of pornographic literature as his legacy in life.

The Aruntas and Farouk are two extremes — survival vs. pleasure — in life styles.

Today, each man needs some commitment to survival stresses to furnish him with a sense of being needed if only for the maintenance of his own existence. He needs opportunities to exercise his senses in unique, non-utilitarian ways in order to enhance and stimulate his spirit with pleasure, joy, and fun. He needs escapes, fantasizing time, small drop-out sessions to reassemble his jarred and sensitive self for his next confrontation with reality.

Play is the natural means for fulfilling these life needs. Play is the response through movement and expression by which man affirmatively meets the demands society places on him.

Huizinga, who wrote *Homo Ludens* (Man the Player), argued that man kept work — his basic survival necessity — an attractive endeavor by playing at it. For example, he contends that two lawyers arguing in court are only playing a game invented by man to generate fun out of necessity. Eskimos hold trials by having adversaries shout abuses at each other in front of an audience which hoots or applauds while deciding who out-poison-tongued the other.

2

NEW LEISURE LIFE STYLES

"I wonder what I'm going to be when I grow up?"

There are a lot of mornings for a lot of people when that question hangs in the corner of the mind. It's often in the way of getting up and enjoying the day. Kids can kick off the covers and bounce out into the world because growing up seems a long way off, and everything is new and happening today. Tomorrow . . . well, tomorrow isn't real, just something talked about.

Those who groan and pull the covers over their heads suddenly realize that they have grown up, and it's not such a big deal after all, only routine and responsibility. Today and tomorrows line up and fall like rows of dominoes, just days and nights on the way to the grave.

Other people have a lot of answers to what they'll be when they grow up. They plant their carrots of goals and rotate their crops of commitments so that the blooms burst never-endingly, day after day. They manage to balance life, change their pace, make work and play, if not compatible, at least coexist.

Growing up for many people is arriving at an anticipated destination and having neither plans nor ambitions once they are there. It's really hard for most of us to put our mixed-up wonderings and expectations together for too long a time. That vague discontent, that hollow feeling, wells up regularly. Even when things are going well, there is still a nagging sense that things could, or should, be better.

Keeping up, making life worthwhile, is a frustrating job, and most of us need a lot of outside help. We play life as if it were a pinball machine, leaning our body with the steel balls, hoping through psychic waves to cause them to nudge the right bumpers and light up a score; or, we carefully develop a feel and carefully ease them down the slot; or, we snap the plunger with great, wasted force, driving the steel balls out only to ricochet back to the starting point — until in utter frustration we shake, kick, or tilt the machine. The machine stops playing, and the game's over. Circumventing the rules only shuts the door on one game, or one life; the chances, the opportunities are taken away.

A ten-year-old somewhere in middle town:

"I go home after school and watch TV. I get something to eat and drink and watch a movie. Sometimes I go out and ride my bike with the other kids on the block or play ball in the street, but the cars mess it up and it gets boring with the same kids. The playground has classes and teams sometimes, but you have to sign up and be there every time; it's too much like school, and I'd have to walk home or get somebody to drive me. After I get home they're always mad when I ask to get taken anywhere. . . . It's just easier to watch TV. . . ."

A 14-year-old in the inner city:

"You know, I don't know who I am, what I'm supposed to do. We stick around the playground after school, but the stuff they do there is for the kids; you know, like crafts and playing board games. We talk a lot and mess around with the boys, you know. I get mad, though; there ought to be something more happening. I don't know what, but you're always seeing people having fun in the movies. We just all get mad, we don't know what's going to happen, nothing ever does, so we paint names and words all over everything just so something is happening."

A 23-year-old:

"I mean, you're not adult until you're twenty-three. You're still trying things out up to then. Then you have to make up your mind; you can't keep being a student, and you want to get out and see more of the world. You try a lot of things — a machine (motorcycle), drugs, living with one person, living with a lot of people, a week in the mountains, even reading books. You're just starting to get it all put together by twenty-three, and you gotta get into a job to survive, to start living some kind of real life. Maybe it's because all of the things you're doing for kicks don't seem as much fun any more and you have to pay for everything yourself."

A 28-year-old:

"I've got to make it now. Both of us. That's why my wife's working. I'd

3

like to retire at thirty or thirty-five and then really start living, do all the things we've been putting off. We don't do too much — go to the movies, eat out, go over to friends and watch TV together. I play some golf with guys at work and we collect antiques . . . figure it's a good investment. We're pacing ourselves; the real fun is ahead of us when we've got more security."

A 35-year-old:
"We're always with people, parties, informal ones where someone brings the beer and someone the chips and dip, play a little cards and gossip. We've got a camper; used to have a mountain cabin, but it got boring going to one place. The kids pushed the camper, but they're tied up in dancing or swimming classes, and we have to taxi them everywhere, and never two of them interested in the same thing. I guess we live a lot of our life through the things they do."

A 42-year-old:
"I'm a woman alone with a teenager. So what the hell is my life? Not much. That SOB ran out and I'm trying to scratch for the two of us. There isn't any money to do anything, even go to the movies. So there's TV, and talking to the other women at work and around the apartment where I live. No men; old ones maybe, but they all need too much; I'm the one who needs. I just walk sometimes, look at people, look for people more bored and lonely than I am, then I go home feeling better."

4

A 48-year-old:
"The kids are off at college or married and things are really better than they've ever been. The job takes care of itself, but it's no big deal any more. I've got a 26-foot sailboat and I'm going diving again; used to do it twelve years ago, used the boys' equipment they left. I still have the camper, but we don't use it much. My wife never liked it too well; she doesn't like sailing either. She spends a lot of time with some do-gooder organizations, I think. I've thought about going on one of those tours of South America next year; I want to use my new camera, it has a hell-of-a zoom lens."

A 55-year-old:
"I never thought I'd be wondering what I was going to do with my time, but in five years, if I can just sit patient and not rock the boat, I'm going to retire. I don't know what that will mean. My life's pretty full now: I read a lot, work in the garden, watch TV, go to the ball games with my son-in-law, more of a social thing, take week-end trips to some of the local resorts to loaf around with friends, play some pinochle. Nothing really exciting. I'm in good health, but I can't afford to stay here when I retire. My wife and I will have to find a new place or get a trailer, maybe; travel around and see something, but we can't just do that for the rest of our lives. I wish I had more hobbies that really interested me, that I could afford. I'm really afraid of all that time without being needed on a job somewhere."

A 68-year-old:
"It was hard at first. You just let go, like you've been drugged. Sleep a lot, let things slide; then you realize that one life's over, but you've got

another one to make the most of. The worst is if you try to re-live the old, do the same things, or bore people talking about it. I just got out every day and watched people, got ideas from them, checked on what was happening, free classes and concerts, started writing away for free things to get some mail; got busy with my hands, too. . . Both my wife and I make things and grow gardens of vegetables. We watch TV together, read to each other, take the bus out of town somewhere, especially if we know of a flea market or swap meet, or we drive there and sell. The big thing is we've got the pace slowed down, the little things are important again, and you keep interested in what the damn world is going to do next."

Each of us can find a part of ourselves in everyone else. But each of us is, of course, unique and our approach to life must fit that uniqueness.

The world is comprised of numerous overlapping subcultures. The way we behave in these various subcultures — and each of us may exist in several at the same time — is called *"life style."*

Never before have life styles been so diverse and so distinct. History has been caretaker of the master, slave, lord, and servant life styles until a hundred years ago. The wealthy invented leisure and a way to take care of it — recreation. The have-nots worked and hoped for a day when life would offer them more than concentration on survival.

New economic and social patterns have created a confusion of life styles. The big depression in the 1930's put many back to a basic survival approach to life. But the twist was that with the new common poverty came an abundance of leisure, albeit forced leisure. Probably at no other time in history was so much manpower, intellectual effort, resourcefulness, and experimentation applied to the challenge of undesired leisure. Hard times. The facilities and toys that we accept as a matter of course today were non-existent.

5

From the Depression arose a generation that knew what "making do" meant and accepted it as a life style because it was everyone's lot.

The next three decades gave rise to a wide spectrum of new leisure life styles. Many now moved in a world of abundance and affluence. Things that were once secret desires — sports cars, resorts, country clubs — became necessities, sometimes even tax-deductible. Those who still worked to survive watched and continue to watch with bitter eyes the self indulgence that spins around and taunts them.

Craftsmanship, however, gave way to plasticized volume. Obsolescence was now revered, for it created unlimited productivity. We moved into choice natural regions and proceeded to obliterate the very attributes that attracted us.

This affluence, this abundance, has brought us to panic and violence, bewilderment and boredom.

We are now plagued with non-productive time. Not only must we stop using up natural resources, we must recycle what has been used. We are running out of space, replacing nature with artificiality, stacking up people in population jams that destroy the potential joy and flavor of events, activities, and places.

Many are testing out the subcultures, picking out groups with which to belong, in order to gain special advantage or to salvage some identity in the unending mass of multiplying people.

The new leisure life styles that have developed out of this stress and ferment are not mysterious. They are generational types, marked off by chronological and social restrictions, health and fitness limitations and interest saturation. Within each generational type are a variety of *sub-types*, based upon commitment and economics.

The generational sub-types in the normal population are: (1) Infants, (2) Formative stage children, (3) Socialized children, (4) Teenagers, (5) Apprentice adults, (6) Pre-occupational adults, (7) Occupational adults, (8) Family adults, (9) Change-of-life adults, (10) Pre-retirement adults, (11) Active retirement adults, and (12) Passive retirement adults. This type structuring in our complex, changing society, probably needs review every ten years — a kind of census of emerging living patterns — for these ideal model types are a launching foundation for programming and can be adjusted to fit different regions of greater or lesser sophistication.

Looking at each generational type in more depth provides the best window for a comprehensive view of the new leisure life styles.

(1) *Infants* — Ages 0-3

At this age young explorers are discovering their five senses and creating their primitive, basic patterns of reaction to the world. They need loving one-to-one attention from their parents. Behaviorists now tend to focus much greater concern on this starter time, speculating that it may provide the basis for personality, temperament, and basic attitudes in adult life.

In some societies infants are separated from parents and thrust into structured state centers where group membership accelerates progressive growth patterns and attitudes are officially patterned. Experiments in America may lead us into formal infant programs in recreation programming. These experiments may eventually lower the traditional age for organized recreation and could greatly reduce the concentrated infant care previously required from the mother.

The multiplying tiny-tot programs, pre-school nursery schools, and day-care centers are evidence of society's willingness to program its children at an early age.

(2) *Formative Stage Children* — Ages 4-7

The emphasis in this formative period has shifted from resourceful leisure, where newly acquired skills of movement and thought are freely expressed, to more artificial, formal, and goal-oriented behavior regulated by television, school, and manufactured toys.

In this stage, the recreation programmer must begin to recognize certain overlays; that is, conditions that create differences within each generational stage. The social and economic class structure of American society tends to keep the rich and super-rich more or less invisible to the public and private recreation programmers. By necessity, they must protect themselves and their very young by self-imposed isolation, perhaps to avoid guilt-producing contact with the disadvantaged and to protect their mansions, swimming pools, yachts, estates, and other expensive toys. They are able to purchase parks and playgrounds and fence them in to allow their children to interact only with those of their class. They buy high mobility for their young, whisking them off to elite camps and resorts.

At the other extreme lies the ghetto, the depressed areas, the poverty belts, the welfare class, the slums, and the disadvantaged who are predominantly racial minorities. While these groups now have the bulk of the big cities' public and private non-profit recreation services — a form of compensation and pacification — these services tend to ignore the 4-to-7-year-olds. Bombarded with TV's revelations of how the other world lives, disadvantaged children tend to bitterly destroy their own areas with carelessness, vandalism, and graffiti. Their play area is often one of decaying artificiality, dirty plastic discards, breeding a rougher, more primitive and more physical form of play.

Our third social/economic overlay embraces middle-class America which represents the majority of the population. The true core of the established order, the representative life style of America, really lies with the middle 80 per cent of the population. In many ways it is here that the leisure life styles have most drastically changed for better and for worse. Burdened with a work ethic, protected by law and order, mildly affluent, simultaneously they are trying to keep what they have laboriously gained and to obtain those elusive satisfactions which touch them gently but not frequently.

Their children at this formative stage are creatures of the made-up world of suburbias and planned communities. Their lives, in contrast to the other two extremes, are very predictable, full of responsibility. The middleclass consumers' children are making do with the plastic world in which they were born. Their leisure patterns are designed around fun in cellophane boxes, mass produced toys with built-in obsolescence, and lots of TV. They play in streets where car dodging is a built-in challenge and in small manicured yards congested with a confusion of live-it-up leisure ideas from the Sunday paper's home section. Suburbia's child is not to reason why — or discover and explore — but to be sure that he has a plastic jumbo special whatever just like the kid next door.

7

(3) *Socialized Children* — Ages 8-12

These are boom days for Socialized Children. They aren't treated as real people with identifiable personalities until this stage. There is a basic drive at this point to test everything that has matured *against* others, since both the programmers and culture have stressed competition over cooperation.

At this generational stage, the class differences seem to diminish in terms of play. Highly organized group activities, especially in sports, tend to dominate the leisure picture of all three socio-economic groups. Boys focus on recreation in ceremonial miniatures of professional sports, e.g., Little League, Pop Warner football, Junior tennis. Family Adults arrange life styles to accommodate scheduled practices, games, and classes. Even the girls are swept into this vortex of boys' sports, twirling batons, marching in drill teams, cheer leading, and baking cookies to raise money for uniforms and trips to the finals in some faraway city.

Where there is family involvement the entire life style seems to adjust to boys' sports, and the family car becomes part of the Great American Taxi Company shuttling the kids. The boys identify with male figures such as athletes, coaches, and even fathers; hopefully fathers — if they can make the grade. Those not involved — the less athletic boys and most girls — are pushed away from group experiences toward more solitary, self-directed pursuits. Reading, TV, and studying fill the gap.

Recreation programs tend to support the group pattern by spending dollars and effort to meet the ardent demands of organized boys' sports groups. Classes with culminating events have replaced progressive activity programs at playgrounds and centers.

Leisure life styles at this stage are hectic and over-emphasized for those who join organized activities, while traumatic for those who don't by isolating them from the more prestigious activities of their peers.

(4) *Teenagers* — Ages 12-14

The term "teenager" does not include all people in their teens, but those who have a difficult adolescence because of the expectations of society. Awkward and without wheels, the bulk of them are responsive to momentary fads, sexual desire is beginning, drugs are secretive and forbidden, and experiments take place without thought of the consequences.

The carryover from sports is limited since the glamour doesn't match that of the previous stage. They are not cute in little uniforms playing adult; but they are neither adults nor children. A few try to stay children; others try to play adults.

(5) *Apprentice Adults* — Ages 15-18

This is the high school scene, the period for which people are most nostalgic. It predominates in the responses of adults who are asked, "What time of your life would you most like to live over?" A large number want to relive it because they were miserable, and they feel they would handle it differently the second time.

Sexuality fully emerges with the opportunity of fulfilling it. Groups are "in" again, as a means to find an identity, people, or boy or girl friends.

For all socio-economic levels "wheels" create an abrupt independence from family and neighborhoods. Rapidly approaching or involved in their own change of life stage, Apprentice Adults are self-centered, unsure of the future, and lack understanding about both themselves and others.

The boredom of the previous stage is relieved by periodic "good trips" (from drugs to sex, to a trip to the lake, to riding a motorcycle up a dirt hillside, to a rock concert with big names) but complicated by an anxiety about that puzzling question, "What will I be when I grow up?"

It's a time for adulthood, but the rules keep saying, *"not yet."* Everything is waiting to be tried, and the first time — of which there are so many at this stage — is mind-blowing, like a solid year of fireworks.

It is a time of seeing and being seen, hanging around, gaping at girls, boys, sports for some, studies for others, and sampling grown-up life for most.

The leisure life style at this stage is serious recreation, goal-oriented fun, for it is a play that develops and prepares for total independence.

(6) *Preoccupational Adults* — Ages 19-23

Some go to college, some join communes, but most, especially from the disadvantaged areas, begin to work and pursue the American Dream of success.

An amazing, important development in our churning society is the alienation of youth, the dropping out of many youths from middle- and upper-middle-class families. These young adults — eyewitnesses to the results of progress, technology and bureaucracy who see their middle-aged, unfulfilled parents as architects of a plastic world — have taken up a way of life that seeks basics, a closeness to nature, an end to authoritarianism, a loving and unrestricted expression of self. It often involves sexual freedom and drugs.

There is a large core of straight pre-occupational adults who sample the free spirit of hippie life in moderation. On weekends, these are the Clark Kent types, as Lewis Yablonski calls them, who use the hangouts and life styles of the hippies for a change-of-pace fling without giving up their scheduled preparation for the future.

Others live a work/study, self-denying life, postponing pleasures until the diploma is earned and enough money is made to live the good life. Not many seem able to balance present and future so that joy and promise can co-exist.

Individuals in the working segment of this generation have by-passed the preparation for the occupation stage because they were obliged to support relatives, had early marriages, or were thwarted by school and social failures. They settle into the trades and begin to lock into a pattern of prepared leisure.

(7) *Occupational Adults* — Ages 23-30

Military service or its refusal must be reckoned with by both male and female. Serious mating is undertaken, either in marriage or out of it. Lost years, key ones, tend to accelerate an anxiety to establish a definable and meaningful way of life.

These are "establishing" years: the period of occupational apprenticeship in which men and liberated women must mine their future and refine the crude ore of their potential. Many are trying to do it together with dual careers. But more and more are putting off deep mating commitments until they are established and making some money. People from the lower and middle socio-economic classes try to move toward the traditional American goals of material acquisition and security.

The leisure life style for the early marrieds stays pretty much a penny-pinching, planning-for-the-future life, with movies, TV, and groupings with friends for a great deal of self-directed, passive recreation. The singles pick up on the group affairs and save up for big weekends at resort areas or a big night on the town with a friend who will pay his own way.

(8) *Family Adults* — Ages 30-40

The desire to compete in the mating merry-go-round generally gets stopped at this stage. Coping with careers demands what youthful energies and drives are still available. But there is a wisdom that says they shouldn't be wasted.

The leisure life-style best suited to provide men and women with the least interference with careers is some type of permanent relationship, which in our society has been traditionally the family unit with children.

For most Americans, the career is on the track and material things are at hand, if not paid for. If the job is fulfilling enough, the family can participate as active partners in leisure pursuits. But if the job fails to fulfill, people accelerate their leisure, trying new diversions while desperately seeking commitment and fulfillment. If the job is demanding but not fulfilling, people often occupy their leisure by vicariously living through the involvements with their mate or children.

This is a difficult decade and the Family Adult often needs outside help, professional counseling to get through it with his psyche intact, his ego in balance, and the ability to handle a change of life without regret or panic.

(9) *Change-of-Life-Adults* — Ages 40-50

Arrival time. Now it is usually all in place; the career and the ultimate

9

position achieved, recreational skills learned, and interests locked in, children on their way, a comfortable and predictable marital partner . . . .

But there's a crack in the antique mirror of the 40-odd years of life, a sour nip in the taste of middle age, a gaping vacuum in the inner resources. There are the regrets — what has been missed, what could have been better, lost youth, untried adventure, the routine, the continuing debts — and the path ahead leading to old age.

The change of life is a mental condition, a stark self-analysis brought on by boredom, physiological changes, slights at work, and the realization that one may well have used up all the goals and commitments, snuffed out the incentives. The reckless energy and bubbling expectation that youth expends in all directions isn't easily aroused again. Everything — the movies, the novels, the resorts, the amusement places — all seem designed for young people. What happened to the slim-hipped cowboy movie star? Now the horses look like they should be riding the fat, old, girdled veteran actor.

Long-established job and marriage commitments come tumbling down at this crisis point. It is time for change, and many seek guidance from trained professionals in order to cope. Career changes are drastic dents in one's feeling of security, but they have been successful surgery in many cases. Social changes, such as divorce, are even more detrimental — not only to individuals, but also to society. Replacing one partner with another of the same vintage is very complicated; personalities and habits are fixed and collide without compromise. Chasing lost youth through a partner of another generation can be a fool's folly, a temporary relief from existing doldrums and anxiety, but quickly creates a new set of complications, stresses, demands, ego bruises, and self-doubts that far surpass the original set.

Leisure life-style is the least trauma-producing change area. Change-of-life Adults often make travel the central way for creating a new outlook to avoid damaging the marriage or career. Only the disadvantaged can't structure an exciting planning, going, and reminiscing leisure program, whether it is tenting or touring. The opportunity to travel is one of the great social phenomena of this era. Travel provides many of the new experiences that a change in life style is supposed to provide — new people, new places, new opportunities, and new roles.

Education is another direction for Change-of-life Adults, picking up special knowledge or skills that always intrigued them but escaped them because of the press of career and family. Such education may permit career changes, spark a calcified marriage, or enhance travel plans.

The Change-of-Life generational stage is a brutal challenge. But change of life is really a second chance, and more and more people are being counseled into sane and delightful anticipations of the years to come.

(10) *Pre-Retirement Adults* — Ages 50-60

By this stage leisure life styles are modified by awareness and acceptance of physical and financial limitations. It is the planning age for retirement — that ultimate reward of the working man. For many retirement is the ultimate curse, which has made pre-retirement planning a focus of concern for many in their 50's.

Leisure is spent in preparing. Travel is aimed at finding a place where one can live comfortably without unnecessary financial stress. Finding the place is important and looking is fun. The place will have to provide opportunities to pursue the less costly recreational activities which the Pre-Retirement Adult now enjoys, or he will have to start learning and acquiring new leisure interests in order to adapt to the place.

(11) *Active Retirement Adults* — Ages 60-75

Total leisure is thrust upon many of us at this age. There are predictions that retirement will come at an increasingly younger age. Medical advances will give the retiree a chance to play vigorously.

A human being will atrophy if he isn't pursuing useful purposes. Being actively retired, doing things, being interested in life, is becoming a major concern of society.

We have made play a childish pursuit because our ethic is work, production and success. We encourage senility and childish reverie if we do not generate respect for recreation, to value it as highly as work has been valued.

The actively retired are working in their gardens, lounging around parks and golf courses, engaged in do-it-yourself chores around home, traveling, and watching the world they worked to build. The leisure life styles of this generation are bittersweet with the doubts and paradoxes of leisure without the balance of revered work.

(12) *Passive Retirement Adult* — Ages 75 and over.

Spectator time. The porches of convalescent homes, seedy little hotels, clapboard little cottages, and even some big mansions are filled with the generation which sorts through memory collections and watches the new generations on their way to some mystical, ultimate destination.

This charting of generation types is only a limited interpretation, a rough attempt at summarizing a massive collection of individual life styles. It should serve as a guide to personal discovery and evaluation of specific regions and situations.

11

THEORIES OF PROGRAMMED PLAY

The balancing of play activity in life styles means systematically and intelligently ordering and directing its use. Recreation is the refined control of play behavior to best fulfill the needs of individuals through structured group experience.

It is important to examine at this point some of the pioneer theories that have helped us understand the meaning of play in human behavior. Most of the early attempts at understanding play focused on children, but were one-dimensional opinions falling short of full theories. Nevertheless, some useful foundations emerged.

Educators, psychologists, and sociologists have all made some play analysis because wherever they tried to uncover the secrets of man, there glittered the nuggets of play.

The first theory is one we may call the *Surplus Energy Theory*, which maintains that man and all animals are active organisms expending energy to sustain life. Animals low on the evolutionary scale expended all their energy to obtain food and to escape from enemies. Man, however, figured out systems and inventions and survived without depleting all his energy, diverting the surplus to non-life-sustaining activities called "play."

Not unlike the above view of play is the *Catharsis Theory*, which sees play as a safety valve for pent-up emotions. Man catharts, unloads his hostilities, frustrations, and other bottled-up emotions created in one situation by kicking, punching, or outwitting another.

A closely related but newer theory, is the *Compensatory Theory*. It is derived, in part, from sociological theory. In this theory, man seeks self-expression, but if a direct attempt in a selected arena — say work — is met often by obstructions, indifference, or superior competition, he moves to another arena, preferably a similar one, very possibly a play activity. He compensates by expressing himself in the substitute situation.

There is no real error in any of these concepts; perhaps, together they approach a full-blown theory of sorts. They all say that man moves of his own will to fulfill internal forces that trigger his behavior. The three seem easily accommodated and synthesized in our Dominant Needs Concept.

Another extremely popular theory and one dear to the hearts of all educators is the *Instinct-Practice Theory*. It was most easily applied by the pioneer thinkers in dealing with children, for their time was involved with non-life-maintenance play activity. But why were children so motivated? The instinct theorists believed children were practicing for adulthood. They imitated adult behavior in order to prepare for it. This theory has been discredited over the years because there are many unrelated, almost non-sensical, play activities that find no counterpart in adult work life.

Some authorities feel that childhood is a gift of time for higher animals to prepare them for an increasingly complex life later in which each will have to sustain himself. The preparation, they believe, is not specific, but general, leading to general physical, mental, and emotional efficiency. Low-order insects, which come into life as fully automated, mature robots with fully developed instincts ready to use in a short, uncomplex life, do not play because they do not need to be educated.

This theory explains the play motivation of some adults and children. We play to prepare ourselves for work and other life situations. In childhood, life styles are full and complete, with all the realities and tensions a person of any age feels. Adult life is no more ultimate, meaningful, or valued in the scheme of human existence. The adult has padded his part by treating childhood as a less-than-human prelude to life and play as frivolous outbursts of non-serious impulses.

It is in one other theory, that of *Recreation/Relaxation*, that we find a treatment of play on an adult-focused level. It originated by explaining not only play as the opposite of work, but also as an opposite of surplus energy insofar as play is a recuperating, recreating, renewing, and energy-recovering process. It recognized that sheer idleness is not the best way to recuperate; rather contrasting activity, a change from work, was potentially more effective. This theory is quite important in the architecture of our currently more complex analysis of play insofar as adults are included in the study of play. From this, a new word — "recreation" — emerged to serve more fully in treating the life styles of man.

We might accept these major concepts in somewhat of a unified,

12

conglomerate theory. Put together, they might say that play, when purposefully organized, serves man by providing activity arenas in which he attends to his inner drives, unfulfilled needs, and renews his energies and spirits, and practices survival behavior without jeopardizing his existing or future work participation.

MORE ON PLAY AND WORK

"Stop playing games . . ." is a serious rebuke nowadays.

No one ever passed a law saying that work could not be fun, but, for most of history, man's whole waking period was taken up in work — a work that constantly utilized all man's energies just to meet basic physical needs.

Trial and error learning stimulated the inventors; streamlined methods took more pressure off; producing survival didn't take the whole 24-hour grind. Early man began to repeat the fun aspects of work, even though the tasks provided no addition to the productive goals.

Yet even today, when occupational involvement for some makes up less than half of the active available time, we tend to feel guilty if our efforts lead to no materially measurable goal.

Says the lawyer: "How do I have fun? Well, there's this got-bucks client, we climb into his Mark III, roll over to some classy restaurant, have three or four drinks, talk some business, some bullshit, order a filet mignon after a couple of hours . . . I like it, and it's good business."

Says the college student with a pro football contract: "Even if I'm playing badminton or taking a walk, I make it count for getting in shape for playing. It's always been that way. It's hard to do anything unless I feel I'm able to make it pay off."

Says the college student without the pro football contract: "I go to this joint, they have beer and dancing, everybody goes there on Wednesday night, it's a place to meet chicks, but really it's a place to unscrew, unwind, forget about school and studies completely so you can get your strength back."

What are they saying? That they play because it contributes to work efficiency or achievement, or that play allows an escape from the pressure of work, a necessary escape to rebuild one's work potential.

The process of surviving, that obligated time in its pure form we call work, has kept man on edge about using his free time. His broad economic spectrum of standards for surviving — from daily bread to a color TV to a yacht in the harbor — have further complicated each man's decision about what his basic material needs are, and when he can turn off work and tune in play without guilt.

Recreation programmers work against this continuously. It is frustrating. It makes play difficult to encourage.

RECREATION'S ROLE

Play has permeated human affairs from man's beginning. Leisure is historically old for the aristocratic few, but is a new invention for the masses of the more affluent countries. Recreation is organized society's formal and orderly way of blending play and leisure into something more than idleness. Recreation must actively produce program activities that coincide with the needs and interests of people.

Accommodating activities of outside groups by merely scheduling facilities or providing neat grounds for free play for the walk-ons are subsidiary service of recreation programs, but they do not constitute genuine recreation. Program is what recreation as a field is all about, and the only performance deserving recognition as recreation is the recreational activity initiated, promoted, and produced by trained personnel of the agency. The above establishes a pure model, but it does not mean that partial involvements or support effort are unimportant. Medicine, however, did not build its status on taking bows for every headache cured by an aspirin tablet from the local supermarket.

Recreation is more difficult to find clearly delineated than the other arenas of group work, commercial amusements, therapy, and education. For example, education is the formal, organized production of learning, which in turn is defined as changed behavior. Learning, like play, takes place in all phases of life, but it's pretty wild and unpredictable. Education, like recreation, claims to be able to structure teaching and learning into a shortcut to fulfill an individual's needs. It is scientific, has system, can save time, predict results, and synergetically amalgamate resources into a force greater than its parts — at least, that's the idea. Recreation has a partial role in education, but it is hard to find unless the school announces recess. Actually, as with other service arenas, recreation is used as a tool to achieve established objectives. Thus people play through an organized recreation program in order to facilitate learning (education), rehabilitation (therapy), adjustment (group work), or product satisfaction (commercial amusement).

So far we have stepped erratically over recreation in various forms. It exists in adulterated forms, serving goals beyond the participation in activity itself, blending into other functional areas of society so that the people who work with it lose their identity as recreation programmers and become educators, therapists, or group workers. But there is a pure form of organized recreation which may be described as *the scientific production of organized experiences that fulfill social needs and interests of individuals in order to achieve an immediate sense of joy without reference to survival necessities or delayed rewards.*

It is important to mention at this point two strong trends that have given organized recreation's role new dimensions. Strongly in the foreground is the professional conglomeration of recreation/parks/planning administration envisioned as a catalyzing agent. The concept arose for several possible reasons. Recreation failed to catch hold of the people's "pride movements" (general public efforts without government interference) which ran new activity programs like Little League up the flagpole, causing the erosion and demise of traditional agency programs. You might say the amateurs took over and the professionals, after a struggle, decided to join them in a support catalyst role. Another possible basis for this view is that it's a lot easier and cheaper to let program come to you as an expression of what the public thinks it wants, rather than trying to finance and manufacture it from raw beginnings. Perhaps one other reason for this current swing is the ambiguity fostered by a field that has been notoriously tongue-tied about what it actually and uniquely does. Being a "catalyst" for recreation and related community happenings leaves the recreator uncommitted and available for all sorts of general odd jobs. As a coordinator of resources and organized groups, the catalyst concept recognizes the key idea of organization, which sets the good recreation man apart, but it creates a disservice since it implies the role is that of a public relations liaison aide.

More in the future, but indelibly set in recreation's horoscope, is the expanded area of recreational counseling and guidance. The training and application will differ from the traditional role of program producer. Ideally, the greater inclusion of recreation into the social sciences will produce a well-versed recreation programmer with counseling technique who can match individual needs to existing scheduled activities. Glimmerings of this development are seen in counseling on camping by urban recreation agencies and the half-way house bridge between institution and community.

Whatever concomitant tasks organized recreation takes on, however, the production of activities is indispensable and is the unique, primary role that justifies recreation's claim to identity as a special and specific functional field of service.

ENVIRONMENTAL FIELDS

Where an event takes place has an enormous impact on our feelings and emotions. The environment where recreation takes place has important differences from other environments, not so much because of the physical aspects, but because of the nature, philosophy and atmosphere that create the environment. A good program works in a jungle or in a neighborhood street or a phone booth, but the environment dictates which good program.

The environment has the potential of becoming a caustic or enhancing catalytic force at any time. To acknowledge this is not to be dominated by it, but rather to be prepared for it. The recreation programmer must know not only the characteristics of a specific neighborhood, hospital or base, but he must also be able to grasp the technological, ecological, and sociological nature of the larger community within which the smaller unit functions. The recreation profession must know the territory in order to produce a program with the least resistance.

There are several general considerations that apply to almost all environments and are worth identifying before we categorize the nature of specific environments.

1. *People expect recreation programs to happen at specifically designated places* like recreation centers, resorts, parks, playgrounds, beaches, or social rooms. When people arrive at a place where recreation is expected, they have a readiness for it; they generally come equipped, and physically and psychologically prepared.

Soldiers go to the base canteen, college students to the union or campus recreation center because the very nature of these places inspires play. It indicates that those who come there are looking for fun. Recreation programmers should take advantage of the structured readiness provided by the environmental places that suggest recreation to the public.

2. *Environments expect traditions and ground rules to be followed,* conformity at the expense of creativity *sometimes.* The concept of *indigenous leadership* — the use of locals familiar with agency quirks, neighborhood folkways, technical knowledge — is vital in this era. A word of caution, however: inferior recreation programming skill is never compensated by territorial familiarity.

3. *People in isolated environments* or institutionalized settings, shut off from other sub-units of society, may have no alternative to the recreation program offered. There is nowhere to go but inside oneself for the prisoner, the soldier, the astronaut, the ship's crew, and even the tourist at a remote resort. Such forced attention often deludes the programmer into expecting active participation. What probably will happen is withdrawal to uninspired, self-directed, superficial amusements.

4. *Environments set a mood* for having fun, they inspire an individual to excel or take risks. It's hard to express your best talents in a Disneyland where the rides are fixed; but people will do incredibly goofy things swept up in the hoopla of a company picnic at a country park. You want to ski when the new snow sits on the perfect slope before you, or skin dive when you look down from the surface through clear water to the bottom corals 60 feet below. Hands flex and itch to make something in the cheerful crafts room festooned with well-done, completed projects.

The cry of "this is the place" has been the verbal reflex of the satisfied customer, which suggests that the environment is important in the overall joy of the moment.

5. *Pursuit of the environment may overshadow the recreation activity itself.* The old miner or the backwoods logger, who lives in isolation, heads for the city's bright lights to break through cultural atrophy. What he does there is not as important as just being there. In turn, city people, saturated with smog, pressure, fast pace, crowding, or a climate of cold, snow, and rain, make going to the outdoors an end in itself.

6. *Space is one of our major concerns.* We are forced to live closer and closer together. Some of that space is lost because of pollution. Our concern for privacy and personal space has risen to the top of human need priorities recently, and space as an environment in itself cannot be overlooked. The failure of a basically sound program activity can often be traced to the space problem. But while crowded contact destroys effective programming, it also enhances activities such as cocktail parties and rock festivals which take on a more fervent, action-laden nature necessary for success. Nothing is more chilling than a sparsely-filled auditorium for a special event. Space is a two-edged sword in the environmental picture.

7. *People respect an environment in which they feel they have a stake.* People's parks are historically old, but modern times have shown how much effort and protective care can be given a place that the people really feel belongs to them. It's part of the belonging need, the community spirit. Rizal Park in Manila, Philippines developed and run with donations, large and small is unscarred and immaculate, amidst a city of ravaged and vandalized public facilities.

Tax-supported, government-operated public facilities are part of the dehumanization of the threatening future world. They are resented, and the alienated leave their identifying marks in negative ways with spray paint and knives.

There is a hazard in too much of the amateur human element, too. A recreation place can be poorly put together by the people, badly constructed and designed for the immediate present without concern for the survival and effectiveness in the future.

Where people pay to join they also feel they are buying a piece (of whatever) and tend to protect their investment. The more they pay, the more they seem to care for the environment. Private recreation facilities generally illustrate this assumption. Fees and charges are often based on the philosophy that they make people respect the place. But this often excludes the poor and racial and ethnic minorities. There is a backlash effect as well of which programmers must be aware. Coin-operated toilets are a classic example in which resentment toward fees causes both hostility and vandalism.

The recreation programmer does seem to gain a greater participative effort from those who feel a pride, a sense of belonging, a stake, a sort of ownership identification with the environment where their activities take place.

8. *Any change of environment can give a lift to program,* even if the change is downward in terms of sophistication, neatness, maintenance, or refinement. Take a craft class outdoors and rough it on the grass or a dance group to the roof of a tenement. The toughest and most popular summer basketball in the U.S. may be, according to many old pros, the New York three-man league played outdoors on asphalt with netless hoops. Perhaps just change itself is an undeniable excitement that enhances everything, especially recreation activity. Making do, being resourceful with less than usual, is another exhilaration that adds a different challenge to activity if correctly programmed by the leader.

9. *Recreation programs without a space/structural identity have to try harder* to create identity, attract participants, and launch activity. Boys Clubs are recreation center buildings in the eyes of the public and so are YMCA's. This wasn't always true, of course, but when each built personalized environments the job of programming really took off. The Scouts and Camp Fire Girls or most of the special interest clubs today operate untethered to facilities or play areas that belong to them. A lot more ceremony, uniforms, rituals, and progressive development systems are necessary when environment doesn't serve as a foundation for program. The public is more inclined to accept the idea of a facility or recreation area enduring than a storefront program; they'll invest more time because they feel a building is insurance that a program will endure.

Various Categorization of Environments It is possible that you could take a well-trained programmer, blindfold him, spin him around, march him into the middle of a village of head-hunters or a pit of man-eating lions, tell him to start running a recreation program, and he'd come up with a workable operation. A good program man is a skillful mechanic as well as a humanist and social scientist. Give him the ingredients and he'll put together something that will fly.

But in an age of increasing specialization, we prefer our mechanic on our

VW to be a Volkswagen expert. Similarly, for example, in hospital recreation or boys club work, the indoctrinated-to-our-environment recreation programmer is sought.

Environmental fields of recreation are important to categorize for preparing for employment in the field. The differences are based upon multiple factors, with great overlapping and duplication. We can make no attempt here to justify the separate status of each field nor guarantee that political and professional associations which identify themselves as spokesmen for each field would agree with our interpretation, let alone being assessed with a function identified as recreation. We can only claim logic on our side and not field veteran's experience in each case.

The fields as we see them now in operation are:
1. School Recreation (Campus-School Playground)*
2. Public Recreation (Municipal)*
3. Commercial Recreation (Amusements)*
4. Armed Forces Recreation (Military)*
5. Group Work Recreation (Youth Serving)*
6. Therapeutic Recreation (Medical)*
7. Resort Recreation (Travel)*
8. Company Recreation (Industrial-Employee)*
9. Institutional Recreation (Prison-Custodial)*
10. Private Recreation.
(*Other Titles in usage)

18

The following are various differential overlays with which to analyze these fields and to determine how they uniquely function.

Exposure Overlay This refers to the period of direct contact that an agency programming recreation has with the people in its community. This may range from a fleeting moment to a 24-hours-per-day life sentence. On the as-needed basis, in which a participant comes to a recreation activity as he needs and prefers the exposure, the burden of promoting participation becomes quite heavy. With the inmate, those confined for health, rehabilitation, shelter, or punishment, a captive participant is available continuously, basically unscreened. Recreation program must serve both the needs and interests of the participant and the goals of the agency.

The water ski instructor who gives the half-hour lesson, a pet parade at a shopping mall, an art show at the county fair, a guided scuba dive are all short-term program activities that generally need no follow-up series or progression sessions. If follow-up is programmed, continued participant interest is a constant problem for the programmer. On the other hand, recreation program is used in prisons, hospitals, and detention homes to serve many purposes for a population that is resident. 24-hours-per-day without competing recreation programs, but with the responsibility for covering all of the leisure.

Another aspect of the exposure overlay is the projection of contact — the length of time in days, weeks, months, or years — for which the agency has to program individuals. In some agencies such as juvenile halls, which are way stations, youngsters are detained for indeterminate periods from a few days to weeks or longer, awaiting judgment. A progressive program that follows a series of scheduled sessions leading to a climax, gives way to single one-shot activities that begin and end in the same session. People leave hospitals unexpectedly, military men are transferred, and this kind of transience and rootlessness complicates and demands a different program format.

The Goals Overlay Agencies use recreation program as a tool for obtaining their objectives. Some goals achieved through recreation are:
1. Discipline and control during custody.
2. Development of morale, *esprit de corps*, positive attitudes and loyalty toward an agency.
3. Avoidance of boredom.
4. Filling leisure in positive, active ways.
5. Providing interests and skills for later leisure life.
6. Teaching citizenship and socially-accepted attitudes toward people, laws, and the environment.
7. Promoting physical health.
8. Promoting mental health.
9. Making a profit.
10. Premiums or prizes in sales contests or promotions.
11. Helping cure or adjusting to physical and mental handicaps in order to achieve a functional role in society.
12. Rehabilitation through creating new interests and skills so a lawful, positive new life can be pursued.
13. Leading into new occupational opportunities.

19

The Locale Overlay Some agencies' programs arise from their very environment. For example, the urban setting spawns a profusion of youth groups, work clubs and organizations, because cities create the problems that these agencies are set up to solve. Resorts depend upon the natural locales that have unique features. The application of this overlay is of descending importance, but nevertheless a help to understanding the nature of the fields. The various locales — and their related climates and weather — are urban, suburban, rural, mountain, beach, desert, and lake. Additionally, some fields focus either on the outdoors or indoors.

The Exclusivity Overlay An open door to all the public is an ideal for which a democratic nation strives — and other styles of government, too. But some fields of recreation can function more effectively by limiting their services to those most in need, specific ages, or economic classes. The more specialized the recreation program becomes, the more exclusive and effective it may become by concentrating on a smaller target. Private operations have narrowed their challenge by controlling who participates by user fees.

The Involvement Overlay Involvement in this case, an area ranging from participation as a spectator, to actively playing, to directing the play, does not differentiate fields as much as analyzing the types of programs they have. It is unlikely that any of the fields would ever concentrate on any one extreme of involvement to the exclusion of the other, but the danger is ever present.

The Economic Overlay The degree of wealth generally channels people into specific environments. In America, there are three major environmental separations: the poverty belt, suburbia, and millionaire's row. There are shadings, areas of more or less economic power, that fall between or beyond. Resorts, for instance, belong to the upper two levels while the group-work operations are most likely to be found in the poverty areas.

The chart on page 21 relates these overlays to the ten fields and lists for a column specific agency operations that fall into each field.

CLASSIFICATION OF ACTIVITIES

"Football would be classified under 'Sports,' right," we said to the class explaining our classification system for recreation activities.

"But why bother to classify, what's the point?" came the practical, relevant reply.

These are the moments when those neat, structured lecture notes seem absolutely and discouragingly foolish. We then try a free approach.

"OK, what is football?"

"A game played with eleven players and a ball on a field . . . a sport with goal posts. . . . Well, you don't really need that many players . . . or the goal posts. . . ."

"How does 'sport' help to define it?"

"Because we think of sports as physical activity with rules and competition, and that's football . . . and baseball, basketball, wrestling, weight lifting, golf. . . ."

"Let's take golf. Does practicing your swing in the backyard still qualify as part of golf as a sport?"

"Sure, practicing something is still part of it, it's the learning part, improving yourself so you can compete better."

"How about someone teaching a beginner how to swing a golf club, is that person also engaged in sports as we're trying to define it?"

"No, teaching something isn't playing it . . . of course, learning isn't playing either, but it's more of a lead-up to playing, more directly a part of playing."

That's pretty good thinking and we're going to jump ahead a little, to where this discussion will eventually lead through a long series of small discoveries. First of all, a classification system is merely a shorthand code that makes it easier for us to understand the meaning of things in order to communicate our concepts without constantly redefining words. If we can agree that a word like "sports" covers a distinctive set of activities that have common characteristics then we can move on into a more advanced analysis of things, such as what happens to the personality and health of the participants. That's our real goal — one that hasn't been achieved too well, if at all, in these many years of organized recreation programming — understanding how these activities fulfill the needs of people.

The following are the classifications we will use in this book: Sports, Cultural, Social, Special Events.

	Environmental Field	Exposure	Goals	Locale	Involvement	Economic	Agencies Identified With Field
1.	School Recreation	Partially continuous, rooted	Educate for use of leisure	Varied	Active participation	All levels	Public and private elementary and secondary schools and colleges.
2.	Public Recreation	As needed, rooted	Balance life — leisure need fulfillment	Urban/Suburban	Active	All levels	Park and playground recreation centers
3.	Commercial Recreation	As needed, rooted	Profit	Urban/Suburban	Varied	All levels	Amusement centers, bowling lanes, golf courses, private gyms, movies, and sporting events
4.	Armed Forces Recreation	Continuous, rootless	Balanced life	Varied	Active	Middle economic classes	Special Services, USO, and Red Cross
5.	Group Work Recreation	As needed, rooted	Develop individual in citizenship and social interactions	Urban	Active	Poverty belt	YMCA, YWCA, Boys' Clubs, Girls' Clubs, Scouts, and other related youth groups
6.	Therapeutic-Medical Recreation	Continuous, rootless	Therapy and balanced life	Urban	Varied	Not significant	Hospitals and Mental institutions
7.	Resort Recreation	Continuous, rootless	Profit	Lake, desert, beach and mountain	Varied	Upper economic classes	Hotels and auxiliary recreation services
8.	(Industrial-Employee)-Co. Recreation	As needed, rooted	Morale and loyalty to organization	Varied	Active	Middle economic classes	Industry-businesses-employee associations
9.	Institutional Recreation	Continuous, rootless	Balanced life, some rehabilitation	Urban	Varied	Not significant	Prisons and detention homes
10.	Private Recreation	As needed, rooted	Balanced life and some profit	Urban/Suburban	Active	Upper economic levels	Condominiums, private communities, special interest clubs, country clubs, and Athletic club

Let's return to *sports* as it was being discussed. Sports deserves a kick-off position because it dominates recreation life styles wherever organized program exists. It's important to remember that our concern here is not with amateur, do-it-yourself activity, but the organized efforts of professional agency staffs. About 70 per cent of the numbers participating, budgets, and special facilities are devoted to sports.

Two other words immediately arise in examining written programs of agencies: "games" and "athletics." "Games" will appear in several other classifications, especially social and sometimes special events, but those games that are designed primarily to provide physical exertion and to develop prowess and coordination for more advanced sports are best categorized under "sports." "Athletics" is a school-oriented term and, while in some quarters representing a more strictly organized form of sports, is redundant for our purposes.

It is easier to explain what does not belong under sports and why, than explaining why football, basketball, and baseball are defined as sports. Card playing has rules and competition, but physical exertion is missing. Gardening has physical exertion, but neither universal rules governing play nor competition during the activity itself. Card playing would be included in our social classification because of the need it primarily fulfills; gardening is difficult to categorize because it is a personal, self-directed activity; but its emphasis on creating something, making something with one's hands, makes it better classified under the subsection "arts and crafts" of cultural program.

In light of the difficulty in classification, it is easy to understand why in the past men have tended to call lists arbitrary. One has to like crossword puzzles or be a dedicated researcher to enjoy setting up classification systems.

There is another difficulty about sports which should be cleared up: There are three arenas of participation in all sports, and they are part of organized programming. They may each serve different purposes and fulfill opposite needs, but they are part of all program packages. They are:

The Learning Arena — which covers class programs, the practice sessions, and other types of preparatory activities leading to actual competition in which scores are kept.

The Performance Arena — in which the participant competes against records, his own or others, and opponents. Or he uses the skill and knowledge to effectively engage in an activity for the sheer sense of fulfillment involved in it.

The Mastery Arena — which has to do with champions who demonstrate their mastery in exhibitions or utilize it in instructing others. It is the sometimes lonely high point of participation in any activity and carries with it a sense of great achievement but also a sense of having gone as far as possible, thereby diminishing future incentives for accomplishment.

These three arenas are part of all programming which can be analyzed better after we understand the motivations behind participation, which will be discussed later.

Have you got sports locked in now? It's all the physical games, their practice, performance, and mastery.

The literature to date has treated water-related activities as a small element of sports. But recently there has been an enormous increase in popularity of organized aquatic programs, Aquatics. Activities encompassed by Aquatics — swimming, canoeing, skin diving, sailing, water skiing (and we'll put fishing here too, just as hunting belongs with sports) — are sports, with the small but important qualification that the unusual environment of water is vital.

Aquatics is a very significant part of the numbers game for all recreation operations. For example, attendance figures at any area with a pool soar astronomically in the summer. Surveys demonstrate that swimming is the all-time best mass activity ever set up for the people. Admittedly, a lot of that is just splashing around in the water, but even eliminating unstructured bathing, aquatics from the active participant standpoint is big recreation business. We would estimate that it takes up 30 percent of that 70 percent figure we tagged on sports.

In the future, a classification entitled Special Environment Activities may be in order, separate from Sports, e.g., snow and winter pursuits, vehicle recreation and certainly aquatics.

Cultural Programming is a potpourri classification with subclasses of arts and crafts, music, dance, and drama. Education tends to describe these areas of activities in terms of performing arts and fine arts, but then other sub-units of society define them as communicative arts, creative arts, aesthetics, or folk art.

If there is one important characteristic to help assign activities to this classification it would have to be the *communications* aspect.

Social Programming is traditionally part of the folk lore of the recreation profession and although it usually lacks substance, we will use it to cover some activities that defy manipulation into other categories and seem to have their origins and justification in the socialization process, almost to the exclusion of all other aspects of play theory. Much special-interest club programming should be treated here as well as a great deal of the programmed spectator activity.

Special Events are merely large editions or combinations of the activities of the other classifications. There might be a few exceptions insofar as an event may cover an interest that has not been programmed on a regular basis but which could be. Pet shows are an example since there is usually not much happening in regular program with animals. A beauty contest is isolated from any regularly scheduled program.

Special events are referred to as "frosting on the cake" in recreation literature and conferences. Special events give prima donna recreation programmers a chance to honk a lot of horns in public, but special events take guts and organizational skill.

We are a people who will often settle for one supercharged blast once in a while rather than steady, regular emotional arousals. A good programmer should produce both. But if you're limping along with the weekly offerings, it's amazing how a special event can skyrocket your support and probably fulfill a lot of needs for a lot of people for one glorious moment.

Before accepting this classification system it is necessary to discuss several classifications used in other studies.

What about hobbies? First of all, it is an old-fashioned word dug out of old normal school pamphlets, early *Readers' Digests*, and craft kit manufacturers' promotional literature. It is derived from "hobbyhorses", something you get on and ride with intense involvement. A hobby seems to be a deep and committed interest to something outside of the job. Many creative activities, such as painting, are classified as hobbies, but we have included them under cultural programming. The diehards complain, "collecting stamps and coins or autographs . . . you can't really call them anything but hobbies." But we will, under "cultural programming."

Outdoor recreation and camping are difficult not to classify separately. But it is redundant to make an activity classification based on environmental setting. Recreation often takes place, however, in the outdoors, and much of the appreciation of nature takes place indoors. We cannot find something special and unique in the activity line that is completely and uncompromisingly tied to the outdoors or camping, but building a fire is the closest we can come.

We have not ignored, eliminated or slighted camp program in this book, but we don't want to have to say something twice. Better said once and understood as universally applicable.

Volunteer service is another classification of program activity that is an operational involvement by recreation agencies. Many lists of program classifications include it, but interpreting program in light of individual needs it is better to handle it as one of the ten basic need areas and present its involvement in recreation program as a part of the need fulfillment potential rating section of program activities.

24   We are convinced that recreation has performed nothing so well as it has the programming and production of leaders with organizing ability for society at large. It is one of the few places where people can try themselves out by helping others in activity where the mistakes don't lead to business bankruptcy, family breakup, or loss of career. It deserves careful, conscientious professional supervision.

If you run across other classifications that work, use them. But for now, this classification system is the language we will use discussing recreation programs.

Chapter 2

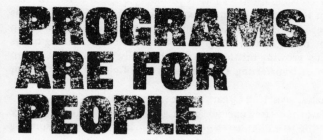

PROGRAMS ARE FOR PEOPLE

Doll tea is where little girls play mother and bring their dolls like children to a mock party. Wouldn't it be strange for the recreation director at San Quentin to program one for his grizzled convicts.

That's a rather extreme alignment of dissimilar elements. But degrees of unrefined program-to-people applications remain one of the major professional lags in the recreation field.

Programming should never treat the general public as an homogeneous mass that must adjust to whatever program professionals decide to put on. In our field's primitive times, if we staged football or a dance activity, it was for whoever came through the door first.

The following list suggests some goals to keep in mind when dealing with a diverse public.

1. Take advantage of ready-made interest and skills to facilitate the promotion of participation
2. Be able to prepare the instruction, leadership, facilities and materials to best serve the specific nature of the identified public
3. Protect the participants by adapting the program to their health and safety requirements
4. Determine the objectives the participants wish to achieve
5. Schedule a balanced, broad, and non-overlapping program for all individuals
6. Simplify organizational control by working with small compatible units in both the planning and operational stages.

The process of differentiating may be illustrated in the following example. Insert the English sport of rugby, which is much like our American football. We'll assume we're convinced of its worth for programming, although we've never played or run it before. What kind of people can play it, will want to play, and should play it? Program is produced for people, certain people, and finding out which ones is every programmer's starting effort.

25

The bone-crunching, bodily-contact nature of rugby indicates that it is for men. The physical limitations of women suggests that rugby would be dangerous for most women and allows us therefore to narrow participants down to men. Then, of course, there is the supporting, if unenlightened, rationale that rugby is traditionally for men.

There are other considerations. There is probably a specific age for best playing rugby, when the proper blend of experience and physical prowess is at its zenith. If we are dealing with Americans with no previous experience in it, our starting point might be college-age men who have neither young bones forming nor old bones growing brittle, who are physically tough, able to learn quickly and capable of transferring knowledge and proficiency from familiar sport activities.

Now we have males, ages 18-24 years as our target public.

At this point, we have to consider some geographical boundaries very carefully. What is the community to be served? If we're programming recreation at a Girls' Club, rugby has already taken a nosedive. We have to assume that the first two characteristics, age and sex, exist in our service community.

We will discover also that there is a skill factor to be considered. Although we assumed we were starting a new activity, as we set out to analyze our community we discover people who have already had some experience, either from a college or from living in England. Each skill strata creates a separate public which must be considered in the program planning. Participants can then be separated into novices, beginners, skilled, and even champions. Skill joins age and sex in shaping our public.

Progressive recreation departments have assisted their identification of publics by obtaining interest inventory surveys which superficially indicate what people are interested in participating in an activity. Such expressions of interests, however, are a long way from actually participating as we have all learned from program bombs that were founded on paper images of people's momentary enthusiasms. Interest may be discovered through the initiative of individuals, but more significantly and more reliably through the requests of special-interest groups or clubs that already exist. The latter groups are often supported in a vast area of co-sponsored activities that make up an important segment of many agency programs.

It is also important to determine the level of aspiration and, in relation to this, how far the participants ultimately wish to advance in the program. These are individual objectives. They change constantly, but they do serve to help structure the publics, especially for long-range planning.

Handicapped Recreation are significant programs that have created new publics. There are large numbers of people with major, incapacitating handicaps, who are now getting a chance to try everything. Often, however, they do it only under the pressure of keeping up with others with similar restrictions. It is a public with which we identify with our hearts as well as our minds.

Another separation is the polarization of rich and poor and ethnic and racial groups. These categories serve as important indicators of how a group of people will respond as a public to recreation programs. For example, Mexican-Americans prefer soccer over football. Foxhunting, of course, never caught on in the ghetto. It is perhaps the least desirable way of defining publics, because it tends to negate the individual approach that this book advocates as the most enlightened system for quality programs.

The measurement of social needs fulfillment gives us the opportunity to make program truly reach and serve each individual to the fullest; it also allows the recreation programmer to compute social needs as he produces programs for publics seemingly as vast as individuals themselves.

LEVELS OF ASPIRATION

Did you ever toss rope rings onto a stick? That's what they did in an old-time game called "Quoits." But it was also the testing procedure in a famous study series on motivation from which the idea of *level of aspiration* developed.

When someone sticks the quoits in your hand, five of them, how many do you feel you can toss over the peg? Big ego, lots of confidence, you're sure you'll get 5 out of 5. You try but only ring two. Five was your level of aspiration, what now? The reasonable thing to do to avoid frustration is to adjust the level downward to a goal of maybe three, one above your current record.

Now you ring three, and the temptation is to hoist the level of aspiration up to four or even back to five. But suppose the second try, you fall back to one ringer. Crash! Down comes your confidence.

The level of aspiration is a constantly fluctuating psychological regulator that can be the major influence at any time on the success of any activity in producing participant satisfaction. Up until now we have indicated that aspiration is involved with actually performing a skill with some proficiency. That is the best way to understand it, but the concept envelops other facets of participation as well: ranking, acceptance by others, and identification.

For some, it is not how well the game is played, but how much better you can play than your opponent or perhaps your rank among many competitors. Others rejoice in making the team and just riding the bench. Some are satisfied to identify with a particular dance group or with a specific art center regardless of how lowly their participant status may be.

There is a marvelous ability of the human psyche to rationalize failure in achieving expectations. Not only can the participant adjust his level of aspiration upward or downward in cases of competing against one's own record, but he also can substitute aspirations, change the calibre of his opponents, or the environment against which he measures himself.

Not that this is ever easy. Many participants need guidance and leadership that will facilitate adjusting. Rapid deterioration of interest in an activity is often found in the "loser type" who sets up a self-deprecating pattern, expecting to do poorly, tending to set lower and lower expectations to avoid disappointments until he has phased himself out of participating altogether. At the other extreme is the desperate, frustrated, high-aspiration participant who can never settle for less than five ringers out of five attempts. Such perfectionists are nursing dangerous compulsions that tend to make recrea-

27

tion program become work ordeals, pressuring rather than refreshing.

Levels of aspiration can be established on a group basis. It is an ideal strived for by teams, businesses, and organizations of all types, when group success represents individual success. Sociologically it is called "congruency of goals," but it is rarely achieved for more than a moment. The recreation programmer must become adept at the continuous process of helping to maintain achievement satisfaction and interest in an activity by analysis of individual levels of aspiration.

Recreation program is like Russian roulette because it does not have a technique for measuring individual needs. Like double-talking snake oil salesmen, programmers have tried to fit the individual to program, instead of fitting the program to the individual.

If personality is the sum total of life's experiences, that means each individual is unique and each person will have his own unique set of needs to be fulfilled during work and leisure. The recreation professional recognizes the impending hiring of recreation counselors. Using the term "counselor" implies one-to-one investigation of leisure. How are these new counselors going to determine needs? At this time there are no measurement instruments available in the field. We propose to introduce one here. It will be incomplete and somewhat primitive but could provide a large enough target to lead others to search for an ultimate device for determining the quality of program.

A Human Need That which is required by the organism for satisfactory emotional and physical well-being. It can be intense or weak. It is the force that stimulates feelings which change conditions.

Controversy over human needs started with William McDougal and his "instincts theory." Dunlap used the term "desires" and Gurnee spoke of "motives." Each new theorist reduced the list, added a new need, or changed the concept. All were criticized, altered, discussed, or renamed. W. I. Thomas called his needs "wishes," and limited them to four: response, recognition, security, and new experience.

Maslow and Murray wrote about the "hierarchy of needs" and the "need concept." They were challenged by Lewin's "field theory," and Lewin was challenged by Leeper, Brunswik, and Householder. The challenges and changes go on and on. This is hopefully a process toward understanding. Should we stand dead center waiting for agreement between social scientists we would never get started on a measurement instrument. We will select from the social scientists those ideas that seem applicable to recreation.

Need Conflict Since needs are combined to different degrees within the same individual, it is difficult to look at them as separate entities. Needs that are working at the same time within the individual will translate first into action the need which is most intense. When an intense need is met the pattern changes and the individual becomes needful in another area of intensity. What it means is you never win or beat the game of human needs since they are constant and changing.

After examining an original list of twenty-two needs, we settled on the following ten as the most meaningful for recreation programming. These needs are, in no special order, as follows:

Human Needs

1. New experience
2. Relaxation/escape
3. Recognition
4. Security
5. Dominance
6. Physical activity
7. Mental activity
8. Creativity
9. Response/social interaction
10. Service

New Experience Adventure, exploration, discovery, challenge, and seeking the unknown.

If you drove to school or work today without remembering it, you are like Pavlov's dog insofar as you have become conditioned to the experience. It is possible in this automated world for one to live twenty-four-hours-a-day and still draw a blank if asked to relate the experiences of that period. People become habituated despite the fact that repetitious behavior creates apathy, atrophy, and boredom.

As the opportunity for change decreases on the job, the fulfillment of the need for new experience intensifies in leisure activities. The human cries out for a change of pace, a different scene, an escape from empty routine. In our technological society, man is forced and shoved into mechanized behavior. He needs new experiences to test himself to be sure that he exists, has an individual identity, and can cope with challenge.

Relaxation/Escape Blank mind, forgetting, running, fantasy, removing stress.

Physical labor is being phased out of our society while mental occupations increase with their accompanying stress. Family structure has weakened, divorce rates are up, relationships are transitory, pollution has ruined our cities, unemployment is up, and stocks are down. Loneliness is the common denominator. Modern America embraces escape. Escape in any form, be it moving to Australia or curling up in a fetal position on the floor of a mental institution. Run, hide, and forget. When the organism can no longer tolerate the environment it either mentally or physically removes itself to catch its breath.

Here is where recreation can perform a positive social role by creating the atmosphere for rejuvenation, by harboring the battered psyche, by relaxing frayed nerves, and by recharging the physical man.

Recognition To be verbally or materially rewarded for achievement. To rival

29

and surpass others by overcoming obstacles and have it acknowledged. To receive attention.

Once, for twelve hours, a nude man stood on Golden Gate Bridge, wearing spats and a top hat shouting, "Now see me." He got his moment of attention. That is the need for recognition turned sour. We all have it to some degree. What varies is the intensity of the need and the ways it may be satisfied. Some may be satisfied with making the best pickle relish at the fair, while others will settle for nothing less than superstar status.

Every individual fights for some form of identity. If you have an opportunity to go through an estate, look at the things people treasure enough to keep. Recently we went through a trunk and found carefully wrapped and preserved a ribbon which read in faint gold letters "Third Place Winner Rose Show 1912." Almost sixty years of preserving a ribbon because no one else could ever be that at that time and in that place.

Security To avoid pain, physical injury, illness, emotional hurt, and death. To be free of concern about thirst, food, or warmth. To feel needed, necessary, and safe in the environment. Comfort.

To some degree we all need a security blanket. Social pressures prevent us from sucking our thumbs, feeling our blankets, or hugging our "teddies." From the careful man wearing suspenders and belt to the daredevil motor-cyclist, all of us have some need to feel safe.

It is important for the recreation worker to know the intensity of this security need. The response to new experience, the unknown, is often a chorus of avoidance excuses. Children feel a need to go to the restroom, throw up, giggle, or cry.

What we deal with is degrees of security, and what the program planner must have is awareness of those degrees to avoid pushing the participant past the point of tolerance.

Dominance To take charge and control of one's environment. To direct the behavior of others by manipulation, orders, suggestion, or persuasion.

There are some individuals who are uninterested in participating if they are not in charge. Often the recreation leader is challenged by a rogue-elephant leader until he relinquishes power. An individual may seek power above anything else in his interaction with people.

The danger of an intense dominance need is that if it is not utilized in a positive way it easily becomes a negative force in the group. If a group or club has more power-oriented individuals than it can cope with, it will splinter.

The positive force of these "take-charge" individuals is that they do make things happen and they provide the vitality and change within a program.

Remember, with all of the various needs, we are talking about ideal constructs or pure models. Needs modify each other so that the pure dominance need is seldom encountered as all-prevailing and uninfluenced. If the need for dominance becomes destructive to the program, other identifiable needs could serve to replace it and prevent disaster. It takes a clever programmer to manipulate this.

Response/Social Interaction To relate and reach to individuals and to have individuals react with you.

We often find our essence or identity reflected in us by others; it therefore follows that everyone will have some operative need for social interaction.

An extreme need would be characterized by the individual who can never stand to be alone. A person who is traumatized by criticism or rejection may need constant, superficial social interaction. Such extreme cases may not be able to manage a trip to the restroom in a public place without someone to accompany them. They often function as yes men, comics, court jesters, and free baby sitters, all in an effort to fulfill their basic need.

Most people will fall between the extremes of a totally gregarious life and the life of a hermit: needing human contact and intimacy but cautious about deep involvements. There is contact, but no risk of intimacy in a crowd; there is risk in the intimate one-person involvement.

Mental Activity The rational ability to perceive, interpret, and understand various alternatives. Mental concentration as opposed to sense perception and emotion.

Everyone is capable of mental activity. People who have as a primary operative need mental activity are often indifferent to physical activity. These are the bridge players, chess players, discussion group leaders and intellectual planners. Creativity is dependent on mental activity, but not all intellectual activists are creative.

The mind, like the body, must be used to stay functionally healthy. It should be challenged and stretched. Unused, it slips into a kind of limbo, deteriorates, and loses its potential for perceiving, interpreting, concentrating, and deciding.

31

Creativity Creation of a new image, construction, idea, or product in contrast to a copy or imitation. Original. The ability to see and express concepts never consciously encountered.

For the purposes of recreation programming creative need is best described as the internal drive to express oneself in a visual or verbal form that does not already consciously exist in the participant.

Creativity has been one of the most difficult phenomena in human behavior to isolate and define. As a basic need, it takes on added mysticism. Explanations are attempted but ultimately fail.

The best approach toward explaining it for our purposes lies in contrasting it with general mental activity. Both are related in the sense that one cannot have creativity without mental activity, but one can have mental activity without creativity.

We tend to see creativity as the final refinement of the mental process. It evolves from a great store of knowledge which sets the stage for constructing an original product or concept — new and original in terms of being unknown to the individual.

There is a paradox to the premise that creativity exists at the peak of intellectual effort. Many authorities cite spontaneous self expression in children as pure examples of creativity. There is logic to this idea insofar as children, not having had time to store many known concepts, are constantly uncovering what is new and original to them. Unfortunately, much of their creative expression ends up in the trash can.

Creativity, in terms of it having social status, seems to be derived from superior knowledge and mental conceptualizations attained through culture. Creativity may even emerge as a separate dimension in itself, a process entirely unrelated to the use of the mind to solve problems.

Service to Others Altruism, humanitarianism; contributing, helping, assisting and concern for the well-being of others.

This need may be based on a negative motivation such as guilt, the desire to be superior, or even may be interwoven with needs for response or recognition. But it doesn't matter what the clinically precise reason is as long as we recognize that there is no pure altruism. Often the "Do-Gooder" is getting much more in the area of need fulfillment than those he or she is serving.

We can probably draw our extreme model of the service-to-others need in the volunteer instructor or leader who stands in for professional staff. A medium potential for fulfillment is found in dramatics or music, which tend to entertain, thereby acting as service to others. There is most often no harm done by the using of service for one's own needs, and most programmers recognize service as the backbone of their volunteer program.

Physical Activity Provides release from muscular tension. Fitness, physiological health, the response to the internal flexings of any living organism.

It is to move, jump, run, sweat, pant, and strain. It is the control and awareness of the physical self. The fulfillment can be exhilarating to some, torture to others.

32

To those who get up early in the morning, pull on a sweat suit, run two miles and return home to a body-building breakfast, physical activity is a way of life. To the plump matron huffing and puffing through a ten-minute set of exercises, it may just be an alternative to fat hips.

All that tissue and muscle is restless and feels threatened. Unused, it atrophies. Used, it is greedy for more.

It is the umbrella activity need for the greatest number of recreation participants. Sports is its chief agent for fulfillment.

The Origin of the Need Indicator Test

When this test was undertaken, the various researchers and authors who managed to get an elbow or a word in were friendly and somewhat harmonious in their understanding of needs for recreation program.

It wasn't because any of them had a really good system for measuring people's needs or the need fulfillment potential of activities, but because they were working on it and thinking about it. They had a confidence that once they sat down to it, put their beliefs in a common hopper, a shiny new revolutionary and scientific programming miracle would emerge.

The following test was developed at Los Angeles State College for the purpose of defining individual needs. Developing the test was a frustrating battle.

Respond to each set of words based on your immediate comparison reaction. Work quickly, filling in the circle under the column which best indicates the degree of attraction to one of the compared words. Equal attraction or no attraction directs you to indicate this by using the neutral column.

		Strong	*Moderate*	*Neutral*	*Moderate*	*Strong*	
1.	sacrifice A	O	●	O	O	O	indulge B
2.	tender A	O	●	O	O	O	tough E
3.	give A	O	O	●	O	O	play E
4.	serve A	O	O	●	O	O	participate E
5.	soft A,B,J	O	●	O	O	O	hard C
6.	entertain A	O	O	●	O	O	enjoy B
7.	comfort A,F	O	O	●	O	O	relax B
8.	ambulance A	O	O	O	●	O	mini-bike E
9.	teacher A,J	O	O	●	O	O	student D
10.	decorate A	O	O	●	O	O	announce C
11.	canvas A	O	O	O	●	O	donate F
12.	freedom B,G	O	O	●	O	O	responsibility C
13.	tranquility B	O	O	●	O	O	vitality E
14.	blend B	O	O	O	●	O	attention J
15.	release B	O	●	O	O	O	hold E
16.	dream B	O	O	●	O	O	plan G
17.	leisure B	O	O	O	●	O	occupation J
18.	silence B	O	O	●	O	O	life F,A
19.	tight I	O	O	●	O	O	loose B,H
20.	security I	O	O	●	O	O	relax B

33

21.	book D	o	o	o	o	o	barbell E
22.	study D	o	o	o	●	o	perform A,F,J
23.	investigate D,H	o	o	●	o	o	accept A
24.	circumvent D	o	o	●	o	o	follow I
25.	lock I	o	o	o	●	o	unlock D,F
26.	rational D	o	●	o	o	o	emotional F
27.	puzzle D	o	o	o	●	o	move E,H
28.	checkers D	o	o	●	o	o	ball E
29.	argue D	o	o	o	●	o	leave B
30.	explore H	●	o	o	o	o	observe D,G
31.	surprise H	o	●	o	o	o	know C,J
32.	unknown H	o	●	o	o	o	familiar I,J
33.	mother I,A	●	o	o	o	o	father H,C
34.	challenge H	o	●	o	o	o	agree F
35.	excitement H	●	o	o	o	o	safe I
36.	rape H	o	●	o	o	o	masturbation I
37.	hidden H	o	o	o	●	o	exposed J,G
38.	air H	o	o	●	o	o	earth I,G
39.	lost H	o	o	o	●	o	found A,I
40.	superior C	o	o	●	o	o	subordinate I
41.	decision C	o	●	o	o	o	indeterminate G
42.	charge C,E	o	o	o	●	o	compromise F
43.	address C,J	o	o	o	●	o	listen F
44.	fame C,J	o	o	o	●	o	happiness G
45.	respect C	o	o	●	o	o	love F

46.	win C,E,J	o	o	●	o	o	draw I,F
47.	control C	o	o	o	●	o	participate F,H
48.	hot I	o	o	●	o	o	cold C
49.	money I	o	o	o	o	●	fun C
50.	circle I,F	o	o	●	o	o	line C
51.	center I,J,F	o	o	●	o	o	side D
52.	anchor I	o	●	o	o	o	drift B,H
53.	belong I,J,F	o	●	o	o	o	observe D
54.	near I	o	o	●	o	o	far H
55.	invent G	o	●	o	o	o	copy E
56.	abstract G	o	o	o	●	o	concrete D
57.	art G	o	●	o	o	o	technology D
58.	pragmatic C	o	o	●	o	o	hypothetical G,D
59.	make G	o	●	o	o	o	buy F
60.	design G	o	●	o	o	o	trace I
61.	experiment G,H	o	o	●	o	o	accept F
62.	write G,J	o	o	o	●	o	read D
63.	puzzle G	o	o	●	o	o	dice H
64.	feel G,E	o	o	●	o	o	think D
65.	sweat E	o	o	o	●	o	cool C
66.	run E	o	●	o	o	o	sit B
67.	hustle E	o	●	o	o	o	cease B
68.	peddle E	o	o	●	o	o	coast B
69.	push E	o	●	o	o	o	lean D
70.	conversation F	o	o	●	o	o	observation G

71. window J	o	◉	o	o	o	fence I
72. public J	o	◉	o	o	o	private C,B
73. crown J	o	o	◉	o	o	hat A
74. headlines J	o	o	◉	o	o	listing A
75. salute J	o	o	◉	o	o	tag E

Score Key

A ...... Service to Others	F ...... Response/Social Interaction
B ...... Relaxation/Escape	G ...... Creativity
C ...... Dominance	H ...... New Experience
D ...... Mental Activity	I ...... Security
E ...... Physical Activity	J ...... Recognition

Under each word the assigned needs are indicated by the letters listed in the key. All the marks in the strong column are worth 2 points; in the moderate column there is a 1 point credit. Marks in the center neutral column are 0 or no credit. Total points for each letter. Example:

36

							Total
1. sacrifice A	●	o	o	o	o	indulge B	2A
2. tender A	o	o	●	o	o	tough E	0
3. give E	o	o	o	●	o	play E	1E

Key: Total Points

36–30	High need indicated
30–20	Moderate need
20–15	Less need indicated
15–0	Not indicated for programming

There are certain grouping of needs that appear together with greater frequency than others. We are presenting them in the hope that it may give short cuts in programming. However, the diversity of people tends to make these groupings overlap. Exceptions rather than these pure models will predominate. But the models are the most common and usable for recreation found in our studies.

CHART OF FOUR FREQUENTLY CLUSTERED COMBINATIONS OF NEEDS

Temperament Classification	Needs	Goal	Characteristics and Descriptive Behavior
Leader	Dominance Physical Activity Recognition	Power	Projects self into sur- roundings Indifferent to others Initiator Dogmatic Opinionated Doer
Follower	Relaxation Response Security	Love	Projects self into sur- roundings Supports others Tries everything Flexible Fad follower Open to persuasion
Tactician	New experience Relaxation Mental activity	Challenge	Dissociates self from surroundings Well-organized Manipulative Thoughtful Neat Challenging Aloof
Autonomist	New experience	Accom- plishment	Identifies with causes Sympathetic Humanitarian Hard worker Vicarious Draws attention to self

Chapter 3

PEOPLE WHO MAKE PROGRAMS

INVOLVED HIERARCHY

There was a time when a simple product was made by a simple man at his work-bench. Those were the good old days for some people; they are the good days now for others in by-passed corners of the world.

Life has become very complicated. Technology, arising from progress and industrialization, has pushed us along a compulsive trail of over-needing. Luxuries have become necessities. It is often cheaper to get somebody to do something for you than to do it yourself. Man has become a very dependent creature, persuaded to need and desire beyond his basic drives. He handles this situation by dropping out and returning to basics, or by creating more intricate systems for meeting the challenge.

Recreation as a service field, which faithfully imitated education and social service, has become a separate entity: recreation has developed what we might call an "involved hierarchy." Under the questionable but popular assumption that size is achievement, recreation organizations have established hierarchical functional positions in order to produce recreation program. The hierarchy runs from policy makers on boards and commissions to administrators, to line and staff supervisors, to local leaders.

A hierarchy is merely a way of taking on more work, expanding horizontally by covering more territory and people and growing vertically to create specialized jobs that supposedly create both greater operational efficiency and better products. The old shoemaker bought the leather, made the shoes and sold them — very good shoes, very good service. Recreation as a service field was like that once and still is in a few slow-paced, volumeless operations. Now recreation has gone big league, subscribing to the upward mobility incentive as a success goal.

Has recreation improved as a result of this expansion? The answer is yes and no. Yes, we have proliferated recreational opportunities for people as leisure, discretionary incomes, and social therapy needs have increased. No, our result, a balanced life with need fulfillment exceeding frustration, has not kept pace with the life style — or, rather than keep pace, which implies following, recreation program has not set the pace. Bureaucracy absorbs the energy to do so.

It is at the leadership level where the ultimate responsibility and power to set this pace must reside. The generals and officers may create and manipulate the logistics of a war, but only the front-line combat soldiers can make it work. The small war, the containment type of guerrilla warfare, parallels the small recreational service areas — rec halls on bases, campuses, institutions, and neighborhoods — because the leadership is not identified with planning and procuring, but with the direct confrontation of participants.

A good product sells itself eventually and the people who use it will help to improve it. Somehow, recreation program leadership has to acquire a new prestige and support. The very best program producers should not be rewarded by flight up the hierarchical ladder but reinforced with status and material benefits at the local level. Perhaps the kind of status given scientists in the Soviet Union — a privileged elite while producing results — is the arrangement social services, especially recreation, should experiment with.

At any rate, we seem to be stuck with organizational hierarchy as a means of making recreation grow within current society. If that system can yield greater resources and evaluative devices for planning and the removal of secondary pressures from the program leader, then the hierarchy can serve rather than frustrate the attack by programmers and leaders on unhappiness and boredom.

40

THEORIES OF LEADERSHIP

One of the ways to understand leadership is to identify whom you consider a leader and why. It's a nice, simple game but the results are quickly dated for the clay in leaders' feet crumble with time. It is disillusioning to name a crusading anti-pollution politician one day and have him indicted for double-billing his expense account the next.

Specifying a particular individual helps us to analyze the ingredients of leadership according to our own experience and even may lead to the discovery of theories of leadership that may be almost universal. If you have difficulty identifying a leader on a grand scale, perhaps you can recall someone in your personal life who is or was a leader for you.

Don't be surprised if you come up with an old coach from the past or a temporarily forgotten recreation director — and for some of us who have been in certain environments, the non-com or plant foreman may appear. These are rather common listings on our surveys.

The following dialogue was from a group discussion about leadership:

I asked Charlie why he listed Knute Rockne, who coached the great Notre Dame football teams 40-odd years ago. "Well, he knew a lot about what he was doing [superior knowledge], and he inspired the players to want to win, you know, those dressing room fight talks, 'win one for the Gipper [inspiration].' "

Grace named John Kennedy, who was often at the top of lists identifying leaders both during his presidency and, like Lincoln, after his assassination. I asked her why: "President Kennedy had a magnetic personality [charisma] — the way he looked and talked — and he seemed like he really believed in things [dedication], like peace, and helping the poor and stopping racial discrimination."

Someone objected to Kennedy at this point. "That's just an image they created about him. How do you know how he really felt? The other party thought he and his brother were ruthless, rich opportunists. His public relations people told him how to dress, comb his hair. Just like Lincoln, if he hadn't been shot, his mistakes might have caught up with him."

Grace replied, "But it doesn't really matter as long as what I see is a good leader. If he was rotten to the core, my impression of him, his ideas, I suppose, are what's important, not any speculative muck-raking."

Pablo listed Zapata and Pancho Villa, and a high school counselor. "You know, some of these guys who were leaders may have been real bummers, bandidos, but they led a bunch of men and got good results for a lot of people. I mean, a lot of people followed them, and in a way we're following what they stood for today. But I got myself straightened out talking to a counselor. She got me to read some books about places where I lived, and it really hooked me on reading, that seems like some kind of leadership."

Grace questioned several points; "I don't think leadership is happening when you force people to follow out of fear, and I don't really know about Villa except through what I read in what I suppose you'd call the WASP culture books and films, but a man with a gun to my head doesn't give me the impression of a leader. And I don't see counseling on a one-to-one basis as more than a technique of leadership, but not leadership of any dimension. Maybe it's some low form of leadership."

41

Truman named Malcolm X and Ralph Nader. "These two guys started something, they really believed, sacrificed a lot of creature comforts and money, because they really had deep committments to some exact goals. They knew what these goals were and could be articulate about them [communicate]. People fell in line and wanted to be part of whatever they were pitching because they seemed to know where to go and what to do. Sometimes the leader seems to be just a tool that a group uses to pull things together and explain in words how they feel and what the hell they're doing."

It's funny how the traits indicated by this discussion have never been given universal validation. The military studies of combat leadership, in which life and death hangs on the physical presence and proficiency of the leader, have only found one common denominator with any real frequency: leaders are tall, they stand above the group. The message from this is not to look for 7-foot ex-basketball centers but to realize that we are dealing with different types of leadership, determined by the needs of the group, as well as a self-imposing leadership that identifies and directs need fulfillment opportunities.

Some leadership traits seem to be the following:
1. Serves the needs of group over personal aspirations
2. Has superior knowledge about the group's interest

3. Inspires by creating positive group spirit and motivation without use of threat or fear
4. Is fair in treatment of individuals in the group
5. Recognizes individual differences and can unite for joint effort
6. Has clear concept of goals
7. Can clearly communicate information, give direction, and interpret goals
8. Has integrity of purpose, procedures, and principles of model behavior
9. Is sincerely dedicated and committed to group needs and goals
10. Projects a physical image of trust, confidence, capability, physical well being, responsibility, and personal care
11. Gets results in terms of group goals
12. Self sacrifices in interests of cause

Most of these traits directly relate to "Personal Power." — which is what the word "charisma" seems to be all about. That magnetic, dynamic, mystical power that a person can project to get others to do something or feel someway is labelled "charisma" but when unmasked, critically analyzed, appears to be constructed from many of the twelve traits.

It is personal power that is sought in leadership. Artificially, we can give power, symbolic power, to anyone in terms of authority. We can give political power through a title or position. Others inherit such position and power by rule of family or organizational tradition. But only personal power works without dependence on coercion — power, threats, or reprisal. In the classroom, failure in school is used to force group obedience; in the military, the firing squad; in the hippie commune, group ostracism.

When we place someone in a position of power by election or appointment, we try to select the individual with the most personal power for the specific group. The amount of personal power is inversely proportional to the amount of coercive power that must be allotted to a leadership position.

There are several cliches about leadership that must be given attention.

The first, "leaders are born, not made," is a fallacy. There are certain physical and emotional characteristics that set the foundation for leadership, but leaders have been made just as we have trained people and counseled people into new careers and life styles. The fallacy lies in accepting charisma as a mystique rather than analytically understanding its basic process.

The second cliche has a bit of controversy to it. The job of leadership is to train other leaders and thus generate more opportunities for activity and fulfillment. Related to this is the idealistic "good leaders inspire confidence in them by the people; great leaders inspire confidence of the people in themselves." The message here seems to be that great leaders are magnificently unselfish and non-indulgent while meeting all of the 12 traits and more, who willingly work themselves out of power by developing power elsewhere. If we expect power to be given away by leadership, then we must substitute positive reinforcements to replace it. A leader will magnify himself through others.

There is one final, comprehensive theoretical guideline to be remembered:

Leadership itself is a life style assumed by individuals to fulfill their personal needs and, if properly managed, provides greater opportunities of fulfillment for others than they could manage as individuals on their own.

LEADERSHIP ROLE IN RECREATION

"Who needs it? Leadership in recreation? I self-direct, run my own leisure play activities. I turn on my own TV set, go to spontaneous parties, pick up a tennis game when I want it. Just put the facilities there and I'm a free agent. Who needs somebody lock-stepping you through ritualized program?"

The pro in this business hears a lot of this independence articulation from all directions, all ages. He gets patted on the head and told that he's probably needed on the playground to keep the kids from killing each other.

There isn't any role in recreation services for bad or mediocre leadership. When we first emerged in the various environments to supervise and insure the proper use of facilities, people were glad to see us. Some talented pioneers of recreation programming organized experiences that added huge dimensions to play beyond what individuals could put together. But people can do for themselves when they're really stimulated to do so and occasionally the self-directed participant activity is better than what trained career experts can do. We are not denying the magical power of a grass roots, personally-motivated movement that follows from an individual's independence.

But professional leadership performing at its best can accomplish the following: (1) keep activities interesting only to a small segment of the public from becoming dominant, to the disadvantage of other interests and people; (2) assure a predictable quality and continued progress of program along scientifically validated and approved lines of health, safety, and personal fulfillment; (3) control selfish involvement of participants in the leadership of program that creates unprincipled bias and harm to others.

There are many who would describe the leadership role of recreation as a community stimulator, catalyst, someone who stirs up latent, existing brews. The role is seen as a facilitator, non-directive counselor, a match-maker of existing resources and interests. Such a role is seen as basically starting from where people are, what they're ready for, and assumes that they know what they want.

We agree with that concept of role, but it doesn't go far enough. It assumes too much about people and their ability to put their leisure lives in order. Roxy, the famous theatrical producer, said, "Don't give people what they want, give them something better." What they want is only a starting point, for there seems to be a tendency to want only what they expect from experience and know is possible. If you never have tasted sweet spring water, you never thirst for it. If you have never been skyrocketed to peak exhilaration by total absorption in a colossal professionally organized recreation activity you remain satisfied with diluted imitations of the real thing.

Recreation can play a gigantic role in creating the rewarding, balanced life only by forcefully creating and mounting magnificent programs. It has the direct production role of beginning an activity from scratch, creating interest, and making sure, by scientific and experienced methods, that the program will be successful in fulfilling people in its jurisdiction. That's leadership at its full, wide-open, flying-high best, and it is the role, the only role, that can be played if recreation is to achieve its place in environments where it may flavor and enhance life style.

Principles of Leadership

None of us wants to be doomed to repeating what has gone before. To avoid boring routine we often lead others by hunch, spontaneously reacting to the situation. And a creative leader might prosper by leading a group directly to its goals.

Most groups which form to pursue a mutual goal have some common characteristics. They consist of people, their needs, and a mutual goal that is more easily achieved in combination. If we believe in planning, then there are also ways of doing things that may be stabilized and repeated to give us predictable results.

Beyond charismatic leadership and a personal repertoire of techniques, are principles. Principles are not precisely leadership methods; rather they are guides to action. They help shape the individual acts of leaders in light of the experience of others. Professionals predict rather than speculate. Recreation leaders guided by principles may be surer of the results of their personal style and techniques.

We are by no means talking about conformity to tradition. Principles are not universal truths but beliefs which change with society. They serve society, the recreation field, the agency, the group, and the leader by guaranteeing progress and improvement. Without principles we would keep re-inventing the wheel each time we wanted to build a new vehicle.

Here are some of the more significant principles that a recreation program leader will find helpful.

1. *The type of leadership should fit the group needs.* If a group of mature adults convenes to plot the course of a car rally, a number of alternatives will arise out of the experience of the members. Leadership in this case can be only a moderating force to maintain democratic order through directing non-partisan communication.

A group of six-year-olds learning leaf printing in a crafts class may need a pretty heavy hand of authoritative leadership. The recreation leader here must teach some exact procedures and skills to prevent the wasting of time, materials, and equipment.

In these cases, the professional leader enjoys an assigned role of leadership. Since the power does not originate out of the group, assigned leadership can be easily rejected unless the correct style is matched to the group and situation.

2. *Leaders plan* with *rather than* for *people.* This principle should not be taken to mean a leader cannot devise a plan based upon indirect contacts and surveys of the group prior to consulting them. Groups respect the prepared leader who has done his homework and are receptive to his ideas. But they can not be bypassed or talked down to if the greatest support and effort is to be mustered.

We are talking of involvement here. When we leave the participants out of the planning process, either by failing to consider them or physically avoiding them in decision making, we cultivate the autocratic power and resistance to it. How much and what type of involvement? The group members must be capable of handling the responsibility. A good leader allots the amount of involvement they can successfully handle.

3. *The leader must know clearly at all times the exact goal(s) of the group and be able to relate and adjust them to the policies, philosophy, and procedures of his employing agency.*

It is often the most important function of the leader to be able to state and restate the goals. He keeps a clear and understandable target in front of the group. In doing this, he evaluates the impact on his agency of the achievement of the group's goals.

4. *The leader must recognize individual differences in people.* Each person is unique and requires individual consideration even if a leader is forced to use mass methods because of the size of his group. The talented should be allowed a chance to excel while the low achievers are left unpressured but aided. Everyone should achieve fulfillment to the point of his individual capacity and expectations.

Pre-testing situations help distinguish differences. The need profile analysis presented in this book is one effective way to categorize the differences.

5. *Leadership sets up an organized pattern of effort, a system by which the role of each group member is clearly defined and the means of achieving group goals are outlined.*

A system may consist of anything from the drafting of a constitution to working individually with each member on a rotating system until each can function effectively on his own.

6. *A leader recognizes that individual goals and group goals must be made the same to obtain cooperative effort.*

This is perhaps the greatest secret of all organizational success. As each individual is different, so are his goals. Hopefully, the leader learns the individual goals and attempts to harmonize them with a group goal. When they are congruent a group enjoys loyalty, cooperative behavior, pride and *esprit de corps.*

This is the leader's most difficult task. Conformity to the group means giving up deviant but creative behavior and ideas. The cult of the individual is a powerful force, and the leader must realize that program must be planned to accommodate it. Such program may have to be separate from the group activity to avoid ruthless, law-of-the-jungle competition. Dominant types of individuals often can not adjust to the group process and imposed leadership.

7. *A leader develops other leaders so that he can move on to different projects.*

The professional recreation leader often finds himself threatened by strong lay people who emerge in the course of activities. The volunteer leader especially presents a threat to the program careerist who sees him as a competitor for his status and job.

Such threatened leaders are generally unwilling to face new experiences or put out effort in a new undertaking. At such a point they may cease being leaders and become caretakers and protectors of their established power. Obviously program and projects are robbed of a chance to grow and improve with the infusion of new, different, and enthusiastic leadership.

"Work yourself out of a job" is an ageless guideline that applies here.

Keep replacing yourself and someone will find a more important position for you to expand your potential.

8. *Leadership opens up new interests for people besides fulfilling their expressed desires.*

Leadership that doesn't race ahead to pull people into new activities and interests is failing its most challenging assignment. People can easily self-direct themselves into established, stale recreational routines. Indeed, they never realize what joys lie undiscovered until led into an opportunity. Everybody's happy with hot dogs until they've had steak.

People have no compelling urges about things they do not know or have not sampled in their best form. This has been one of the great tragedies of recreation's development — the redundant programming to meet demand rather than exploring, experimenting, and creating demand.

9. *A leader anticipates difficulties and prepares for them.*

Nothing is more destructive to a well-meaning program activity than an accidental injury. Safety has to be a primary consideration for all programming. The point is not to let extreme concern for safety eliminate program possibilities but to prepare the activity in order to be reasonably safe.

A thorough leader studies past programs and investigates new and unknown projects. His ability to foresee hazards is one of the attributes of leadership. He issues special directives and devises equipment and rules to avoid upsets. He is successful because he makes as much happen as possible without deliberately endangering participants.

10. *A leader knows his own leadership objectives and continuously evaluates their achievement.*

Leaders must evaluate themselves along a continuum of points between complete success and complete failure. An objective may be met in part and the reason for the partial success identified. It is better to find a degree of success rather than accepting anything short of complete success as failure — the half-full glass versus the half-empty glass outlook.

Growth and improvement is a constant and demanding process and must have the benefits of conscientious evaluation.

11. *A leader maintains a broad repertoire of activity ideas and continuously adds to it.*

A good leader cannot simply be charming and compatible with people. He has to be encyclopedic about the lore and ways of recreation activity. He needs to understand and appreciate all forms of play expression, continuously working to be conversant with the new and unfamiliar. One way this is done is by establishing a need profile analysis on such activities.

But a recreation leader needs to know how far any activity can be carried in its advanced stages. For this reason the repertoire should have several interest areas in which the leader's knowledge and skill plunges deeply. To some extent he must be an expert and become thoroughly absorbed in some activities that will reveal in depth all the possibilities from novice to master for programming. He then can transfer this depth framework to any of a broad spectrum of activities he carries in his repertoire.

12. *The leader is concerned with people first and what happens to them as a result of activity.*

There is a tendency for recreation programmers to fall in love with super program ideas and force them to work despite the participants. It's possible for them to work out well if participants rise to the occasion.

But people should come first. Their readiness at a certain level of skill or understanding is the real guide for good program leadership. The level can be altered by special adjusting program — classes and practice — but the leader gambles on losing momentum if he makes people fit the program he prefers.

13. *A leader takes pressure off participants so that playing is made easier and more comforting.*

The job of a leader is to make everything easier for his followers. He doesn't achieve this by placing great stress on them, setting up impossible goals, or driving them to upgrade skills and knowledge through fear.

It is through the art of leadership — the manipulation of incentives, compelling devices, persuasions — that he helps participants move easily and comfortably through recreation experiences. Since leaders desire great achievement for participants, they are always dangerously close to the line. One careless instance of pushing may push them out of carefree, joyous play into pressured work.

But we walk that line very closely because deep commitment to any activity must naturally woo the same demons of the human psyche as labor does. The deadly seriousness of children's athletics is one place in which we have teetered dangerously.

14. *Leadership is an opportunity to serve others above any vested interests or ulterior motives.*

A leader exists because the situation and people involved in that situation need direction. The job and reward is in being needed to serve others. A leader generally fails when any personal interest beyond service predominates.

These principles are a mere handful from long lists compiled for leadership success in recreation. Lists tend to end up filed in notebooks somewhere, never handy when needed most. But they must be read at least once, and from them a way of thinking established.

So, put these principles in your cerebral blender and make your own frame of reference — but get one.

47

Techniques of Leadership

All leaders have their own ways of working with people to accomplish things. If we were sure there were precise ways that every leader could use we would call them methods. They aren't that exact, however. There are many ways that work for some and not for others.

Since any of these ways might work with your leader personality in a particular situation, we will describe a few here. You'll have to decide whether you want to experiment with them and build your own style. Not being exact, but individualized, we refer to them as "techniques."

1. Building Advance Support

Divide and conquer might be the negative way of looking at this technique. Most leaders get rattled when they look back and see the troops running in the other direction. The situation has to be one in which you're convinced by fact and experience that your direction is right in terms of group good. If so, isolate the group opinion leaders in advance and convince them if you can. One additional ally can do the trick and keep the group from resisting because they feel the leader is imposing something on them.

Take a teenage dance where the participants want as little light as possible. The reasons for restricting the participants in their wish is more easily imparted on a one-to-one basis and you can create a supporting confederate by the confidence you've placed in him.

Speak to an influential peer leader and advise him of any safety law that conflicts with the lighting wanted by the group. Let him sway the group.

2. The Leading Question Technique

Leaders can railroad but not ramrod. By this we mean that a leader usually melts resistance if he doesn't try to force one idea on a group. The system is to provide two or more alternative choices about an activity or project and avoid the group hassling about the doing or not doing of the activity at all. It takes all of their energy to make the choice.

The leader bypasses the decision about the total project and gets the participants involved in choosing how it is to be done. For example, a leader has analyzed a need for a dance activity at his center and asks the eligible individuals if they prefer square or modern dancing, avoiding the public decision on having a dance at all.

3. Inventive Involvement

We all want to be needed. To be a spectator, an outsider, a sheep, in any activity has a demeaning quality. Pre-mix baking recipes still let the cook break an egg. Good leaders invent roles for every participant by a wise distribution of existing tasks. The clever part, the real technique, comes in making the most trivial involvement seem important.

For example, after a craft class, no matter how much individual cleanup is encouraged, there is still a mess. Try appointing monitors or assistants — titles do wonders for elevating trivia — from those who aren't getting much out of the class. It's the old passing *hors d'oeuvres* at a party trick or creating equipment managers for ball clubs. Passing out things, keeping score, even shagging balls, can involve many who feel like a giant unwanted thumb in activities.

4. What's-his-name Avoidance

Everybody is somebody. As a leader, you don't have to like them but you'd better be interested in them.

Many of us are terrible on names. Most of us are if we are lazy about it. If a name has escaped you or never was captured, it probably wasn't very important to you.

The leader who has to play Mr. Mumbles or call "hey, you" when addressing people is probably not interested in people. What the self-centered, activity-centered leader has to do is develop a recognition system.

First of all, explore everyone with whom you spend time. Dig for something that interests you: What is the person's favorite book of all time or what person in history would he like to be? Somewhere there is an identifying quality that will lock him in your memory. Don't associate the person with the situation in which you've encountered him since you will forget who he is when he shows up in other circumstances.

Actually, the single individual is easy. In recreation we take on large groups all at once. It's part of recreation to take time to make a game out of the name and interest investigation. It helps to take notes on the exact pronunciation of names, identifying physical aspects, and unique interests. Writing the name down helps to lock it in memory.

This all takes practice. Do it every chance you get. Don't miss any opportunity to address someone fully, such as, "Ok, Charlie Broomspit, the spoon collector, let's see you roll one." If you dead end, stall. Just say, "Oh, you're —" and when he fills it in then come on strong as if you knew it all the time.

5. Plead Ignorance

There is no excuse for not knowing everything about everything in recreation. That is, if you're a top notch leader and keep boning up all the time.

If you get caught in a situation in which you don't know the skill, the rule, or whatever and the group is looking on intently, take the human route. Plead ignorance without feeling put down.

If someone in the activity is clued in, then let him shine — but control the glow. Show what a good interviewer you are. You can actually make it appear as if you were dispensing the information if you take command with penetrating, professional questions.

On the other hand, maybe no one in the group knows. Don't bluff on anything crucial or there will be a backlash later. Don't bluff at all if you want to be a true leader. Instead, meet the situation with an organized, sincere plan for discovering the missing information. Once again make a carry-over game out of it, and go on with the activity using some momentary ground rules or substitute skill.

People like to discover that the whole system isn't rigidly memorized and that there is room for error and imperfections.

We're talking about the exception here. A veteran leader builds his repertoire, and he continues thoroughly to know all activities after he leaves his face-to-face duties and becomes a master programmer.

6. Firing Enthusiasm

Nothing lights our fires like an enthusiastic leader. His zest keeps saying, "Let's do it," whatever it is.

You can't fake that kind of enthusiasm, although back-slapping extroverts may manage to ho-ho-ho their way on occasion. Enthusiasm is simply honest interest. It's not even professional.

By that we mean professional in the sense of objective systemization and coolly predictable behavior. Exuberance, however, can make a participant out of a leader — to the point his personal needs and ego prevent his helping real participants.

A good leader has to live through the joy and activity he brings others. It is vicarious, but it's also a feeling experienced by a chosen few. A leader is a leader when he is able to experience enthusiasm because those for whom he is responsible are excited about their activities.

Part of the technique for sparking enthusiasm is to keep an activity balanced and timed. "Balanced" means mixing in different experiences to keep all interests ignited. "Timed" means beginning an activity when the participants are ready for it and stopping it before they quit enjoying it. There are no precise signs to tell you when an activity is going stale. You must watch the mood of your opinion leaders, for if they drop out the group goes, too. It is better to stop too soon than too late — leave them wanting

49

more, and next time enthusiasm will be an automatic response for the group.

7. Short-term Dictator/Long-term Catalyst

This may not be a technique at all, for it is a full-blown principle if begun correctly. Then again, it has much to do with styles of leadership.

The one-shot or short term experience doesn't permit the development of leadership from the group. In such cases a very directive style must be used.

The long-term activity provides a chance for participants to take over responsibilities of leadership. The leader moves toward a catalyst role, stimulating hidden, untried talents among the participants.

The technique that best accommodates both situations is to survey in advance what results are expected by participants. Unless wholly spontaneous, short- and long-term activities can be anticipated and the participants analyzed. An advance file on every participant might be a heavy duty for a one-session terminal activity but the clues for pacing leadership are enormous.

Carry a profile card on every participant into the activity, and body language and alienated behavior will be interpreted easily. A leader may want to make notes on the card to guide future contacts with the individual participants. An outside visitor is another valuable source of information to add to such files, especially regarding his observed reactions to the leader's style.

8. Discipline and Control

Recreation is by nature a loose arrangement, subject to people's voluntary participation. The more rigid an experience becomes, tightly bound with rules, the less it seems like play.

That is the dilemma. We strive for a relaxed, freely expressed happening, one that is ideal for chaos and disorder. To exert a harsh, forceful control over behavior in the recreation situation is to make it restrictive, like work.

Discipline has become more program than activity in many recreation situations. In some cases this has been unavoidable because of the surrounding environment, but in others we have lost good program to discipline management requirements because effective discipline techniques were not employed in earlier activities.

Discipline is required when some participant behavior threatens injury or prohibits the achievement of group goals. The leader has a responsibility to protect other members in the group.

Liking and having a rapport with the participants is a good foundation for keeping a light-handed order. But there must be an unambiguous explanation of all ground rules so that participants know what behavior is expected. Usually this is sufficient.

When it isn't, the leader has the choice of several techniques to maintain an orderly system.

You can isolate the trouble factor, the person creating the havoc. Remove the person from the activity so that it can proceed normally. Don't leave it at that, however. Find out the causes of the behavior and try to resolve them if you can.

Another way is to let the group resolve the trouble. Explain that they have the choice of cancelling out or shaping up. Gyms have blacked out because the participants couldn't put together an orderly environment. If only a few are making the trouble the peers might force order if the responsibility is thrown upon them, since group pressure is a powerful technique.

In some cases, recreation leaders use loss of privileges or punishment to handle problems. It works but not without creating new problems. The leader must be sure it is not levied vindictively. The punishment should bear a relationship to the offense and follow it closely in time. For example, a craft class that misuses materials or paints the walls can be asked to scrub clean the entire craft center or be denied participation again until they do so. A word of caution: taking activity away from a disorderly participant may be giving him brooding time to manufacture a grudge or cultivate more of the problems behind his bad behavior. Punishment is a technique or discipline that easily backfires.

Brute force has become popular and practical in many crisis centers of recreation. It becomes an expeditious if temporary technique for squeezing a bad situation back in shape. In a way, it works on the bigger-bully concept. The leader maintains control by muscle power but that only lasts as long as he is around. It is a technique whose lasting value is questionable and certainly limited to young male activity, if acceptable at all. It is presented here because it exists as a reality, a technique being relied on for short-term control but perhaps creating even greater problems for the future.

Problems are not easily resolved by any techniques, only contained for the moment. The worst action by a leader is to have to bring in a higher authority, either his supervisor or the police. He has probably dug a grave for his own authority in the future.

Nothing prevents disorder like a good leader employing good principles and techniques to stage an activity that has participants too busy playing to disrupt.

We found techniques harder to uncover and relate than principles, perhaps because techniques are personal and individual. It's situational problem solving in the final analysis, i.e., common sense. If we've been able to nail down a few techniques as formulae, it's only because we can recite actual cases out of experience and thereby define them.

The Volunteers

They come for the best of reasons and they come for the worst of reasons. Too often the professional uses them without caring what the reasons are. People always come forward to help without expecting a salary. These are the pure volunteers, the eager and easy army of people who like to serve others. They should constitute the most valuable resource of any recreation program, but we can not be naive in assuming a goodness about all volunteerism.

Historically, helping friends and neighbors was part of a large social framework to accomplish ends that one individual or family could not do alone. Barn raising and crop harvesting required community action to beat the weather. It was both a way of life and an organizational technique. It was fun. The work was interlaced with singing, dancing, horseplay, food, and games. Some of our best big events today follow these same devices.

But modern society is specialized, and today's congestion makes man seek privacy by avoiding informal involvements. If he can, he hires things done for him; if he can't afford services, he resents and is suspicious when they are given to him. Because of this suspicion, volunteerism is no longer the good-natured, spontaneous outflowing of goodwill it once was. The red tape and screening thrown up today often makes the act of volunteering an insulting ordeal.

Professional recreation programmers have recognized this situation recently. They are paying attention to this service-to-others need in a much different way than they did before. Now they are treating it as a valued end in itself, an actual program activity area that serves some people who are not adequately provided for in the standard program based on self-indulgence.

Reasons to Program

But along with this enlightened programming of volunteerism as activity in itself comes the shallower reasons for using volunteers: cheap labor. But penny saving through the use of incompetent amateurs can cause dollars' worth of damages.

Some pros weed out the challengers from the participant pack by making them volunteer aids. It's an age-old technique to reverse pressure coming from a vocal wise-guy, a self-propelling expert, and turn the irritant into a buffer. Some participants outclass their peers in knowledge and skill, having become involved by accident or intent. They can destroy an activity, event, or meeting from within unless they are dumped or placed in a different role. The pro who decides to share the throne and let these super participants share some of the fire directed against him could be giving power to someone wholly incapable of using it for the good of the group or sponsoring organization.

One programmer, when asked about his success in isolating trouble-makers by placing them in vulnerable volunteer staff positions, gave this caution, "You're rewarding bad behavior, of course, when you recognize an attention-seeking individual as someone special. It could encourage some latent resistance to authority in others of the group. The key to it is isolation. Get the difficult prodigy into a situation not affecting the whole group or situation, where he can't poison the whole barrel if his motives turn out to be malicious. Let him help someone falling behind in the class or activity. It takes care of two extremes that way. But keep an eye on him because only close supervision can prevent a runaway disaster."

Another reason behind the use of volunteers is a valid if precarious one: There's no better training ground for a career recreation programmer. In fact, like most social services, recreation was entirely in the hands of volunteers in the pioneer days. Academic training programs for recreation focus a great deal of importance on volunteer field work experience. The precarious aspect is that serious harm can be done by a bumbling amateur. Medical students first try cadavers, and engineers build scale-model bridges. In recreation we use case studies, but we all know that the real experience is the master teacher. But while recreation programming is emerging as a respected field, we can't permit error in the interest of training.

Reasons for Volunteering

It is with the volunteer himself that lies the clue to our methods of handling him. If you are concrete about the abstract notion of altruism, a rational analysis is possible. Noble acts can frequently be traced to a need to express something or compensate for something.

One of the most important motivations in behavior is the need to discover one's own identity through the needs of others. It is proof that we exist when others call out for us. Devotion to abstract causes, things, or animals can not be felt by many as strongly as fulfilling the needs of other people. Whether it is a self-sacrificing love for others, or a lust for power, or a combination, the volunteer at the activity leadership level receives an identity reward. It is not selfless, but it is not necessarily selfish.

A second reason for volunteering is to pursue a recreation interest in a deeper, more meaningful way. When one's dedication to a hobby or sport becomes nearly obsessive, every outlet for participation is usually exploited. Fanatics about an activity or an event will fall upon envelope stuffing or master instructional techniques with abandon. Just as jockeys too large to ride the races shovel hay to stay close to the track, ex-competitor performers stay involved through volunteering services. "The smell of the greasepaint, the roar of the crowd" syndrome is a mighty magnet for attracting effort and support.

A third incentive for volunteering comes from people preferring non-monetary rewards, such as special benefits and privileges. Volunteers are permitted to go into sections of a facility from which the general public is excluded. They may use organization equipment and materials for personal purposes after normal operating hours. They wear identifying uniforms and badges and call professional staff by their first names. Each organization, however, differs in benefits allowed volunteers. Special privileges, though, are a valid reward if they do not detract, destroy, or take money from the operating budget.

From another reward standpoint, the "paycheck" for services is issued somewhere else. Students serve to get grades at school or pad their job resumes. Various clubs and service organizations conduct merit systems that require members to volunteer time and effort in order to rise in the organizational hierarchy. The Boy Scouts have made volunteer service an integral part of their program through their merit badge program, best illustrated by the classic scene of a scout helping an old lady across the street.

Status beyond any merit system may be another less important reason. Lonely people will sometimes volunteer to do almost anything to be involved with people.

To understand the motives of the volunteer is an important task for the programmer who wishes to master this massive energy resource for program expansion.

53

Recruitment and Selection

The world is a house of cards, full of con men and hoaxes. The good professional can't plead ignorance if he's used volunteers without carefully screening them.

Most pros get soured on volunteers because they often must invent work and organize special situations for people they can neither control nor depend upon to be regular.

The first step in a system is to list those functions in the program that can be entrusted to volunteers, that is, those functions you can afford to have fail. In doing this, a programmer organizes himself as well by setting up priorities and deadlines. The following is an example:

First priority tasks:

1. Publicity releases (staff)
2. Poster distribution (volunteers)
3. Equipment inventory (volunteers)
4. Inventory reports (staff)

Second priority tasks:

1. Bicycle owners' survey (volunteers)
2. Bicycle trail budget (staff)
3. Regional bicycle safety conference (staff and volunteers)

There is no exacting format, and each programmer must use his own knowledge and discretion. The major point is to have the tasks in readiness to assign. A rule of thumb might be to designate as volunteer those functions and tasks that enhance the program, but which do not have the organization's basic operation dependent upon them.

Ordering priorities should reveal special programs that either you've wanted to try or which are defunct because the necessary special leadership disappeared. Ordering may also show some rather general and continuous tasks which do not appeal to the professional staff and consequently never have been done correctly, if at all. With these dimensions in mind, good recruitment decisions can be made.

Many programmers use newspaper releases to call for volunteers for specific activities. Special sections of newspapers often serve as bulletin boards for bringing projects and volunteers together. Special interest clubs and service clubs are ready reservoirs of talent, usually seeking project involvement. Parents of participants in youth activities have always been prime targets and make up the bulk of the taxi service so necessary to keep recreation's transportation systems operating. Most programmers sample their own brew by watching for leadership potential in their own program activities. Using people already involved with your program gives you a head start on analyzing potential volunteers. It also means generally that such a volunteer would already have an orientation to the agency and its programs. There are of course the schools which, with their novice student recreators, do a fair job of bringing new leaders into the field.

Selection procedures are a matter of situational choice. Obviously, if a very special skill is demanded, such as knowledge of ceramics, a very strict guideline is set up automatically. What we might be able to universalize is the character of the individual and his ability to relate to people. At this point, most of our expectations of professional leaders is applicable. The volunteer, of course, is usually not expected to be involved as broadly or intensely with program and people as the career person.

The following are a few general considerations that may serve in a selection system:

1. Personal resume on volunteer
2. Interview with all concerned staff
3. Police check for criminal record
4. Observable try-out experience prior to any commitment

If you're satisfied with the volunteer's potential, discuss exact arrangements with him. If possible, set a short-term commitment with a definite termination date since you don't fire volunteers as you would professionals. The waters stay muddied for a long time when agency/volunteer associations go bad because volunteers generally are from the community, so that any hostility permeates the environment.

Training and Reinforcement

Actually, a volunteer ought to receive orientation to the job and agency on par to that of a paid employee. This should be true for training also, although professionals will already have advanced knowledge and skills.

Training should place special emphasis on safety and liability, discipline procedures, and the limits of their authority. It is generally around these negative areas that volunteer services go afoul.

Volunteers may undergo changes in their motivations after a number of months of service. The original glow of being part of a meaningful enterprise may become mundane. The first elations about power, status, and special privileges often become diluted with regularity and repetition. Some professionals solve this problem by constantly altering jobs and assignments, using a progressive system of awarding privileges. They may also stage recognition events, ranging from mentioning a volunteer's name in a news release to an annual banquet honoring volunteers. Certificates of service are always good, but nothing serves as well or as unfailingly as the sincere *thank you* delivered at the right time — as close to the act as possible. It's a phrase that never bores anyone by repetition. Professional programmers should be sensitive to the volunteer's needs.

There is one very difficult decision that the professional probably must make at some point with all volunteers, i.e., whether to hire them or fire them. Volunteers begin to compare their situations with the salaried staff. They feel disadvantaged if they discover that they are doing parallel or superior work to the paid workers.

A good professional will try to avoid this situation by programming his volunteers and keeping them satisfied. But even with conscientious supervision, he will probably have to sever or seduce.

Seduction usually means a paycheck. The volunteer changes spots and is hired, which is tricky business. If the pay is token in all likelihood the ex-volunteer will turn into a disgruntled employee. The situation produces either a restless volunteer or an underpaid worker. No volunteer should be hired because he was a good volunteer, but because there is a good paying staff position to be filled which he can fill.

55

To sever is to drop the volunteer gracefully. If termination dates are long past and the volunteer is causing the agency difficulty because of feeling unrewarded, then the professional must let the volunteer go. This is never easy, but sometimes discontinuing the volunteer's activity for a short period will take away the stigma of firing him. Another possibility is to hire someone really superior in all ways — a recognized professional meeting all agency's personnel requirements — to operate the program controlled by the volunteer.

The greatest hazard is to have a volunteer who can not be topped and who has established a personality cult and power base in the agency which protects him from any attack. It should not reach such a point under good supervision, but if it has then the agency will have to live with it. The powerful volunteer's program should be isolated, at the least, and permitted to roll without contaminating the rest of the programs.

It is not absolutely necessary to use volunteers. If you don't use volunteers, however, three dimensions are shut off for your program. First, growth and expansion will always be limited by the dollars available. Secondly, an excellent staff recruitment opportunity is denied And thirdly, many people who receive their greatest fulfillment from serving others will be denied that fulfillment.

Chapter 4

PROGRAM IS A PLAN

INTRODUCTION TO PLANNING

Planning is an extremely difficult subject. It's not the exclusive methodology of recreation programming, for it is a vast technology of its own.

We will not handle it in depth here; we will discuss those aspects that pertain directly to recreation.

A plan is just an orderly system, thought out in advance, for doing something. It's often a better plan if it's written. If planning as a process is thinking ahead to predict and control events, then the plan may be described as a map to direct the production of the recreation experiences.

There are three ways that a plan comes into being for program. First, there is the *reaction plan*. This is essentially a passive approach in which the programmer waits until people come in with ideas, demands, and complaints. He reacts, leans with the wind, and conforms to what the demands seem to be.

The second plan is the *investigation plan*. This is derived from active research, from trying to learn people's desires and building a plan from those expressed desires. Interest inventories have formed the bulk of recreation effort in this approach. Only in a few cases has there been refined, in-depth probing which seeks deeply seated attitudes and needs rather than the superficial expressions of the moment. Typically, a recent local survey of teen-agers showed horseback riding as their primary recreation interest. Yet none of them was riding at the time, and when riding was finally programmed only three youths in the community enrolled.

The third plan is the *creative plan*. It has elements from the two preceding, assimilating expressed demands and analyzing propensities and desires in depth; it also importantly adds the programmer's expert and comprehensive experiences. With the creative plan, the programmer constructs a program that meets people's needs and exceeds their expectations.

Only gypsies and hippies have been able to put together a functional system of living life as it comes. Most of us are neither trained nor talented enough to cope without a master plan in one form or another. We need to determine goals which will produce the best lives possible and identify the means for obtaining those goals with the least waste of time, energy, and emotions.

We advocate a blue-sky idealism; shooting for the stars, dreaming up the super program as a starting point to master planning, i.e., the creative plan. The flaw to this approach resides in the programmer himself: Can he keep reaching for the perfect program without becoming discouraged? Because there is no set format for the universally perfect program, many recreation programmers try to pacify by using second-rate social functions to manipulate people's muscles and minds to ready them for the more serious game of life, work, learning, and therapy.

The perfect program is not the long printed list of possible activities — the massive collection of games, hobbies, and fun things — that have been associated with recreation programs in the past. This is only one source of guiding information. It cites everything but says nothing. But we have a start with those lists. They remind us to investigate possibilities that we have not yet programmed.

To make these lists meaningful it is necessary for the programmer to exercise his social scientist function. Each listed activity must be measured to rate its value in fulfilling the needs of different individuals, its seasonal and geographical appropriateness, and its group size effectiveness. Ultimately, some valid, acceptable charts may emerge from the research to serve as effective tools. But the programmer uses his experience and personal research to set the values.

The master plan begins with the complete, unabridged, encyclopedic collection of every possible human experience that may be improved by programming and which falls within the leisure category, i.e., which is non-survival-oriented, freely chosen, personally constructive, socially acceptable, and pleasurable.

The master plan is rarely an operational plan or working model; rather, it is an ultimate goal kept in the top desk drawer to remind the programmer of *what could be* rather than what is. The master plan should be as great and as perfect as the best creative mind can imagine. It represents maximum expectations rather than minimum requirements.

To strive for less than the perfect program is the individual programmer's concession to mediocrity. No human enterprise moves ahead by its directors standing still or walking backwards.

The Overlays — Major Limiting Factors

We may have overwhelmed ourselves with our super program since our analytical listings of experiences might easily resemble the telephone directory of a big city.

The job now is to become a kind of mapmaker. We must plan program to meet specific situations. The place, the people, and the time are broad areas of differences that determine the scope and nature of the program. Because there are many other differences that influence our planning, we will simplify the course of action, as in mapmaking, by using these differences as overlays. When one wants to locate the parks of a city, a plastic overlay with imprinted symbols is placed over the master map or, as in this case, the master program plan. In this way, we concentrate our analyses on one element at a time.

Needs There are no established sequential priorities in considering these overlays, but we believe that we must place the need profile of the people in the community service area first and foremost. If there is an existing need from which interest may emerge the ambitious programmer will make the program happen in spite of other limiting factors.

Budget Scratch an administrator and he'll bleed budget. Budget is the major problem for people who manage recreation services, both profit and non-profit ones. This is always an easy rationalization for not attempting greater program expansion and improvement — lack of money.

The money in question might be for the programmer's salary, or the administrator's, or other activity personnel; or for special facilities, equipment, special insurance, or extraordinary promotion. It *is* important, and any programmer with carte blanche resources is surely blessed. But recreation program sincerely desired and based on clearly identified needs can be financed by various manipulations.

The manipulations are something that have to be worked out within the agency's policy and managing authority. Doing without essentials or even refinements is not the best device for overcoming a small budget. Inferior attempts that are doomed to failure and that could discourage future efforts may be worse than no attempt. The best approach that has emerged recently for non-profit agencies is the participant or use fee which finances the programming. It means a program can be activated on a self-sustaining basis with those who use it paying the tangible costs incurred beyond normal operating expenditures. These costs may involve outside specialists, the leasing of facilities and equipment, or the cost of supplies.

The profit-oriented recreation service is definitely more limited by budget because its operation is already based on a fees-and-charges concept with the cost of facilities, management, and other intangibles pro-rated into the fees — fees that must be reasonable enough to compete with parallel non-profit programs and still yield a profit.

Recreation agencies, whether profit or non-profit, need to recognize the public relations and goodwill dividends of certain deficit program activities. Such activities may be worth programming at a loss in order to boost public awareness, attitude, and support that in the end cultivate financial backing for the total operation. Additionally, the profit and non-profit agencies must be intelligently aware of each other and not create destructive competition which confuses the public and makes the job for each other tougher. The solution in many cases is a compromise, with the profit agency conducting the program in cooperation with or on behalf of the non-profit organization.

Facilities The big problem for most recreation services is investment in some type of recreation facility or facilities. A recreation department that inherits or builds itself around an elaborate multi-sports facility is pressured to maintain a program that puts available facilities to optimum use.

If there are swimming pools, golf course, tennis courts, or dance studios with mirrors and bars, it is considered gross negligence not to fill them with programmed activity. The seaside cities are only now recognizing the ocean as a dominant facility-area in the life styles of their citizens. Surfing and open-water swimming programs are booming.

The major difficulty for most agencies is building to a trend or current conditions. Once an elaborate, one-interest, specialized, costly-to-maintain structure or development goes in, it places a demand on programming that can run counter to other major factors, such as population needs and budget. A community gets very big, or very small, becomes a ghost town, or the mean age distribution shifts from senior adults to young children — such changes can render a facility obsolete. Trampolines had a boom period and permanent installations were built on a commercial basis; today only vacant lots with rectangular holes remain. Many a softball diamond has been uprooted to adjust to the specific dimensions of youth baseball.

A safety device has been to design multi-purpose fields and buildings, making them adaptable through use of artificial turfs and mobile installations. But a neuter impression may emerge from this, with the facility-area losing the glamor of being a special place exclusively designed for one interest.

The programmer's single-minded effort has been to obtain as many special places as possible to add importance to activities. But a good programmer can make anything do, adapting weedy space and bare-wall rooms and asphalt parking lots to a program he believes in and really wants to put on despite space and place limitations.

60

Personnel We exhausted a chapter on leadership. Boats don't sail themselves and gymnasiums don't become orderly by fulfilling wildcat activities. Program at its absolute best depends on professional leadership — the personnel of the agency.

Personnel must have leadership ability or the agency will fail. Program planners must know the talent, knowledge, and skills that the regular staff possess. When all support elements are saying "go" for an activity about to be programmed, the absence of a knowledgeable, skilled, and interested regular staff man may delay or even derail good intentions and efforts. It is a fine, precarious line that employers walk in hiring the generalist programmer who has a broad repertoire or the specialist who is capable of mounting only an intricate, high quality, large participation, single activity. The dilemma forces many agencies into short term, seasonal hiring practices if their programs are highly sensitive and susceptible to changes.

But whatever the procedure followed in hiring — permanent generalist, permanent specialist, or short term combinations — the programmer must look to the personnel overlay in deciding on activities. In some instances, shaping program to the leader available has had splendid results. Inspired, enthusiastic personnel who are fresh and deep into a new recreation interest for them, or experienced old veterans of an interest who can relive the joys through others — these leaders can produce exciting experiences that will attract and hold participants despite the adaptations that must be done with the other elements.

An interested leader who possesses all the techniques of leadership will give you a winning program activity built around his interest. If all of the other elements are going for an activity a specialist is not an absolute necessity for a smashing success. An inspired generalist can pull it off.

Equipment There are many activities that require elaborate uniforms, equipment, and facilities. What is a bowling center without bowling balls or the copper enameling class without a kiln? Bridge sessions really need cards and card tables, and it would be best to have chips for a poker night. Youth tackle football requires a vast, involved array of pads and protectors, jerseys, and helmets. The tumbling class needs mats for safety.

The trend with equipment parallels the facility/activity use fee insofar as the burden is placed on the participants. They furnish their own tennis racquets and balls. Basketball players buy their own shoes and uniforms; baseball teams furnish balls, bats, and uniforms. The dancers buy leotards, the party goers bring their own bottles, noise makers, and pot-luck food. People expect to provide their toys for personal play.

There is difficulty in participant provision caused by poverty or the failure to bring equipment to an activity. Then there are some weird items that an agency must provide to insure standards of unbiased participation, such as a discus or track hurdles. Or a lathe in a woodworking group or a piano for the dance class, where one item can serve the entire group.

Equipment is a less restrictive overlay, overlapping with budget and facilities to some degree. But it is frustrating when the programmer is not sure he'll be able to get a big hawser rope for the picnic tug-o-war, the horses for the trail ride, or tools for the leather-working class. Someway, somehow, the good leader can resourcefully dredge up get-by equipment, but there have been horrifying disasters when the equipment failed to materialize at zero hour.

Climate Every so often there's a film director who has Indians do a rain dance for a scene, and then it rains the whole production out.

Recreation programmers press their luck in less dramatic ways. Campfires at high noon in summer programs can be scheduled, and they often work out well, but beware of places like Death Valley or even Palm Springs where 110° can be regular. Big-city activities are learning to respond docilely to smog alerts, when the physical sports program goes into hibernation and passive indoor experiences are substituted.

There are an amazing number of climatic conditions that fry, wilt, freeze, dampen or wash away the participatory spirit. Unless you're striking for membership in the Polar Bear Club, a dip in the northern regions' cold waters is an absolutely paralyzing experience. Mid-day in the humid southern regions may be good for siestas but little else.

For safety reasons, for health reasons, for property-damage reasons, and for mood reasons, a planner must realize that seasons and climates are harsh regulators of the super program plan. Play on a soaked field and you not only jeopardize participants but do long term damage to turf and equipment. We open our swimming pools to the biggest attendance program of them all — in the summer season when the sun makes water the best escape environment there is. We ski and ice skate when the snows come, one of the climate/

61

seasons that we await for positive reasons. March winds are positive too, and we plan our kite making and flying around them.

There is no escaping weather, seasons, and climates. They're vaguely predictable, insofar as we have a general awareness of a period when we set up cancellation-and-postponement procedures or operate under a rain-or-shine-we-play policy. The good planner sets up alternate activities and moves in and out of doors mentally in his planning of activities, subject to climatic conditions.

Calendar There are certain times that are dictated by the calendar when activities are traditionally expected and responded to. Halloween, for example, is a prime recreation happening, red-lettered in to take place October 31, rain or shine. There are many holidays which inspire certain activities which celebrate them. The wise programmer capitalizes on the blooming spirit of festivity inspired by holidays to unfurl his big, extraordinary efforts, i.e., the special events.

But recurrent, regular activities are also traditionally calendared, and it is rare to see any agency attempt to activate football, or baseball, or basketball out of their normal seasons. There's a danger, too, in letting recurring programs, classes, and activity series cut into holidays when people generally change the pace and nature of their daily routine.

Besides the calendar, which coordinates planning on a yearly and seasonal basis, there is the clock, which establishes certain times when specific activities have the greatest potential for success. This is very situational because each community has a time lifestyle, perhaps three different sets of peoples whose leisure shifts run morning, afternoon, or evening. Their work and sleep patterns affect their time of readiness and availability. The planner who assumes a norm can end up neglecting large segments of the population.

There is strong support for a right time and wrong time for certain activities, based not so much on participant availability, climate or promotion, but rather on emotional atmosphere. Adult parties work best at night, perhaps because people expect to be indoors when it's dark. Story hours click best after a lunch period, housewives' bowling leagues thrive in the morning, and baseball games are at peak excitement in the afternoon. Maybe there's no magic at all to timing, just cold hard facts of given communities' life styles, but a planner has to keep all doors open to possibilities.

Local Customs Wherever you plan a program you must know the territory. Your repertoire of activities, your super program plan, is headed for its Waterloo if you ignore local customs.

A hard-line church community — and there are still a few of those left — is going to resist any wild Sunday programs you decide to initiate. There are still many places where Saturday is walk-gawk-and-shop-downtown night, and any scheduled recreation program fires a blank. Cruising, driving cars up and down a designated street to see and be seen, is a Friday night way of life for many teenagers almost anywhere.

In ethnic sections there are Catholic holidays, Old Country philosophies, strange foods, crazy rules for common games, fierce pride, fanatic patriotism, free love, street brawling, extreme discipline, and local events that have been around for fifty years or more.

You can do everything right in your program planning, but it won't be successful if the local situation has customs in its life style that reject it. It is best to ask around on local customs before drafting final plans.

Male/Female — A Fading Overlay Differences are beautiful. They pave the way for change of pace and unique programming. They are undesirable if they tend to promote a sense of inferiority or restrict the opportunities of anyone to explore all recreational outlets. The programmer is justified and encouraged to apply these differences when they positively contribute to the enhancement of program.

Recreation program has undergone repeated surgery with the changing position of women. As quickly as woman rejected traditional restrictions, threatened man invented new restrictions, as flimsily constructed as movie sets, giving a false front of stability and reality. When the tedious home chores of children, cooking, and cleaning were reduced by machines, and women found mobility by hoisting their skirts and entering industry, recreation had to recognize woman's claims. No bastions are left unstormed today, and only caricatures of past male supremacy burlesque themselves in a world grown up. A few sweat and liniment gyms or grimy pool halls hang by decaying teeth to the male myth, repulsing all but a few insecure spittoon types. Even McSorley's, the last male-only New York bar where, for over a hundred years, trespassing, red-faced women exited to thunderous male applause, succumbed when a female task force sat down and replied to the objections with wet Bronx cheers.

Poker parties, boys-nights-out, the smokers, and stag parties are carried out in sheepish fashion; the all-male get-together now has more chance of being viewed as gay rather than heroically masculine as the male and female stereotypes are liberated.

But male mastery and double standards are still afloat and will continue to plague the programmer who has an all-comers approach. The Puerto Rican *viernes*, social, Social Friday, when males, married and single, spin wheels, belt booze, and try to establish or reestablish a men-only recreation existence is one of the remaining strong examples. Traditional Anglo-Saxon males now express their sex prejudices more subtly.

Laying social tradition aside for the moment, assuming the programmer is aware of cultural carryovers but does not necessarily accept or promote them, attention must be given to the possibility that physical limitations may be a basis for different programming of the sexes. There has been extensive research applied to this possibility and there is organized support for recognizing limitations, which says that a big bosom and throwing things aren't compatible. Menstrual cramps don't contribute to record-making physical outlays. But then these are foreseeable handicaps, perhaps more psychological than physiologically restricting. A fat boy doesn't throw too well either, nor does a mentally or physically depressed male rise to great efforts in recreational activity. We need to seriously consider setting aside the male-female overlay.

The Unforeseen and Flexibility

It's been said in many ways but it is universally true: *whatever can happen is*

63

going to happen. No matter how well you shape the plan, measuring and blue-printing specifications, the unforeseen springs eternal.

The crowd you didn't expect, the shortage of prizes, the rain storm, the obscure religious holiday, the stick-in-the-eye injury, the out-of-the-blue participant indifference — they could all happen at once. Of course, the tough lock-step planners claim a plan has everything, even the unplanned. To some extent this is true. We keep stand-ins in the wings, substitutes ready, alternative programs penciled in, and generally maintain back-up possibilities for every aspect of program activity in the plan itself.

But even the best program planners have found themselves playing musical chairs with ideas in the actual production of the plan. The unforeseen, the really surprise elements, demand either a very special kind of leadership style, a creative, adaptive kind, or a plan which has built-in flexibility.

How is flexibility structured when we don't know how it will be used? First, the planner needs to walk through every detail of each activity, either through a mock-up situation, a case study based on in-service training, a brain-storming session with the involved staff or, if pressed for time, through a visual think-through process. Each of these exposures offers a play-without-consequences approach, relaxing the planner and allowing him to be an observer outside of the situation itself. The planner can even interject plan jammers to test the plan and reveal weak, susceptible areas.

The input from any or all of these analytical treatments will permit the planner to make some of the exacting, rigid requirements more flexible so that snags which arise will not jeopardize overall effectiveness.

It is a delicate juggling act. If the planner is too flexible the plan becomes only a rough set of ideas to be improvised upon as matters progress. There must be a plan, a set of directions that lead to predictable goals, that insure the least waste. Guidelines may be tempered, but not to the point of chaos.

Lifeboats and parachutes are emergency devices with which we are familiar. They bail us out of trouble when our original means of getting somewhere falters. With each program plan, provisions need to be put aboard that will get you home. Never under-prepare. The written plan should definitely have an if-all-else-fails column.

For example, you schedule a little theatre group production about a great love story and only men show up for the casting. Nobody wants to change and do a prison or army story. A good programmer might end up searching out women for the female roles.

But the unforeseen provides an element of suspense and excitement that sometimes is quite desirable in a program. A nature hike really blossoms when someone stumbles on a snake sunning itself mid-trail. Or someone gets a chance to horse around and experiment with surplus clay left over from a regular project and comes up with clever hip buttons. It happens that way sometimes, but don't count on it.

The cautious programmer who doesn't feel confident in his personal resourcefulness to meet crisis and the unexpected had best come well prepared with alternatives to all facets of his plan, ready to salvage an embarrassing situation or impending failure.

It is with great hesitation that we set forth a list of principles. Principles are described as guides to action, telling us the kind of action to be taken to obtain designated goals. They smack of rules and regimentation, like an instruction booklet for raising the flag correctly.

Important information can be set down in a list of principles, and anyone behaving according to them cannot fail to achieve near-perfect success. But principles have a way of getting syruped over with the moral and ethical values of their authors, or they become so precision-sterile that they resemble a handbook on playing field dimensions.

No one sits down and reads a rule book before beginning to play. We play until we come to an impasse or an arresting infraction. Then we thumb through to find the guidelines. That is the best way to make use of principles. Keep them around to help re-chart a course when the program flounders, but don't get all wound up about memorizing them. You'll be surprised at how many of them are built right into your adjusted master plan through the limiting-factor screening process — and the common sense you've applied through the planning stage.

This book would be remiss if it didn't give you a handy-dandy list of principles. We worked hard to compile it out of the literature, and it may serve the teacher who needs some exacting data for evaluative feedback.

Principles of Programming   65

Recreation program should be based upon a careful analysis and prognosis of past program results. The needs and interests of the public, available facilities and equipment, and the available leader(s) repertoire.

Category I: Group Centered
  A recreation program should:
  a. Be based upon the needs and interests of the community
  b. Be considered the basic product of recreation; its application and acceptance determines the ultimate worth of the field
  c. Be cognizant of momentary trends or interest fashions of the day in constructing program
  d. Encompass in planning, the consideration of public, private, and commercial offerings within a community
  e. Be adapted to the time schedule of the community
  f. Augment and enhance rather than compete with other community activity
  g. Be planned for all ages
  h. Be planned for both sexes
  i. Be planned for all ethnic groups
  j. Be operated continuously throughout the year
  k. Encourage family recreation
  l. Utilize all existing facilities when appropriate
  m. Provide passive as well as active forms of recreation
  n. Provide activities of a progressive nature

o. Provide a majority of activity that is within the financial ability of all people
p. Assure safe and healthy conditions for activity
q. Be designed to serve the best interests of the greatest majority
r. Be provided indoors and outdoors
s. Be planned on the basis of traditional seasonal activity
t. Be improved through continuous evaluation and modification
u. Be weather sensitive
v. Provide for the total group within a specific program activity
w. Involve some long range planning to insure future leadership, finances, facilities, and equipment
x. Make use of all available resources in a community
y. Use standards developed by national agencies if appropriate

Category II: Individual Centered
A recreation program should:
a. Provide outlet opportunities for individual skills and interests developed in school
b. Provide opportunities to advance and develop existing skills
c. Utilize and encourage volunteer assistance when employed staff is unable to handle a specific activity
d. Provide equal opportunity for everyone
e. Provide a wide range of individual choices in a variety of activities
f. Provide opportunities for participants at varying levels of proficiency
g. Provide opportunities for social interaction and fellowship
h. Create an interest in self-leadership so that one can provide his own supervision
i. Be aware of individual differences
j. Allow individual participants to help plan activity
k. Provide opportunity for creative expression
l. Provide for individual achievement and recognition
m. Have flexibility determined by changing individual needs and interests
n. Provide opportunities for adventure and new experience
o. Provide instruction in recreation skills
p. Promote good citizenship

Pitfalls and Hazards

There are a half-dozen bad things of which the programmer must be aware. By facing them in the planning stage one is less brutalized when they occur.

First, there is the *unpredictability of people.* Just when the programmer is getting that rosy glow of feeling all's well and running according to plan, people move off in the opposite direction.

The only explanation for the quick shifting of interest participation seems to be the daily bombardment of the public from persuasive communication forces. The ceramics class looked full with a waiting list on Monday, but on opening day only about one-third of the sign-ups appeared. Half-way through a season of bridge, the Saturday group dwindled from six to two tables because of a brand new roadshow downtown.

The competition for peoples' leisure committments is immense in the urban centers and growing rapidly in the suburbs.

The unpredictability is probably more than just the proliferation of tempting alternatives. We should never take the public's response for granted for it is composed of individuals with individual preferences and aversions.

The second hazard is the *water hole poisoner*, the individual whose presence tends to undermine the entire activity. It can happen at a party, in a class, a club, a tournament, anywhere, with any interest. Some people poison the situation intentionally, maliciously, while others poison it unintentionally by being obnoxious.

There are participants who believe themselves superior to the professional leader and compete for the group's loyalty and attention. There are participants who enjoy the role of cynic and pessimist and who are negative about all activities. Super critics are always comparing present experiences to better ones they have had in the past, or they ignore the positive aspects and accentuate negative qualities regardless of their triviality. There are the born losers, people who can't do anything right, or are personally distasteful to the group, causing embarrassment and making everyone else want to drop out. It's a painful situation for a leader who believes in open opportunity for everyone.

We are stuck with water hole poisoners, and no one knows how to handle them well.

The third hazard is the *out-of-the-blue* rival. There is no planner who can do anything about a *last minute entry* — except be sure he's really planned toward an event that can't be rivalled.

Unfortunately, the late arrival has the advantage of seeing all your cards face up on the table, can analyze your mistakes, and build on top of them. It frequently happens in business when the first company out with a product is run out of the field by other companies which reap the research and promotion already done. There is much of this in the private commercial sector of recreation, and it is not unknown in public areas either. In most endeavors there's not enough public interest for duplicate service or activities.

Fourth, *cancellation and postponements* of activities are delicate problems that often arise in cases of illness, bad weather, special events, conflicting involvements, and the breaking down of equipment. Superior planning leaves nothing to chance and builds extensive back-up into the adjusted master plan. But regardless of how complete the planning has been there will be crises arising from cancellation and postponements. A cancellation may mean sacrificing a lot of preparation, but it may be the best way to save an agency's reputation. A postponement is more difficult for it means working against a whole new set of circumstances and conflicts. But the rescheduling date should be made as early as possible to retain the momentum already involved in the activity. The immediate, easy way in some cases is the indefinite postponement, but sooner or later the day of reckoning comes and much can be lost in the ensuing time.

Postponement and cancellation are guaranteed happenings for every programmer, and usually there is no way to prepare for them.

Fifth, the *new evidence* phantom strikes in the middle of the night. A city ordinance bars all types of day-time fires and your announcement of a grand bar-be-que has hit the city attorney right in the middle of a bitter smog hassle

67

among civic groups. Or the surgeon general issues an official report on the dangers of vigorous activity for girls entering puberty — just a day before the start of your brand new powder-puff girls' football league with thirty teams, made up predominantly of 13-year-old girls.

There are no clearly established guidelines for this occurrence. It's just another inevitable hazard for which it is impossible to plan.

Last of the dirty half dozen is the *lost plan*, physically lost, vanished, misplaced, chewed up by the dog, blown out of the car on the freeway, or gone to the dump with yesterday's trash. It's happened often at picnics and special events, where organization has to be precision and split second, but because everyone was so nervous they forgot to bring the plan. Or the Sunday program where the written plan is locked in the office and the supervisor vacationing in the mountains has the key. A photocopy mind will certainly help at this point or great creative improvisation ability. It is like driving from Los Angeles to Chicago, arriving there and discovering that the name and address of the people you're supposed to visit was left on the kitchen table at home. Another pitfall where the programmer flunks responsibility but gets a chance to get an "A" in creativity.

Don't despair that unplanned-for-hazards exist. Expect them and rejoice in them when they happen. Some of the best new program ideas have arisen out of crises.

Chapter 5

PROMOTION AND MOTIVATION

PROMOTION — PERSUADING AND GAINING SUPPORT

P. T. Barnum, the great 19th century American showman who made freaks and weird things into the greatest entertainment achievement in history, the circus, was good in his day. His motto was the "public be fooled." He repeatedly did it with extravagant and flamboyant posters, advertising, and staged events. He would have trouble in today's recreation world, however.

It's not that his techniques and methods weren't effective. The problem is that recreation services deal with diverse publics that the old promoters could never imagine.

It isn't enough to have a good product or program. We have to do good things and get credit for them. That means we have to deliberately set up communications with the people we want to respond.

We have discussed getting attention, the first step in the process. Now we must be concerned with the message, what we want people to hear and their feedback, i.e., how they respond to the message.

We have made a major point about the variety of publics, not just one mass public, but many different groupings based on habits, attitudes, and interests. You persuade, gain support, participation and attendance for program by appealing directly to those relevant groups in the public. To be obvious, fat women are going to be especially receptive to a women's slim and trim exercise class. Sports car owners will be a primary public for a programmed car rally. In reverse, the bird-watchers' club is an unlikely group to persuade to participate in a hunters' safety course which features gun handling. Setting up a bicycle drill team in a poverty area, where bicycle ownership is rare, is a failure to recognize the public to be served.

Once a clear profile of habits, attitudes and interests has been established, the programmer should be able to define the activities his potential participants will consider beneficial. One of the major keys in persuading others is showing them how activities will benefit them personally. Once again an understanding of need fulfillment becomes a useful tool. The message which we send in various shapes, forms and packages through the media is designed to strike a responsive chord, one that programmers can predict and identify.

Persuasion relies on fact and emotion to different degrees. Take a scheduled class in Judo that is being promoted. Some people might participate in response to a set of facts in the promotional material that extoll Judo's ancient history, the numbers of people doing it today, its good exercise, or how much less it costs to carry on than skiing. When we use facts, they have to be accurate and they must be meaningful to the participant in terms of some advantage gained.

The best persuader is a combination of fact and emotion. A great deal of sports program evolved out of fitness tests during great emotional war periods such as the Civil War and First World War. Promoters were able to elevate existing, poorly supported recreational physical activity programs into bustling mass enterprises because people feared they were unprepared.

Timing is an important consideration. If you get to people too late for them to make plans they may be unable to participate because of prior commitments. Too soon isn't as bad, but it can mean a great waste of effort and money. Depending on the hustle and stress of the public involved the individual is lashed every minute with conflicting demands for his attention and support. He might receive a message far in advance of a soliciting program date, sincerely intend to participate, but forgets, misplaces the message, or has it blotted out in the interim by the competition. Is there an ideal time? Of course, but there is no formula for discovering it. It's situational, and the programmer has to know his media deadlines, the scope of the program, and the nature of the competition.

What about the media? Rather than present a formal list we will give a series of quotes about it from successful programmer-persuaders.

The Newspaper

"Nothing beats the printed word. It has a solid permanency. It can be passed around, read and re-read, posted on the bulletin board."

"The public newspaper has to be number-one contact with the general public. When there's a newspaper strike, people get out old newspapers to read. They believe what they read in newspapers, like they're stone tablets or something."

"Of course, the newspaper. A big city has a lot of them, not only daily, but various editions. It's a hotline to the people, especially the over 30's, a big American habit . . . "

"You want to use the newspaper for promotion. OK, then read it, know its style, what it uses, get to know the editor, his hobby, his kids. Get his kids in your program. Invite the editor and staff out for your big events, free food, give him a certificate or something in recognition of his help . . . "

"The newspaper isn't a charity. They won't just print your stuff because you're a good guy or because recreation is good for mankind. You have to dig up news, find something really unique in your program that everybody will be interested in reading about. Write news releases to promote an activity like it was the report of the plague breaking out, not like a classified ad . . . "

"I file news releases and keep a scrap book of the clippings when they're used so I can see how I'm doing. Try for the columns, or you might even try writing one for the paper yourself if you've got talent. Pictures are good, too. Try to key them in with releases, shoot your own but try to get the photographer from the paper, too."

Word of Mouth

"Word of mouth is the best way of contacting and convincing people, no peer in sight. When somebody likes what you've got, and tells others, that's beautiful testimonial, man."

"Word of mouth, having people tell each other, isn't predictable or controllable. Sure it's good, but a promoter can't count on it. It's just a bonus you get when you're successful."

"I don't know. We send people out, encourage them to tell others. We even get them to knock on doors for our program, participants and staff. You can organize it. Use the concentric circle theory where you tell a few people, and they in turn each tell a bunch of others until you've got big rings of information spreading way out from the original circle."

Television and Radio

"The new people, the new generations are all visual. They don't read, don't have to. It's that electronic box that does the big persuading today. TV is instant and covers the mass public like nothing ever has or probably will."

"Recreation agencies can use it, but it's an expensive resource and not easily obtained for public service or commercial use. The procedure changes all the time and a promoter just has to find out anew every time he decides to try and use it."

"Recreation's best chance is to get on the talk shows somehow. You need an angle, not so much news information as with the newspaper but something kooky and entertaining. It can be a lot of bother and do more harm than good if given phony treatment."

"We've had them send the news staff out to film an activity, but that doesn't help us promote the activity unless we stage something in advance of the thing we're really trying to push."

"You can write news releases just like you do for newspapers or radio. With TV and radio they have to be timed for 30, 20, and 10 second spots."

"The radio has made a comeback. It hits a special set of publics, the car radio at traffic hours, the transistor youth crowd. It's a lot easier to score with radio than TV, and it hits right on a specific population segment."

Posters and Bulletin Boards

"Posters are eye grabbers, big colorful messages in prominent places. People see them and they read them. They're the best buy there is. They get seen over and over again, just one big piece of cardboard up on the board."

"I like the hand done poster better than the commercially printed one. It looks like someone is giving tender-loving care to the activity it's promoting. Of course, we're talking original art work and that means dollars. But it's OK if you've only got a couple of places to post."

"We run a contest for posters at the recreation center, give a prize, and use the best ones in promoting our programs."

"The toughest thing is if you're posting a whole region. Getting them out and getting approval from places you're posting them can take a lot of effort."

Flyers and Direct Mail

"When you want to paper the place, you know, put a notification in every potential customer's hand, then mimeo or photocopy off a couple hundred, a thousand flyers. They're cheap."

"The big problem is distribution. Unless you're organized to get the flyers out with a system, it's a waste. There's lots of ways, stuffing car windshield wipers, school classes, mailed with the city water bills, door to door. The best and surest way is using master mailing lists, set up to cover exactly the publics you've determined are the best potentials."

"A flyer is controlled by you, the promoter. It's no speculation like the newspaper, or TV, or word of mouth for that matter. It says just what you want to say, more than a poster usually can, and nobody else cuts anything out."

The promoting of program is a continuous process, but obviously the most vital time of need is in the beginning, when the activity must attract its participants. Defining the publics, knowing their response patterns, and selecting the most feasible and effective means of persuading them must all give way eventually to the carrying power of the activity itself. The gentler art of reinforcement and public relations then becomes the programmer's concern.

MOTIVATION PROCESS

Interests, Readiness, and Need Fulfillment

Motivation, the inner drive that causes behavior and excites participation, is the mystique area of programming. We've discussed needs and interest surveys, levels of aspiration, leadership techniques, and promoting people to the brink of active involvement. All these considerations prepare the way for us to see the central gear system that turns the complex motivational machinery.

People are involved and committed to a recreation pursuit because their needs for fulfillment are pushing them to a point of interest and readiness.

The temper of the moment, made up of all those hanging needs and the inclinations, gives the programmer his most meaningful function. If he can determine interest and its ripeness for activity, manipulating systems and devices can initiate vigorous, dedicated participation.

Environment Influence

Lead someone to a polluted pond and make him jump in. He will probably go in feet first, holding his nose — and you will have to push him as well. Next, place him near a crystal-clear, sweet water spring and he will dive in headfirst without prodding. The physical properties of the environment produce an almost automatic response in any motivational process. It would be possible to take the swimmer through the whole aquatic repertoire at the spring.

One of the most dampening regulations that ever thwarted programs for teenagers, or any age group, concerns lighting at dances. Because of moral prudery, we light the gymnasium or recreation hall like holiday living rooms, expect joyous social interaction to happen, but end up with wax museums. The youth seek their own dark environments away from the professionally programmed places.

A party explodes into being when the balloons and crepe hang high, the music whips the pulse, and the lighting beams "whoopee." The party programmer sets the stage, an atmosphere, an exciting environment, and then people have a good time. A shoddy environment drives everyone away.

73

Status

Fishermen don't buy yachts, and polo players don't buy campers. Truck drivers like to bowl and booze, and the society set likes to play bridge.

This sounds like one of those stereotype lists used to illustrate the narrow-mindedness of bigots. Unfortunately, participants in recreation program, as elsewhere, tend to be directed by status. It has a lot to do with the needs of belonging and recognition, but it also is a phenomenon of its own that deserves special consideration. It is a cluster of basic needs resulting from advanced civilization and urbanization.

In striving for identity, we constantly adorn ourselves with symbolic badges. Uniforms are the classic means of associating ourselves with an activity that impresses people for whom we care. It's not that we love these people, it's that we care what they think of us.

Besides uniforms, many recreation activities have distinctive equipment, which can be carried or strapped on the individual or behind his car. The surfboard on the car roof can be driven past hangouts or parked at them, where people who count will say, "You're one of them, wow!" A hand-carved ivory chess set carried under a tweed-sleeved arm gives an air of cerebral prowess. It's amazing the amount of ski paraphernalia that is accumulated just to sit in front of a fireplace at the lodge.

A story illustrates the complexity of status-directed recreation. A few years ago, when scuba diving was in its boom period, the sales and instruction records showed that the bulk of participants were in the professional category of doctors and lawyers. This, of course, had something to do with the cost of the equipment and the ability to travel to special places where the water was clear and inviting. But there was also an aura of technology and gentleman adventure built around it that created status.

Then the news media hit with a series articles about shark attacks. Scuba diving suddenly took on the look of a blood and guts activity for young dare-devils. Overnight, lessons and orders for custom-made colored wetsuits and colored equipment (color was reported to attract sharks) were cancelled by the professional. But business didn't drop at all!

A whole new group of people responded to the new image. Clerks and truck drivers, using payment plans, streamed into the diving centers. Overnight, scuba diving became much more of a mass interest pursuit. Although the intensity of the shark scare has diminished, the risk-taking impression remains high. Professionals have returned, too, but for different reasons than the original one which had much to do with class status.

Each activity does have its status in society. The public tends to give great identity support to the participants who can establish their involvement. Certificates, membership cards, uniforms, or merely displaying the equipment prominently, are status indicators.

No programmer can afford to overlook this powerful motivating force of modern society.

74

Somewhere, a long time ago, the troops got restless. Perhaps it started with primitive man.

"I don't want to practice spear-throwing any more."

"But we've got to get in shape for the next battle, that down-wind tribe is restless again."

"You said that last year; anyway I think I'm ready enough."

As millions of chiefs have done since, an artificial success system was built into the practice sessions. Eventually it became part of the activity itself. After all, a war could drag on for years before anyone won and a sense of success was possible.

There is an impatience to receive recognition as things progress, every day if possible. If the effort someone exerts becomes difficult to relate to some distant, final goal discontent and disinterest arise rapidly.

Planned progression systems have been one of the best answers to this very human problem. The merit badge system employed by the Boy Scouts is probably a classic example. The badges are a lot of small carrots acting as on-going incentives in a broader system that provides a hierarchy of ranks or titles, each a little more difficult to obtain. At the pinnacle is the grand achievement of Eagle Scout.

The planned progression approach to motivation is a form of structured growth. Like any organization we must keep growing or atrophy and die. It is natural to lose interest in doing anything when no sense of change, improvement, growth, or progress is felt by the participant. The programmer must devise ways that growth can be sensed and tangibly observed by the participant himself.

We use first-, second-, and third-string rankings in team sports that use substitutes as part of the game. One strives to make the starting team then to become all-league, all-city, all-state, all-American, all-pro, all-hall of fame, and if there's some other badge beyond, then that too. It's a way of measuring ourselves, something we all want, even if it sometimes hurts.

It takes a good programmer to set up and deploy a progression system that exerts enough pressure to keep interest up and tension down. There is no formula for this skill. The great difficulty occurs because if a system is used it must be applied equally to everyone. Many of us can't handle the stress of it, and yet we want and need to be a part of the activity influenced by it.

Overall, recreation has done well with its progressive measurement motivating. Some fine examples are the YMCA's swimming progression classifications where polliwogs strive to become sharks through a series of tests and ranks.

In recent years, the commercial classes in Judo and Karate and related self-defense activities have employed the ancient belt system to keep them coming back. The black belt, unlike the blue ribbon, comes to the achiever, not the winner. Perhaps this is the best way to understand the different motivations involved with achievement and award. When a progression system is set up, a participant can keep trying, continue striving, make errors, but never really lose. Frustrated, yes, but not finally and irrevocably defeated.

Progressive achievement systems are ongoing, more of the nature of regular program. Award systems revolve around special events. Obviously, there is great inter-relatedness since the black belt is a symbol of achievement and is an award in the technical sense. Perhaps some of the overlap may be avoided by describing those recognitions involved with progression systems as achievement awards and those given when one defeats an opponent as competition awards.

The drive to move to a first-class rank from a second-class one is strong in most of us, and the progressive achievement system in program activities allows us to know exactly what is required to get there, and leaves the timing and amount of effort up to the individual participant.

75

Competition

Competition happens whether or not a programmer plans it in his activity. Animals strive without thought of how well they are doing since only the goal matters. Humans make sub-goals designed to obtain approval from others. They, unlike animals, compare efforts and results. With animals the reward, the winning, is associated with the act, the effort; humans, however, tend to be more concerned with the concept of self and how others perceive them.

The whole game situation is based upon this dependence. People need continual reinforcement to assure them of their worth, that they have a valuable identity. At the animal level, where survival is the primary concern, there is neither reason nor opportunity to be concerned with more than the ultimate goal. Primitive man feels the direct relationship between his every act and the fulfillment of his basic needs — the killing of game and the relief from hunger. Given leisure and relief from constant survival effort man wonders how important he really is. He senses in technological civilization that his role is fragmentary towards achieving survival. He will survive for others will see to it. He doesn't need to compete desperately, in fact, society often rewards those who cooperate rather than those who aggressively compete.   Cooperation is the lifeblood of recreation activity. It must exist to have activity, to play games and to make things. It is the essence of the club approach that we have discussed elsewhere as an organizational pattern.

Cooperation exists even in war between bitter enemies, for there are rules outlawing atrocities. Certainly a group or team that has set a mutual goal needs cooperation. A football team may compete successfully with other teams, but it does not follow that it will compete best if its members are in competition with each other.

With cooperation everybody can succeed and feel equal satisfaction with the outcome. It is an ideal to which industry and education pay great tribute, although they seem to fall back on competition to maintain productivity and learning curves. Recreation also has failed to accomplish its finest hours through cooperative activities. Competition creates an artificial set of exciting challenges that make life both interesting and unpredictable as we go along without waiting for any final achievement as the payoff. Cooperation exists when the goals are unlimited, but competition occurs when they are limited. Some must fail and some succeed.

The programmer must carefully balance competition and cooperation. It is a juggling act that requires great concern because of the effects on the individual. If great competitive stress is placed on participants, destructive consequences may happen to some individuals. They drop out, withdraw, escape, struggle in frustration, cheat, or abuse the rules. We live in a world where stress is often condoned and sports heroes/leaders say things like, "Winning isn't everything, it's the only thing," or "Nice guys finish last." When we make defeating someone the only goal then any kind of failure is devastating to participants. Nor can we afford to create a recreation jungle where cooperation within a group or on a team is achieved at the expense of developing great hostility toward all others.

A lot of locker room pep talks, whether in the sports or cultural area, overflow with "hate, hurt, and kill." It is often found in the psychology-of-champion studies that star performers psyche themselves up by manufacturing hates that are not left in the arena but are carried into the total life style.

We need great awareness of the dangers of competition carried to extremes and improperly managed. It takes great, insightful, trained programmers to avoid the possible traumas. The following guidelines have been helpful in using the motivational potential of competition:

1. Analyze the individual personalities with special attention to stress thresholds in activities in which competition is overlayed as a planned format.

2. Provide a broad program where there are equal opportunities to select both competitive and cooperative experiences.

3. See that the reinforcements provided are not only for winning but for effort, performance, sportsmanship, and cooperation. Recognition is often given for the best team player. A number of the group work agencies, especially the YMCA, give symbolic awards — pennants of the same size and quality — for sportsmanship and prowess.

4. Adjust the competitive situation so that participants strive against those with equal ability, thereby making competition more satisfactory to both losers and winners.

5. Distribute the possibility of winning. The more classes or plateaus separating the abilities for competition the better, as long as sufficient numbers exist to create a meaningful contest. There is a breaking point to this, of course, and motivation can be diluted if the challenge is made insufficient by narrowing the spectrum of opponents.

6. Avoid working only with the skilled few.

7. Handicap those who have achieved mastery and championship status, or they will drop out. Lack of competition breeds disinterest when all other goals of an activity have been met.

8. Competition may run throughout life, and people should be prepared to face it both in business and in love. But recreation program is not the place to condition people for competition. Competition is to be used as an interest builder, adding zest to experiences — a means, not an end in itself.

9. Program must be arranged so that, despite the necessity of a winner in competition, many can experience success. One obvious approach is to expand the number of winners. This can be done by finding other achievements to recognize besides the total on the scoreboard. It has also been an American movement to vertically acknowledge achievement by creating multi-winners through places, e.g., first through fifth place. The premise is that second is better than last, but creating places does make "last" a glaring and embarrassing placement. The one winner makes everyone else a runner-up, and no one participant needs carry the stigma of being the worst. There is no formula for this since it has to be played situationally for the individuals involved.

There is strong feeling today about creating highly competitive situations for children. Some feel it is never too soon for them to start learning what life is all about, while others feel severe physical and psychological trauma can result from stress applied before proper maturity.

The issue shouldn't be whether competition is good or bad for any age, but whether professional programmers are in charge to structure the activity to fit the needs and capacities of the individual participants.

Social Facilitation

Closely allied to the motivational force of competition and the need to interact with others is social facilitation, which means simply that most of us are influenced by others.

In groupings of people there is a tendency to get swept along with what others are doing. We dance at the party rather than being left wall-flowered on the sideline; we even have lynched people because the rest of the mob was doing it.

People are insecure, doubting their status, struggling with their self-esteem when they conform to the actions of the group because it seems the thing to do to find approval. Programmers of special events since ancient times have always recognized the power of a Claque, a group of stooges paid to go to a performance to applaud. Have you ever resisted clapping or standing up when everybody else does? It's a very threatening moment and only a magnificent self-confidence would allow you to resist the group.

Peer approval is one of the most powerful weapons that exists in society. Management people call it "influence without authority." Legal authority can take primitive measures to obtain conformity but in the process creates alienation. When behavior is facilitated by group membership — just the physical presence — the action is less odious to our sense of freedom of choice.

The classic experiment validating the effectiveness of this force is the line choices offered to an individual in a group where all of the other members were working with the experimenter. Of three lines on a blackboard, one was decidedly shorter than the other two. The group all gave the same wrong answer on choice of line that differed in length. Depending on whether the tested individual made his choice first or last, the influence of the group was so strong that individuals frequently choose the same line as the group.

The recreation programmer is not in a position to control groups through peer pressure. But he must be able to recognize it, encourage it, and use it to his advantage. For example, social facilitation has been one of the strong devices of the Alcoholics Anonymous program whereby an alcoholic gains strength to abstain by exposure to others making the effort. The contagious, positive force found in a recreation situation makes it uncomfortable for individuals to stand by idly or resist when the group has picked up on an activity and gives it life. Being an outsider, no matter how righteous, satisfies only the maverick.

Programmers have always employed the snow-ballers, the starter people, to get reticent individuals on their feet and up on the dance floor, or extroverts to initiate participation in the tom-foolery of a picnic, or athletes to try interpretative dance routines. Once the act of participation by a peer member happens, over and beyond the demonstration by the professional leader, the borderline holdouts begin to participate and a chain reaction begins. Each new participation trips the trigger on the next plateau of readiness to play. The non-participant then becomes the outsider.

Some programmers work the concept into the promotion stages of an activity. This helps encourage readiness to participate. Basically, it's the "one more space" trick of promoters trying to bandwagon registrations. You'll have to decide the ethics of each situation, whether suggestions of full enrollment are justified in the interests of salvaging or assuring attendance in good program.

The "closed class-sell out" device is a further extension of promotional technique. There's nothing like having a waiting list for an activity to enhance its desirability and guarantee full support for the next time it is scheduled.

The whole business of following trends or fads is social facilitation on a grand scale. Without any structured programming, surfing took off in recent years and developed a fantastic youth participation. A rugged-individualist recreation by its nature, its appeal got to opinion leaders and they in turn drew the masses in. At one point, it was embarrassing to be a young person within range of the seashore and admit you didn't surf. Come up with a hula hoop or a game like monopoly and the same phenomenon unfolds.

(Eventually there is a leveling off and the dedicated stay on with a continuous feed in of novices.) The magic of social facilitation energizes participation with a power to match any other motivational devices.

Most recreation activity is facilitated by outer direction and while we are alert to make accommodation for the isolates and self-contained individualists, our work thrives on the manipulation of group pressure for involvement.

Awards

"This green ribbon says 'Third Place, Fifth Grade Standing Broad Jump, 97th Street Elementary School,' do you want to keep it, it was here with the rest of the junk in this trunk?"

"Let me see that. I remember it well. Thirty years ago. Actually I was first for the boys, there were two big Amazon girls in the class who got first and second."

"But you don't still want to keep it, do you?"

"Yeah, keep it. I was the best at something, wasn't I? I mean, right now, in my life, I'm not best at anything, right? So keep it awhile, it reminds me . . . reminds me of something happy."

On mantles, in windows, on desks, in closets and trunks all over America, colorful ribbons and shiny trophies stand guard over fragile identities. They are strings around the fingers to remind us that once there was a Camelot and for a little while you and I were king.

Nostalgia is not the reigning reason behind the use of awards in recreation program. Nostalgia is a by-product. Programmers don't trust the potential of activities themselves to bring participation and create fulfillment. Awards are a crutch.

But a realistic one. We would be unquestionably naive if we put down awards as a bad, weak practice. Our society is glued together by material payoffs. Just as most of us fall short of being self-contained, we also need recognition for our achievements in some hard, substantial form that we can hold in our hands to show others who we are and what we've done.

The major danger of all material or extrinsic awards is the replacement of activity interest with award interest. The mark of the good programmer may well be the ability to have activities that draw and satisfy in themselves even though the great bulk of human experience is embedded in the competitive process. Competition and awards are blood brothers. Like competition, awards are not bad in themselves, but only in their use and the attitudes and behavior they create beyond those needed to sustain interest.

There are some programmers who feel that awards sweeten the attraction, serve as the bait for bringing in people who wouldn't otherwise get involved. Once in, they suggest, the award seekers become involved in the inherent pleasures of the activities, making the awards incidental. There is much skepticism from experienced programmers about such a reversal occurring. Most practical programmers, in fact, think the opposite. Awards take over the motivation once they have been introduced. They create a whole new set of value systems and accentuate and broaden the failure aspects of participation.

There is general agreement that once awards are introduced at a certain level there is no stepping back. That is, if a programmer announces that he will award certificates for taking part in a track meet or choral group songfest, decides he has ample budget and ends up giving medals, he will never be able to revert to certificates again. He must continue to give medals or up-grade to trophies.

The principle here is that once a certain level of expectation has been set with an activity, the future participants will expect equal or better extrinsic recognition symbols. The programmer must be careful in the use of awards as promotional incentives, for he is stuck with them forevermore.

Additionally, awards are like sound or light. When projected against one activity they spill over and upset the operation of others in a program.

Recreation in its various agency settings has tried to solve inequity in awards by installing broad regional systems. Central headquarters will often unify the level, size and types of awards for various events. Some of the devices used are:

1. A seasonal point system whereby two points are given to winning teams and players, one point for being a participant and sometimes an equal number of points for sportsmanship. This is not to eliminate awards, for the points are still symbolic awards and ultimately lead to material objects, such as medals and trophies. But it delays the physical contact with awards, allowing entire seasons of various activities to go by before the points are totalled and actual awards given. It is a makeshift approach, but it has a successful reputation, especially in intramurals on campuses and at armed forces bases.

2. A central authority can increase buying power by purchasing awards for a group of agencies or recreation services. A higher quality award is then possible for less money, and agencies subscribing to such a system of awards avoid comparative shopping by participants. Unfortunately, local agencies tend to use such systems and then use the monetary saving to add some additional award on their own.

3. Another stop-gap procedure is to demand that all branches of an agency issue ribbons at the local level of awards, medals for regionals, and trophies for all-jurisdiction participation. There is no way to say that a trophy is necessarily more impressive than a ribbon, for expensive ribbons can be purchased that are more impressive than cheap trophies.

There is also the general life styles of people to consider. Professional people like wall plaques and certificates for office walls, many youths like jewelry awards they can wear, apartment dwellers and collectors find ribbons easy to store or display in cramped quarters, extroverts like ornate trophies shining from the mantel or in the front window, and people who entertain a lot like a utilitarian award, like engraved silver punch bowls.

The successful programmer must keep in touch with what's in and what's out as far as fashions in awards. In the sea of awards that inundate many recreation programs the most positive reaction the presenter ever hears is, "Gee, this is different."

4. Another experimental system is to rate various activities as to their award merit. Many programmers feel awards must represent true achievement, progress, a triumph over obstacles or opponents. The classic embarrassment is the little sister entering a Christmas doll in a doll tea show and bringing home a ribbon equal to the one her big brother had won the same

day in a football skills contest. The dividing line seems to be based upon the actual putting forth of personal, individual effort and skill as opposed to merely applauding ownership.

We still maintain a rather primitive way of handling awards despite their traditional role in the recreation process of motivation. We are great gamblers and tend to spin the wheel with the eternal optimism that the right number will turn up occasionally. Awards work, that is, they do promote interest, hold interest, and lend a distinct and separate aura of excitement. There is need, however, for scientific analysis, systematic order, and indices of danger to keep programmers in control of what happens as a result of awards.

"Extrinsic awards are those that lie outside the activity itself" is an extremely controversial statement. Is the relationship between the 100-yard dash and the ribbon an artificial one? Do you run to get a ribbon or run for what you feel because of the effect of the activity? Can they be separated easily? Is not the ribbon as much a part of the experience as the starting gun, the printed program, and the chalked lanes on the track? What is the important point in this debate? Answer: What happens to the participants. That is a good, common investigative criterion for whatever we do in program. We obviously want character building to take place. If dedication to material gain is a negative development in your system, then awards must be carefully studied.

One key to the problem is what awards actually represent in each situation to the participants. A starting point might be the ultimate extreme — getting paid to play. While money itself is a symbol of survival power, representing a universal medium to be used to satisfy our primitive needs, it is also a symbolic award. What stronger force than to combine the physiological drives of survival with the social needs of recognition and identity.

The professional worker is distinguished from the amateur recreationist in terms of pay. Money has served in sports as the distinction, but the entire picture has become muddled. There is a big difference between someone becoming a millionaire from doing what others do for recreation — a champion golfer or discovered artist — and those receiving a few dollars to cover expenses. As a symbol money has a relative value to each individual participant, but it is a real measure. The millionaire may not be driven to win a five dollar cash prize as a ghetto participant would, but the money does have a fixed tangible value in terms of what it buys.

Money is not especially bad as an award if it remains only a symbol. For example, the millionaire award winner frames the money on his wall rather than spending it. If the intention of participating was to procure survival power, i.e., money, then the individual has moved out of the realm of recreation to that of work.

Any award that is negotiable or easily converted to money has the potential of displacing the recreational nature of activity with a work overlay. The closer one gets to the basic physiological survival needs the more like work the experience becomes. A descending or ascending scale of negotiability of awards might help. For example, paper certificates and ribbons have a low negotiability factor, medals and trophies medium negotiability, and jewelry and clothing high negotiability. It is not necessary to make such a scale, but an understanding of its significance is essential for the programmer.

81

An item with low negotiability, like a ribbon, should represent the activity if not the participation more exclusively than jewelry. The meaning of the award should rest with the prestige of the activity, not with its spending power.

One of the best ways to keep an award associated with the activity, reinforcing participation for its own sake, is to design or inscribe the award in order to make it unusable for any other purpose. The more distinctively identified the award is with the activity, the more exclusive and the more heightened is the sense of identity with the participant. The Academy Awards Oscar is an example of this.

One clue to the future of awards may be in a growing need to be identified apart from the mass. Recognition is an important means for achieving this. Growing affluence tends to make awards of negotiable power less important, with exclusive awards, such as the American Cup in Yachting gaining in demand. The programmer should be less concerned with bigger, more ornate awards with a money value than with different awards more directly related to each activity.

Awards are not a necessary evil. They're not an evil at all if they make people happier and have no depressing side effects. They can be a legitimate and integral part of programming in competent hands.

Intrinsic Reward

82

Should programmers initiate motivation through the methods we have previously discussed, or should the participant seek out that which intrinsically interests him?

When we speak of "intrinsic" we simply mean the inner workings of a person and how he directly responds to an experience. Motivation means the energizing force that makes a person behave in certain patterns. This energizing force, even if heavily activated by external sources, is only operative because there exists in the person established *basic drives.*

These primary drives, when directed toward fulfillment goals, take on the characteristics of *motive.* External environmental sources stimulating drives are called *incentives,* which we have already described. The *goal* is the conscious realization of what will satisfy a drive. The *motive* is the thought or feeling that makes one act and is a prevailing force for a period of time.

Motive creates *interest,* the emotional state that accompanies participation. When interest is focused on an experience, *attention* results. Programming is the arrangement of experiences to achieve the type of *participation* that leads to goal satisfaction.

So when we deal with intrinsic rewards, we cut deeply into the cluster of basic drives within each of us. *There can be no motivation without some basic drive.*

The child learns to expect others to minister to his basic drives because of his dependency. Certain socially-approved behavior is required from the child for the adult to feel and act positively toward the child. The child then seeks *approval, recognition, prestige* and *status* from his parents, other authority figures (recreation leaders), siblings, and finally his peers. But acceptance by peers is in part a function of and dependent upon acceptance by authority figures.

But if we are defining intrinsic rewards why are we discussing extrinsic factors? They are related to each other. Authority figures give acceptance and approval to a person through which the concept of self begins to develop.

Through the process of incorporation a person internalizes standards set up by others and makes them his own, i.e., they become intrinsic. He craves for himself what others expect from him. He develops *self-esteem*, *self-respect*, and *self-satisfaction*. The final intrinsic drive is independence, the transferral of values from outer to inner sources, which is a rare if ever-existing state. There is strong evidence that reinforcement by approval of others is in constant association with all behaviors.

The participant in the recreation experience may be able to intrinsically give value and importance through his own evaluative processes, but at some point seeks external approval. He seeks mastery and success — intangible states of mind that seem to elude the self-contained intrinsic process.

A young camper learns to build a fire in order to cook his meal. Hunger is the primitive need behind the drive to build a fire. He may satisfy himself by building a bad fire and barely cook his dinner. He is pleased with himself and experiences an intrinsic reward. Unfortunately, he overhears *praise* given some of his fellow campers for their mastery in making a fire. As satisfied as he was, the very absence of approval generally is a form of punishment. Only disapproval could have been more shattering.

Regardless of how much we may speak of recreation's noble goals of play-for-play's-sake, satisfaction is a complex process which is not totally derived from internalized motivational force, for the intrinsic is a servant of the extrinsic.

In terms of motivation and reward, the following appear to be true:

1. There is no participation without motivation.

2. Participation must be reinforced through rewards.

3. Approval is more effective than disapproval in creating participant interest.

4. Blame or disapproval has a negative effect, destroying interest and drive in the majority of cases.

5. A programmer has to work with what intrinsically exists and build the extrinsic process upon it.

6. A programmer may have to assist participants establish an intrinsic framework of values based on need fulfillment. Part of this should be directed toward establishing realistic levels of aspirations.

7. Stress is usually undesirable. The programmer should not force participant goals but guide the individuals in discovering and establishing their own concept of personal needs. It is helpful to know the anxiety level and the stress threshold of participants in order that programming doesn't create interest-killing tension.

8. Participants need approval while striving toward ultimate goals. The professional programmer succeeds best when he gives immediate reinforcement to an individual's acts.

Knowledge of the motivation process is important, for recreation programmers too long depended on the expressed desires of the people, fitting those desires into what is convenient for us to do. This is no more effective in developing, initiating and maintaining interest than one-handed clapping.

Chapter 6

SPORTS PROGRAMMING

THEORY OF SPORTS

We've searched with great dedication to find the element that holds together the great miscellany of recreation activities in the field of sports. Sports account for the largest number of participants, capturing from 60 percent to 75 percent of all active involvement. This number may be higher in the spectator classification.

The common element is a challenge which is met primarily through physical exertion. A short dialogue will illustrate this point.

"Does that mean that all physical activities are to be classified as sports?"

"No, dance is certainly a physical activity but its primary emphasis is self-expression, the visual communication of feelings and ideas, which is the general frame of reference for cultural programming."

"Is swimming part of the sports picture?"

"We've been tempted to give aquatics co-billing as a major program arena. The separation from sports of swimming and other water activities promises to be controversial. The numbers participating in aquatics is exceptionally high, consequently distinguishing it from other sports. Furthermore water is essential to make it happen."

"Aren't you obligated, then, to recognize sports that require air space as a separate arena, like skydiving?"

"That's a logical step, but skydiving is the only pure, legitimate air activity that we can think of, although trapeze and flying are close. Perhaps there'll be enough volume and new applications to justify a spin-off arena for them in the future."

"What about fishing, hunting, hiking . . . the outdoor recreation sports? In which arena should these be placed?"

"They're sports if we use the physical exertion challenge. The old activity classifications recognized an area of outdoor recreation which, unfortunately, did little to differentiate it from program activities. The outdoors, as they saw it, referred to the natural wilderness, an identification of environment which does not help us differentiate programs. Most sports are outdoors, so that ruins that idea. Perhaps wilderness sports might be an appropriate term, but there is not only a lot of city hiking, but also plastic lakes in downtown areas for fishing."

"Don't you get in trouble with the physical exertion definition if you talk about fishing since you hardly move a muscle sitting under a tree, trailing a line in the water?"

"Someone with a marlin jumping at the end of a taut line might debate you on the passivity you imply in fishing. But your point is well taken. In fishing, we may have a unique enough experience to be handled as a special activity which cannot be confined to the general sports category. It certainly is one of the five big volume participant activities, if not the biggest. Hunting and marksmanship cause the same problem. Stalking an animal is certainly putting out energy, but sitting in a blind or popping at a paper target are not."

Perhaps we should examine the primitive survival societies to clarify the point. How did sports evolve out of the constant, serious business of life? Habit, even when the game locker was overflowing, sent the hunter and fisherman out on the trail. It was also good practice for times again would be hard and game scarce. He discovered that when there was no pressure, when life didn't depend on his success or failure, he could experiment, compare his skill against others, develop a new style, and do it if he felt like it. It was no longer the burdened necessity of work but the freed joy of play.

He did the same with war. He invented a game approach to physical hostility, a non-destructive finish, with rules to prevent chaos and injury. These organized sports were refined and weapons were replaced with balls and other toy-like equipment until games took on a life of their own.

But even today man understands sports as a compensation for the loss of adventure in his clash with the elements, animals, and his fellow man. These clashes told him that he had important, responsible functions. He was needed, he was tested, and he had an identity.

Our sports, a multi-billion dollar enterprise at the professional level, have become a serious life style. They are used as an outlet to control morale and emotions, to combat boredom, to sublimate social aggression, and to keep man from atrophying in his automated technology.

Sports are the experience of challenge, man against animal, the elements or other men, with physical exertion its primary identifying characteristic. In some instances habit activates the participation, with sports as a substitute for survival activities, or as a reminder of the physically demanding life of our forefathers. Time and a new, less physical world are making sports the only means for adults to keep fit and healthy and to join the youth who have accepted sports as an important component of life.

VALUE OF SPORTS

If we examine sports in light of our need fulfillment scale, we discover a high potential for satisfaction through physical activity. Sports' high potential, however, is lost if the instruments, tools, machines take over effort. Vehicle sports such as car racing, motorcycle hill climbing and cross-country snowmobile runs place man in an accessory category. The whole man and his total physical involvement is fragmented because the vehicle supplies most of the exertion.

We have also noted that the hunter or fisherman who sits and waits for the game to pass dilutes the physical experience. His gun or fishing rod are technological harnassings of power which act as substitutes for the actual physical stalking of animals by men.

These breakdowns in potential are midway between full active participation and passive spectator involvement. This does not disqualify them as sports but does suggest a medium fulfillment rating on the physical activity need area. From a positive standpoint vehicle sports, as well as hunting and fishing, place the participant in the cultural program arena. By their equipment they shall be known and be given special recognition because of it. But these sportsmen also become tinkerers, building and adapting their equipment, which provides high opportunity for creativity and inventive self expression.

Pure sports — such as the big five of football, basketball, baseball, track, and hockey — take us to the other extreme. The sports and culturally oriented sports, i.e., vehicle and hunting, stress the individual; the big five, teams. Track, of course, stands apart to some degree since with the exception of relays, it consists of a series of individual contests. But the team aspect still exists in all five situations.

What does team involvement connote? The opportunity for social interaction, security, and belonging. Making the team is being accepted in a special group, and the player experiences a high degree of belonging. This belonging need is emphasized in its fullest during highly competitive engagements by his team.

The social interaction is most predominant in the less formal team situations. Locker room horseplay provides the broadest opportunity for interaction, with the informality of the practice field next. By gametime, the players are ready to execute by reflex the patterns of the game. They are parts of the machine and the spontaneity demanded for good social interaction is sacrificed for predictable robot behavior that makes the team machine work effectively.

The opportunities for dominance, creativity, and mental activity can be great for a few. The positions played in the game determine this. The captain of a team, the play caller, and the coach have high potential for fulfillment in these three needs because of the decision-making roles they play. The coach, sports instructor, or the master demonstrator receive high potential ratings on the need to serve others.

Each sport demands individual analysis which we are tempted to give here. But that's some of your fun, figuring out the psychological basis of each. As we have noted, sports have a number of values, but they serve man best when they give him a physical life style that was a legacy of his ancestors.

Sports program planning employs all the principles covered under general program planning. Principles, as we have said, are guidelines that tell us how our actions should be structured to obtain the desired results and goals.

We seek to open the door through sports to physical activity that takes on a joyous nature because it is play overlayed with a sense of social significance. We have transferred our restless energy from the vacuum left by the erosion of survival stresses. We have almost come full circle and made the fake life dominant. The imitation of life found in children's games is big business, a respected function.

It is the active participation in sports toward which this book aims. To watch and not to play is to atrophy. Man must move, or he vegetates and becomes passive.

Physical activity is the crown we seek to reach through sports programming. We use teams to achieve social interaction and a sense of belonging. Some sports are excellent gateways to new experiences and, in some cases, recognition.

Accepting this hierarchy of results, let us stress several principles that are particularly important to sports programmers.

1. *The program should consist of various activities to serve divergent publics.*

88

We can ill afford to program intensely at one age level and leave the others suspended in limbo. If we take pride in a Little League then we must take the responsibility to match the effort for all age groups. If we over-emphasize one age level we reflect diminished value on other less accelerated activities. We need to balance the offerings to fulfill the spirit of this principle.

Our planning must not settle for activities for only the highly skilled because they're ready since the unskilled are in greater numbers and shoulder a broader spectrum of needs. Planners tend to fail the individual because of demands for numerical success; the team activities are a much easier route to take. When the programmer does cover the individual, he overlooks the family syndrome. The family remains the strongest primary group membership in our society and, difficult as mixed age-sex-skill sports activities are to conduct, the programmer must expand his array of activities to reach and reinforce family unity.

2. *Participation should improve the character of the individual.*

If we interpret character improvement as strengthening positive personality traits, respect for others' rights, and cooperation, then the sportsmanship taught by sports provides the incubator. The multiple opportunities to take advantage ruthlessly of an opponent in order to win, to crush him rather than defeat him, to act legally but unethically, create the challenges.

We must emphasize that conquest without character creates effective machines, not people.

3. *The program should reflect and seek to improve the culture within which it occurs.*

Our best examples are found in disadvantaged and/or ethnic areas. There are no playing fields of Eton in the congested asphalt ghetto. Not even a vacant lot, just vertical and horizontal walls. Space is a rare and precious thing.

The games are improvised with available equipment: stickball with a fire hydrant as the base; four square in place of net games like tennis. Space and economics dictate. Basketball is probably the most valuable mutant sport to arise out of the original pioneer sports. With a hoop hung high, a ball, and a few feet of space, the most dramatic sports contests imaginable can be staged. Basketball is a truly effective ghetto sport, a product of that culture that must be given a prominent berth in any local program.

But to exclude all other sports except basketball is not improving the cultural climate in which the programmer works. Perhaps weight training, a fitness and body building sport, conforms to but nevertheless enhances the culture by providing an activity element that does not spontaneously spring from the culture. It is instigated by the programmer. It may be carried over to other environments and adds a healthy, cleanliving philosophy to the culture while reflecting the limitations imposed by that culture.

In upper income rural suburbia, horses are a clue for the programmer. In Mexican-American areas, cultural traditions and pride push soccer and a type of handball over the mid-American sports of football, baseball, and tennis. To make additions to the Mexican-American activities, consider moving the soccer interest to rugby football, which has some similarities to American football. If understanding other cultures and uniting our feelings but maintaining our differences are worthwhile goals, then broadening cultural exposures is a move in the right direction.

4. *Program a wide selection of lifetime sports.*

In school there is a hierarchy of sports in which football, basketball, baseball, and track receive the highest status. But when schooling is over, the door clangs shut and the new "adult" is left to find some way to carry on his interest in the upper echelon sports. If he hasn't been given lifetime sports such as tennis, bowling, badminton, and archery to fall back on, he may succumb to vicarious sports, as coach or spectator, and by so doing bolster the hierarchical ranking of the major sports.

These carry-over sports can not be treated as unworthy because they are not big box office. Sports' worth is measured not only by what happens to the participants but also how long it happens. They should have value throughout one's lifetime.

89

SAFETY AND OFFICIALS

The nature of sports, pitting oneself against unpredictable obstacles and placing oneself in physical jeopardy, calls for a disciplined and structured organization of experiences. We can hear the boos and jeering now. Why not just let it happen, forget about trying to regiment what should be spontaneous and joyful abandon?

Boys the world over have engaged in the spontaneous, low-grade game of "mountain," brutally piling on top of a luckless victim in a crunching, bruising stack-up. There are many one-eyed boys groping around from that crude bit of play-war, the rock fight. Sand lot ball and street athletics have produced thousands of crippled victims. If controls are lacking, the worst can happen and often does.

What controls? There are the *rules*, and the people who administer the rules, the *officials*. In the heat of play, with competition a searing flame within the player, caution and delicate behavior are lost in an attempt to conquer the opponent, the past record, or the environment. Such beautiful abandon to the activity is a precious cluster of emotions that deserve protection. On the other hand, blind unchanneled energy is destructive. A ballroom brawl leaves a depressing aftermath in which many suffer.

Rules were invented to temper the sports jungle that seethes with animal urges. High-powered professional sports are controversial today because of growing number of influences, the most terrifying of which is the hate-hurt-kill used to turn participants into feeding-time-at-the-zoo-players. With the pros we are involved with careers, creating a business stress. Unfortunately, the line has been erased somehow and the excessive hate-hurt-kill spirit runs all the way down to the newly-walking sons of retired-to-the-bleachers fathers who seek vicarious experiences through their children. This, plus affluence, has caused a professional sports attitude to permeate the sports of our entire society.

The result has been to shelve the older protective programming patterns which adapted the structure of the sports activity to growth, maturation, and economics, e.g., softball for baseball, touch for tackle football. The older sports program, from child to adult, used to work with a few basic rules, such as you can't run with the ball in basketball, a flip-the-coin attitude when the situation arose.

Then it was an informal participation. But a new dimension for sports has been added, at least in the major team activities. The more popular the activity, the more people want to be a part of it, if only by trying to make it better by changing it and the rules. Highly organized committees are created that eventually become complete organizations, which sit in warm rooms on cold nights and try to refine sports through the case-study approach, studying unusual game situations of the past season and devising rules to protect the participants and set the boundaries of play. To be aware of old rules, new rules, and impending rules demands retentive and creative minds.

Rules are not only a conscientious safety concern, but also a means to make each sport increasingly sophisticated so that games can keep pace with the excitement and demands of other pursuits. The complexity of these rules means a greater demand on the time and capacities of the players, more and better coaches, and expert officials.

The rules are available in printed form from many sources. Organizations representing each sport or sports in general, like athletic associations, fall over each other trying to get out identifying public relations handbooks that furnish "official rules." But the rules can vary tremendously from one organization to another, between age groups, between regions, even from one neighborhood to the next, despite all this sophistication. Pick your rule book and then have your officials and players abide by it.

Players can be plugged into the rules of any sport by the additional programming of clinics. At clinics, rules, especially house and ground rules, are introduced to the team managers and/or players prior to league, tournament, or general play activity through a visual demonstration, i.e., a role-playing involvement process. In a way, participation in a clinic is like a consent contract, a silent agreement to accept and abide by the rules presented. If the officials are present, they have the opportunity to establish their dignity and authority before conflicts erupt in the heat of play.

Officials are the police force we recruit to keep sports life from becoming riots with bats and balls. They keep the wheels of participation turning and keep the play experience from becoming a bitter, argumentative battlefield. They also create better sportsmanship because they approve certain behavior and manage friendship between opponents by giving them a "common enemy" — the rules.

Officiating is big business, a computerized technology in the big leagues of professional sports. There are film records and data on every judge, umpire, referee, time keeper — down the ranks to the simple linesman checking out-of-bounds shots. Some officials become celebrities or colorful performers, and are in greater demand than the players, which has made officiating a status position in our leisure society.

In the good old days non-players were recruited from the bleachers to be unbiased observers and to make decisions if the honor system did not work. In recreation, we involved the bigger kids, created leadership opportunities, and screened our potential workers this way. There wasn't a better way to know sports thoroughly than to have to know more than the players and the coaches.

Professional recreation leaders were often placed on the firing line because officiating allowed them to manipulate unbalanced games so that everyone came away with a shred of achievement and self-respect. But such manipulation is dangerous. It shows up faster today, under the scrutiny of "the little pros," the television-trained students of the game. With adults it generates a damaging attitude toward the recreation programmer because they expect him to be concerned with more important aspects of recreation than simply refereeing. In some ways it is seen as a conflict of interests, an invasion by the boss of the assembly line at lunch. Professional recreation programmers should avoid this precarious involvement except in cases of dire emergency or an absolute draft by the participants.

Where do we get the officials? That depends on the economics of the activity. Do you have funds to cover this refinement of activities, perhaps justifying it in a budget under "supervision of area," or can the participants finance the quality of their own activity? Many of the associations involved with specific sports and the various athletic associations, municipal and school, maintain a stable of certified officials. The higher their certification, the more tests and training specifications they have had to undergo, the more they cost. The best officials are in great demand and are booked seasons in advance for the blue ribbon sports leagues and tournaments. If you know the good ones, it is best to make special requests rather than blind booking. Whether it's your budget money or a self-sustaining league fee for officiating, spend it as if you were hiring an official to control a game in which you would play.

Some agencies attempt to beat the sports empires and the associations, by setting up their own local officials training and certification. This saves

money, rewards local talent, and gives a sense of home rule. But the faceless
stranger in town, who is booked from the regional pool, doesn't get bogged
down in local bleacher politics, personalities, or prejudices.

It's only one step down from the local pool to using a volunteer corps of
officials. Anything volunteer is never professional — and professional means
orderly, conscientious system. Volunteer officiating is short-term, cheap, and
unpredictable, but if you can't afford the train ticket you ride your thumb.
Besides, as we discussed elsewhere, volunteerism properly utilized is good
programming and public relations, but not inexpensive.

Rules and officiating are two major elements that separate self-directed,
chaotic play from organized recreation program that gives orderly, specified
results. The scale of application and the degree of complexity and rigidity in
sports situation is the result of the programmer's craftsmanship, his balancing
the relaxed spur-of-the-moment activity with the heavily regulated, intensely
organized, and highly sophisticated activity of the dedicated fanatics, experts,
and champions.

CLASSIFICATION

Defining sports generally as challenges involving physical exertion leaves us
with a number of sports that meet this criterion only to a limited degree.
Classifications are necessary to refine our thinking about each sport, perhaps
to determine if it is truly a pure sport activity or only a hybrid version
enveloping broad need objectives. Many sports are unique recreational
experiences which defy placement in the sports program as defined here. An
example is hunting, rated traditionally as a sport, sometimes as an outdoors
sport or wilderness sport, which has as its essence the single standard of
killing.

There are numerous classifications, but we intend to cite only those
which are legitimate aids to better programming. A useful classification
should both explain something and guide the programmer in matching
activities to people.

Individual, Dual, and Team

Traditionally we look at sports in terms of how many people are needed to
make the performance of a skill into a game, i.e., an experience that takes
place because of challenges outside the participant himself. All sports' skills
can probably be practiced by the individual alone, but his greatest potential
for fulfillment lies in participating with a requisite number of participants.

Take *individual sports*, which include:

Weightlifting	Bowling	Shooting
Bicycling	Golf	Hunting
Sledding	Ice Skating	Auto Racing
Hiking	Skiing	Rope Jumping
Horseback Riding	Gymnastics	Roller Skating

| Archery | Track and Field | Mountaineering |
| Casting | Spelunking | Sky Diving |

The essence of these activities is that a single individual can engage in it and find a game situation possible. To further explain this, we must first realize that the mere practice of a skill, while it may be enjoyable, does not have the sophistication of the game experience.

A game takes place when a player employs his skill according to specified rules in overcoming obstacles to achieve certain goals. An opponent is not necessary, only a challenge is created by a target, goal, or previous record. This is not to say that any of the listed sports under the individual heading are exclusively individual, only that they can be undertaken as pure, first-plateau game experience, a step more advanced than the basic exercises through which one prepares for competition.

Actually, the addition of opponents and team mates enhances play in any of the sports by creating more complex mental and physical challenges and increasing the possibilities for social interaction. The exception or reverse argument on this is that there are many who seek relaxation through solitude and the sense of self, unaided meeting a challenge alone.

An open-minded programmer can scale any sports activity up and down the range from individual to team play. It is becoming tradition and common practice that we recognize certain sports as individual. There is, however, a trend that indicates decreasing interest in solo participation by the general public. There are perhaps implied guilt feelings if we choose solitude rather than companionship. The loner is an outsider under modern values . . . perhaps always was to some degree.

One of the great supports for single individual play has to do with providing a pure, undistracted concentration, in most cases an opportunity to get close to nature. The presence of another person, companion or opponent, tends to disturb that communion. Hunting and archery seem to fall in here.

Another way of analyzing it is to explain individual play as one person performing the complete execution of a skill within a game context without the need of assistance from a partner or team mates. In track and field for a moment in time a performer is in the spotlight, starring. The shot putter has the complete focus while opponents stand by, but the sprinter runs his race while his opponents are also in action.

Participation in the individual sport provides high potential in the need areas of recognition and dominance.

Dual Category

This arises when two people oppose each other within a game situation, with very little formal structuring necessary. Like individual activities, dual sports allow people to direct their participation themselves. This is not to say, however, that a programmer cannot improve such participation if given the chance.

The contest between two people rates a high potential for fairly intimate social interaction, dominance, and physical and mental activity. Intense love/hate emotions that can alternate in such one-to-one situations probably justify the interference of a third party, a counseling programmer who can structure the play so that emotions are controlled and confined within the game and do not spill into other areas of life. The programmer can also help adjust the serious flaw in all dual sports play — uneven abilities — by equalizing them so that the contests are not so unbalanced as to bore one and depress the other.

The greatest value in the dual sports lies in the fine opportunity for integrating men and women in coed or co-rec play. Couples are able to schedule a lifetime of contests providing they maintain a balance of skill and interest. Since the man/woman cohabitation remains our dominant unit of relationships, dual sports can play an immense role in creating stability into such relations.

Here are some of the sports generally designated as dual:

Badminton	Paddle Tennis	Tetherball
Billiards	Tennis	Curling
Boxing	Table Tennis	Horseshoes
Fencing	Judo	Shuffleboard
Handball	Wrestling	4 Square
Squash	Croquet	Hopscotch

Team Sports

These are the big pay-off activities in recreation, absorbing massive numbers of people. They are complex, challenging programming which require the most expert technology we can bring to bear. The rules of participation are more rigorous because many interests and needs of many players must be served through structuring.

Putting a team together and keeping it together is a difficult process. Strong leadership from among the participants helps, but the real burden of motivation lies with what the programmer produces as activity for the teams.

The pitfall in team sports is, of course, finding enough players from which to construct a team. Each sport requires a specific number for official play if the sponsoring agency is a part of a larger jurisdiction, such as a sports association. Using regulation numbers insures several things: (1) probably the most challenging game experience, since the proper number are playing, (2) less disagreement in the game because uniform rules are applicable, and (3) eligibility to compete with other agencies which also conform to the same standards.

We believe, however, that recreation's greatest achievement is core program conducted locally with a grass-roots breadth that serves every individual. Intramural programming means that a lazy programmer can't merely string together a team and compete in inter-area leagues and tournaments. He has to produce where he is. That's the challenge which usually isn't met without hard work and dedication.

What frustrates the programmer is getting enough numbers together to create regulation-size teams to form a meaningfully competitive league. Competition is the fuel, and generally the more frequently a team competes the greater are its chances of surviving. To meet this numbers pitfall, programmers must be able to adapt play to smaller, non-regulation size team play. Two-man touch football and three-man basketball have been adaptations that have matured into intense, highly sophisticated programs in many areas. The ingenious programmer can cut squad size down to almost dual competition and, by imaginative promotion, field a multi-team intramural competition that generates nearly the same enthusiastic involvement found in regulation play.

The big value in team play is the great potential for fulfilling the belonging need. Even in losing there is a mutuality of feeling, a sense of identity found in the camaraderie and commiseration. The shared elation of winning-team members is a powerful force. Team sports also provide a much greater sense of security for those who want only a small share of the responsibility and for the dominance seekers who accept team leadership roles.

The commonly identified team sports are listed in order of their volume participation in America:

Major Volume Team Sports

Baseball	Flag Football
Basketball	Softball
Tackle Football	Slow Pitch
Touch Football	

Minor Volume Team Sports

Polo	Soccer
Ice Hockey	Lacrosse
Kickball	Rugby
Dodgeball	Volley Tennis
Pushball	Field Hockey
War	Prisoners Base
Volleyball	

Organizational Patterns

There are a lot of people around who think a sports program is a magic happening that occurs simply by checking a ball out. There's no denying much horseplay and self-directed activity comes from the participants' own energies and ideas. No one wants to stop spontaneity, but it is important to remember that it does remain primitive.

"Look, this is my new shuttle system," beamed the college intramural director, "the teams really like it." He fondled the lined draw sheet with an ecstasy usually reserved for antiques or expensive collections, pointing out how a team could lose, drop to the consolation bracket, win, and get back into the championship play right up to the end of the tournament. The whole system was actually more complicated than this, but the point is that thirty teams of rebellious college students received the greatest possible opportunity to play without losing interest because their programmer had made an organizational pattern that eliminated most of the flaws encountered in past programs.

Organizational patterns are the systems technology of all recreation programming and are extremely vital in the competitive sports arena. The systems or patterns fall into three major plateaus of involvement: *learning, competing/exercising, and instructing/mastering.*

Learning

The volume traffic in recreation program passes through the functional area of learning skills presented in various forms of classes, clinics, workshops, and institutes. It is a functional overlap with the educational process in our society. It is necessarily a major enterprise in recreation because schools fail to prepare people for their leisure lives.

Life changes rapidly, rendering schooling obsolete almost overnight if that schooling fails to go beyond facts to develop the capabilities of inquiry and adaptation. Degrees and certificates do not make an expert for organizations tend to retrain their fresh-out-of-school recruits to their particular techniques. Recreation programmers are increasingly realizing that ready-made participants are a myth. Every activity situation is a new one, shaped and altered by a multitude of variables from age to sex to needs to environment to skill level.

We tend to say that all recreation experience is educational, but so is life, and to make a point of it helps us very little. What must be accepted is that recreational sports reach their fullest potential when equally skilled participants play and improve efficiently in a continuous, progressive pattern. If all or even a few lack skill and knowledge the fulfillment possibilities of the sports activity are obstructed.

New recreation outlets which arise after formal schooling has been completed also means that further instruction is needed. This, along with the balancing of skill levels, place the instructional class in a dominant position in most recreation programs.

Such classes generally follow a basic form in which a series of short sessions are scheduled through quarterly seasons. They culminate in some type of evaluative exhibition that recognizes the participants' progress and achievement. The recognition may take the form of qualifying for advancement to classes with more demanding challenges, i.e., from novice-to-intermediate-to-advanced.

The class approach to programming has a psychological edge over other organizational patterns because American society is school-oriented, with many people spending much of their lives in a classroom even as adults. A class with a beginning and an end is well suited for the schedule-directed average American. He identifies classes and learning with self improvement, making it a purposeful activity. Participation in a class doesn't enlist him forever since it ends at some specific period. He is not trapped into making a graceless exit or dropping out when his interest lags.

Unfortunately, the class organizational pattern sometimes extends beyond the learning plateau. By using the progress step plan of novice-to-intermediate-to-advanced programmers tend to make classes the only form of activity. This not only stops short of providing activity outlets for performing the skill, i.e., doing it rather than learning it, but it may create further imbalance in the skill levels of a large segment of participants. This means that people are moved out of a situation where they can participate on a homogeneous skill level into a more advanced level where they outclass opponents and enjoy less.

Of course not all step-plan classes cause chaos if they spread the skill levels at the same time they're adding people to the activity. The next plateau, the performance/exercise one, can serve exclusively the novice, the intermediate, and the advanced student.

There are some general dimensions that are helpful with class programming. Classes should be kept at a reasonable social interaction level, somewhere between 10 and 20 is ideal, fewer diminish the vitality, more affect intimacy to the extent that group members can't relate to each other during the class. Obviously, room or field space, available equipment, instructor control ability, the complexity of the skill being learned, and the capacity of the learners themselves will dictate more exact numerical structuring of specific classes. Another dimension is the scheduling of sessions so that intervals fall between them. This allows participants to reflect on their learning, engage in outside practice, and anticipate the next meeting with enthusiasm. In fast-paced urban settings, service agencies tend to schedule on a weekly basis.

Learning is also provided through adaptations of the class pattern. The clinic is a common one-time learning activity that focuses on improving and reshaping existing skills and knowledge. The workshop is more of an exploratory one-day session in which new concepts and techniques are introduced, attempted, and evaluated. The institute design, a combination of the new and old, generally extends more than one day but concentrates everything into a continuous period of time as opposed to periodical classes.

The clinic, workshop, and institute are in the special event category because of their infrequency and irregularity. Classes are basically standard, regular program activities, recurrent and expected, concentrating on habitual participation.

Sports skills classes in the recreation setting differ from those conducted in the preparation-for-life school atmosphere because the students are voluntarily participating and possess motivated readiness. Their readiness, however, is to get on with it and start performing in the activity with the least amount of formalized classroom ritual. It is difficult to hold the line, to keep people preparing in a mock performance situation, practicing parts rather than immediately doing the entire thing. But the stronger the preliminary incubator learning, the more effective is the initial performance. The power to make participants accept the necessity of training comes from organizations which guard against individuals coming into an activity ill prepared and ending up disappointed with what happens to them. These organizations award the badges and set the participant requirements through rules and certifying tests. These organizations, basically voluntary and representing one specific sport, are the result of the great American desire to organize everything that moves. As power mad as they may seem because of their Czars and elected leaders, they are probably operating under the noblest of motives, i.e., the protection of the participants.

A great deal of assistance in the form of course outlines, standard tests, instructor certification, publications, sanction of facilities and sites, and legislative power can be obtained from such associations. The Amateur Athletic Union probably epitomizes the giant association that has historically governed competitions in a variety of sports, setting the pace for Olympic Games participation. Such control as a matter of course filters down to class operations.

One other major consideration with sports classes is the emphasis that must be placed on health and safety. Each sports activity has unique sets of muscles and organs which are not ordinarily used in normal life. All sports pursued to their fullest potential require above normal physical exertion. Because of these stresses on the participant, even controlled, limited activities in the learning class require careful screening of the participants to ferret out potential distress cases.

Many activities demand medical exams and fitness qualifying tests prior to enrollment. Doubtful cases are advised to spend some time getting in shape before taking on the class work.

The class itself, of course, serves as a screening device for the second plateau of performance.

Tutoring

It is remiss to talk of class patterns and not give the one-to-one tutoring process some analysis. We've suggested that a drop below ten participants begins to dilute the vitality of the group process, and very few budget-conscious agencies permit programming for less than six individuals. But growing affluency permits loners and private-type individuals to learn through individual, highly personalized instruction.

This is fairly prominent in the recreation service areas where profit is one of the major objectives of programming. Resorts in particular utilize this learning pattern because of the short term, free-spending clientele that is served: the person on a holiday is on hand to try everything, *now*, with the shortest possible length of time standing between him and active performance.

People in middle and upper economic classes tend to prefer use fees and charges. They want to pay for what they personally use, no more, no less. Many of them are willing to pay unusually high fees exceeding pro-rated group fees to have the exclusive attention of a tutor. Time is saved, of course, because a good tutor, in contrast to the group instructor, can concentrate his talent on accelerating the learning of one participant.

But tutoring is not simply a one-to-one arrangement, for it can cover a family unit, a couple, or a small group of four or less who have similar learning capacities, interests, and readiness. Tutoring can also be utilized as a spin-off technique for slow learners in group instruction in order to bring their learning pace up to the group's. From this perspective tutoring which accelerates learning, saves time, cuts instructors' and facility use fees, doesn't have to be viewed as strictly programming for the rich.

Probably the most forceful argument in favor of tutoring is that it permits recreation to enjoy a rare moment of concern with the individual, develops a depth of personal understanding, and allows the programmer to better shape harmonious performance activities.

PERFORMANCE OUTLET ARENA

Recreation's core program strength should be in its ability to produce outlet experiences for existing sports' skill and knowledge. In the ideal society, education should fully prepare youth and adults for their leisure life styles, producing ready, eager, and capable players. Unfortunately the school curricula vacillate in their objectives, with recreation consequently being handed either unskilled, unmotivated, sports-sterile people or participants who received an in-depth preparation in activities with poor carry-over.

Recreation has thrived on this breakdown, making learning classes the bulk of program. Other service agencies, especially school, military, and institutional recreation operations that program sports, have relied on actual performance activities in which the participant plays at his present level without being delayed by instruction. If the clientele's stay is unpredictable and usually short, performance outlets are preferred to class programming because the latter can be impaired seriously by the unexpected loss of large numbers of participants.

The patterns of organizing the performance plateau of sports play are many and complex. They range from clubs to league contests to tournaments — all of which are based on competition. These patterns are progressively plateaued, based on participation objectives.

At one pole, programming learned or existing skills toward an outlet begins where self-directed practice and exercise leaves off. The programmer attempts to stage group sessions to accommodate those individuals who can't motivate or discipline themselves to maintain personal, private practice regimen. He also may coordinate facilities and equipment resources to enable the individual to continue privately a sport — a primitive, low-level form of programming technology.

Participant performance at this level is based on trying out skills and keeping physically fit to prepare for a more complex form of sports involvement. The skier works out in the weight room, the swimmer does laps every morning, and the basketball player lobs 25-foot shots for hours alone. Private people, loners, often prefer to stay at this stage, indefinitely avoiding the interactions and frustrations of cooperative and competitive togetherness. Facilitating the opportunities for such practice and exercise, referred to jointly as working out, is an important, primary function of a programmer.

Moving to the next step, the programmer provides the framework for a more sophisticated *cooperative* involvement. He needs some kind of special cement to keep participant interest at a high pitch. He subscribes to the process of social facilitation, the concept that people push people of similar interests. If a fellow fanatic says "let's go fishing" he is more of a catalyst than a recreation programmer whose job depends upon getting some action going. This is where the club organization pattern is important, for it funnels individuals into a self-perpetuating group process.

Sports clubs are set up as combinations of interests or, more commonly now, along one particular sports involvement. We may dispense with the combination club because its format is treated more appropriately under social recreation. The single interest sports club is much more of a pure concept and, although it relies on the adhesive effect of socialization, it can best provide a deep, penetrating, and continuous participation in any sport by those who pursue highly committed horizontal experiences. The club is the ideal route for the new enthusiast who wants to take a sport seriously, lose himself in it, or wrap his leisure lifestyle around it. The club allows one to remain a dedicated participant whether he has the intention or capacities for becoming a master in terms of instructor or champion status.

The sports club membership assembles people of similar interests and provides a communications and inspirational contact point that helps to create and reinforce individual interest. Information is traded, challenges generated — the very act of belonging conveys an identity. There are vicarious fulfillments through members' achievements, and collective group energies can construct competition and outing experiences not easily put together by the individuals. The club has the power to obtain for its members discount privileges on equipment, and admission prices to events. It also may have political leverage through which to gain concessions on access or influences laws pertaining to the specific sport.

The best contributions to sports participation through the club pattern include the motivating power of scheduled group activity, trips, and team competition unity; the cooperative procurement and sharing of unusually costly facilities and equipment; and a system of achievement recognition maintained with the membership serving as a knowledgeable audience.

The club serves the programmer not only by holding the participants' interest over extended periods but also as a handy unit of competition which makes the organization of teams for interplay much easier.

Competition Patterns

If the club is distinctly a cooperative phase for participants moving into a more complex sports involvement, it maintains its appeal by conducting classes in order to recruit new members and provide advanced opportunities for exceptional members by permitting them to instruct. But the club also relies on competitive experiences within and without. These competitive experiences are distinctly a progressive stage for the participant to enter. He may have jumped directly from learning to competition, without the practice and cooperative activity that builds confidence. Many over-all recreation programs prefer this abrupt staging in the fast-paced life style that pushes our thresholds of readiness.

Competition is the equivalent of juggling nitro flasks. Used wisely, some amazing results are possible; used carelessly — disaster! It is at this stage that the programmer is pushed to the ultimate of his organizing potential. Traditionally, however, there are some excellent mechanical patterns with which to structure sports play. The following patterns place the classifications first:

The League Most in tune with the recreational concept of as much play for as many for as long as possible is the *seasonal league* in sports. In its simplest form the team — and it is primarily most effective in team sports — or participants play against every other participant in the league. Its strength lies in the production of the maximum active participation since no team or participant is left with idle time.

The seasonal league is often referred to as a Round Robin Tournament. "Round Robin" is derived from an old English ploy in which nervous protestors signed a petition in a circle to conceal the order of signing. Its application in sports denotes a circular competition which matches every entrant with every other one. Theoretically it is a good method to set up play that keeps everyone active throughout a season. Practically, a team continuously beaten without a chance to win the championship becomes discouraged and may forfeit the last part of its scheduled games, leaving the opposing teams inactive. The whole league then comes apart at the seams. This hazard may be remedied by expanding the basic one round league. We will examine the basic league and then its extension which may compensate for mid-season blues.

Six or eight teams is the easiest number to work into a simple round robin. Let's try eight.
1. Have each entrant draw a number 1—8.
2. Write 1 to 4 in a left column and 5 to 8 up in right column.
3. Play for each entrant is with number directly opposite.
4. The first set of games, four in number, are followed by six more for a total of seven sets (note one less than number of entrants). Pairings change by keeping number one stationary and rotating the others counter-clockwise around it.

Set #1	Set #2	Set #3	Set #4	Set #5	Set #6	Set #7
1-8	1-7	1-6	1-5	1-4	1-3	1-2
2-7	8-6	7-5	6-4	5-3	4-2	3-8
3-6	2-5	8-4	7-3	6-2	5-8	4-7
4-5	3-4	2-3	8-2	7-8	6-7	5-6

5. The same pattern is used for all even number of entries. With an uneven number, substitute a mythical team called "bye" to raise to the next even number and proceed to rotate.

Set #1	Set #2	Set #3
1-bye	1-9	1-8
2-9	bye-8	9-7
3-8	2-7	bye-6
4-7	3-6	2-5
5-6	4-5	3-4

6. Ties at the end of one round of play can be awarded to the team with a direct win during the league over its tying rival or a playoff game or games can be used to decide the championship.

Extending League Play Variations on the Round Robin may be used to solve problems such as mid-season dropouts or the equalization of competition before official competition gets underway.

To equalize competition by determining exceptionally superior entrants the first round of play is used as a basis for splitting into two leagues if sufficient entries allow it or to apply a handicapping system that would insure balanced play despite actual inequities in ability. It is the only practical way of determining unknown capacities, if time allows, and if entrants do not purposely underplay to gain an erroneous handicap.

To solve the dropout problem, one or more rounds are added to the original round so that second and third chances are provided to qualify for a playoff between round winners for the championship.

This is equivalent to the procedure of bringing various local league winners together for an elimination tournament playoff for the regional championship. In a sense the rounds play is a pattern of qualifying teams for a playoff activity leading to the determination of the over-all best.

In the event of a three round league, the same pairings are used so the programmer has only to put three dates over the first round schedule columns. The three rounder can also lead to a team A winning twice and team B winning once. B would have to beat A twice in order to deserve the championship under normal playoff concepts.

102

The Perpetual or Ladder Tournament The ladder tournament is a low-level organizing device to allow teams or participants to generate their own play by a challenge system superficially organized by the professional programmer only in its beginning when names must be placed on a ranking chart. The rankings can be set by chance, drawing names from a hat, or by taking the results of previous league play or tournament elimination.

The play in this type of tournament is much more informal in nature, games taking place when contestants agree upon a time and facility. Officiating is generally by the honor system since short-term planning prevents advance scheduling and the unlimited number of games possible creates unrealistic financial demands. This informality lends itself effectively to dual sports, although abbreviated team sports, such as three-man basketball, have utilized it with some success.

In its simplest form, the ladder is a straight, single-unit, step-by-step listing of ranks. The challenger must contest the man in the step immediately above him. Failure to arrange a contest, avoiding a challenge, or not meeting a legitimate challenge within a prescribed period, such as 48 hours after it is issued, can be considered a forfeit and the challenger trades places on the ladder with the player above. The chart of the ladder can be set up on a chalk board or a board with hooks or slots for name tags. Following one of these procedures enables the scorekeeper to change names easily as the contestants move up the ladder.

Nine Team Elimination Tournament Chart

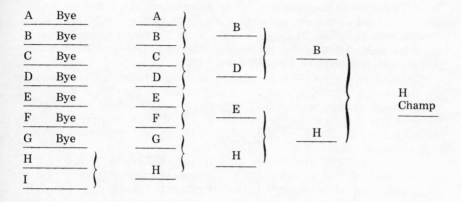

How do we determine who gets the break on the byes? A drawing by chance will award the byes in the most democratic fashion. In established sports, however, certain teams and players are either known to be superior by reputation or are formally ranked by an official association. If this superior ability is recognized when placing them in competition, the process is called "seeding." If byes exist they should go to these superior players in rank order, 1, 2, 3, ... If byes are not required to keep the superior players from eliminating each other early in the tournament, place their names in the brackets so they do not play until the semi-finals.

This is done with two seeded players in an eight-entry tournament by placing number one in the top bracket and number two in the bottom bracket. With four seeded, the third goes to number 5 position and the fourth to number 4 position.

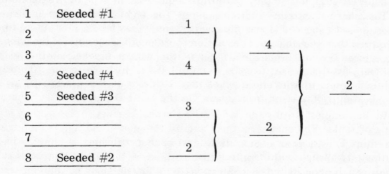

Usually only four players are seeded in a bracket of 16; eight with 32 entries. But seeding should only be used if the records of the players are truly superior and the tournament play will be benefited.

Consolation Tournament This tournament keeps the first round losers from complete elimination from play even if they only have a chance to play for a second, consolation championship. The common form is to run brackets off the left side of round one, continuing play with another single elimination tournament.

A lot of good teams have first round jitters and play beneath their ability. The consolation system tempers the depression.

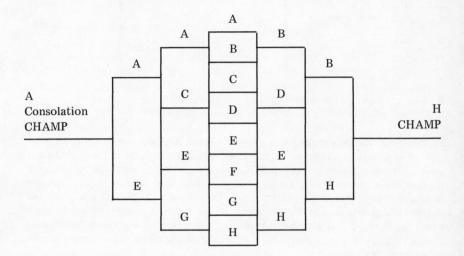

Double Elimination Tournament No one is eliminated until he has lost two contests. On the first loss, he drops to a losers' bracket and if he is undefeated there he eventually plays the winner of the winners' bracket for the championship. A player can lose once and still win the championship, which is a superior competitive play pattern in a quick result type of programming.

The chart illustrates a double setup for eight teams. The increased opportunity to succeed is accompanied by some drawbacks. First, more time is required than the single or consolation tournament. Secondly, if the winner of the loser bracket beats the winner of the winner bracket another game must be played since no team is out until it has lost two games. Thirdly, semi-final losers in winners' bracket have to cross over a bracket to avoid being beaten by the same team again. On the chart D plays F rather than C again.

The Contest Another competition device that provides a simple, basic performance outlet is the contest that permits an individual to try his skill against a number of other contestants. No interference by opponents is involved and generally a measurement determines the winner.

A football pass and punt skills contest represents this type of competition. Each contestant does his best without having any interference. Top measurement wins. Such skills contests are often run as special events to pick up lagging interests mid-season and also to help evaluate existing skills prior to forming a regular league for team play. It is generally designed for individuals, creates opportunity for the non-joiners, and usually concentrates on one skill.

Like most informal devices that rely on participant initiative and self-direction, interest mortality is great. The programmer must watch the progress of play and step in before play activity seriously breaks down. It is best to have a punchy culmination by having the top four rankings play off for a championship at a given time. A new ladder can be set up if the programmer feels the enthusiasm and interest remains high enough to merit another round of play.

Advanced Ladder Tournaments When large numbers of participants are to be served, the simple straight step ladder tournament breaks down. The remedy for this lies in adding subpatterns that create many different opportunities to play frequently. The *pyramid* is the next expansion design, creating layers of several possible challenges graduating from a broad, lower-ranked base to the number-one man at the peak.

Any player in layer A can challenge any player in layer B and so on. If an A layer player loses, he must challenge some other player in layer B next.

The King's Tournament This is a multi-series of pyramids which provides opportunities for horizontal challenging which gives access to higher power pyramids.

The Concentric Circle Ladder Tournament This is based on the same factors as King's tournament but provides an even greater field of play.

All so-called self-operating, continuous tournaments need constant supervision to keep them moving along with enthusiastic support.

Progressive Tournament With this rather simple revolving pattern the programmer shifts his emphasis from extended, long-term play to quick results with an instant determination of a champion. This tournament works well with play days and sports days in which numerous games are played simultaneously on a number of courts.

Teams rotate at the end of timed play periods to new opponents. Winners — with the exception of the winner on court 1 who remains on same court — move to the next lower numbered courts, with losers staying put. A point system can be used, for example, awarding five points for each win and totaling them at the end of day to determine the champion.

This type of tournament is easy, quick, and provides a substantial amount of interaction.

Single Elimination Tournament The classic pattern for the quick determination of a championship is the single elimination tournament. It's also poor recreation structure because half the competitors are eliminated after their first contest. It's swift and brutal but fair.

The system of bracketing the teams or players into paired contests is easily set up as long as the number of players is a power of 2, e.g., 4, 8, 16, 32, 64. Any other number means a rigged first round using byes to make up mythical teams so that the next power of 2 is reached. For example, a nine-entrant tournament would require nine subtracted from 16, which

WINNERS BRACKET

LOSERS BRACKET

A

WINNER

Double Elimination for Eight Teams

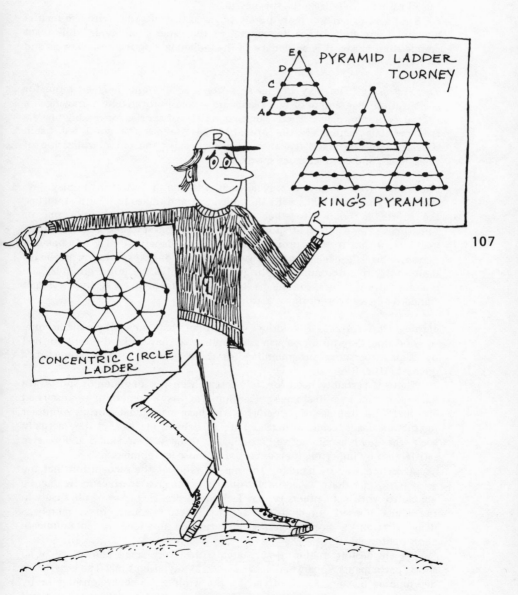

Pyramid Tournaments

requires 7 byes and one contest. This produces 8 for the remaining rounds.

Byes are all put in the first round to eliminate unfair rest advantages and interest lag in the middle of the tournament.

The Meet The track meet and the gymnastics meet are a series of contests involving skills measurement and basically devoid of the game strategies rooted in the other sports patterns. The Decathlon, which tries to determine the all-round athlete, also fits this design.

The meet provides a more purely physical test of skills, with the mental manipulations and chance happenings of the game eliminated. While team competition exists, it is secondary to the individual opportunity to excel and be recognized.

The Play Day The play day is a sports special event designed more for socialization than competition. Teams are generally formed by a drawing at a central gathering place. There can be a variety of sports, for mixing players from various centers is the primary goal. Besides the good fellowship developed by such activity, there is a chance for the cross-fertilization of rules, ideas, and feelings about sports.

The Sports Day This is closely aligned with the purposes of the play day. While the play day works with the individual and mixes him with strangers, the sports day draws together teams that remain intact to play one or sometimes several different sports. This pattern is used to end a season with a grand event, but it often provides inter-center competitive play in a one-day period. This is especially advantageous if costs or transportation problems limit sports to intramural play or confined them to the home grounds. The one-day affair allows the teams to measure themselves against a larger standard at least once during a season.

Mastery Outlet Arena How do we take care of champions? If people become so good that they no longer can find anyone to play with who isn't crushed by their expertness, programming for them becomes one of recreation's greatest difficulties.

There is certainly need for solid research on this one area of sports. We have ideas which we shall merely mention. The first is something we discussed elsewhere, i.e., the use of participants who have mastered a sport as volunteer instructors, leaders, and officials. This, of course, means that they actually leave the field as an active participant, project their skills, and receive satisfaction by imparting their expertise to those less competent.

A second way of handling the master requires the recognition that the great performer doesn't necessarily qualify as the great instructor. He may be unable to work with others or may lack the desire. He has to be physically in the arena himself, even if his activity doesn't count, or is merely a demonstration, a non-competing performance intended to communicate and/or entertain.

We are dealing in the mastery area with a very small percentage of all sports participants, somewhere less than 2% at any given time. The criteria for determining mastery can be fixed by the winning of championships or by comparison with other performers. There are no exact guidelines for this, but there are symptoms, such as boredom with traditionally scheduled programs, challenging the leader or instructor, or a certain amount of showing off that interferes with normal program. We are very primitive with our programming at the mastery level of participation. It is almost as if they have reached the end of a trail, that there is no further place to go and their feelings die; they become pros, getting paid, and what was play becomes work. Others depart and try not to look back. They just have to transfer their interest and involvement to an entirely new interest.

We have identified competition as the major motivating force behind performance in most sports programs. It is the essence of the game situation which, in turn, allows the performance of skills to be interesting, challenging, and constantly changing.

But all is lost if, in the process of motivating participation, we carelessly allow built-in failure and loss of self-esteem to exist. The programmer must use competition as a fine surgical tool, adapting it carefully so that no physical or emotional harm comes to any participants.

While rules and regulations give shape and discipline to sports activities, they can not make a mutually fulfilling experience take place for all participants. People have different skill levels. Champions are bored by amateurs, and weak players have self esteem crushed by superior opponents.

109

There are numerous systems, from the simple to the very complex, that have been used to place individual participants in competitive situations in which the greatest good to all results. The most convenient fixed criteria are age, school grade, weight, height, and sex.

Some programs manipulate a combination of these factors by assigning a numbers or exponent value system. For example, a point is assessed for each year of age, a point for each 10 pounds of weight, and a point for each half foot of height. A 12-year-old boy (12 points), weighing 120 pounds (12 points) and 5 feet in height (10 points) would be rated 34. The concept is to balance differing maturation levels with chronological age. An old, somewhat imperfect system, it is an attempt to protect the small, late developers from those who mature earlier, and in turn to protect the oversized but young and uncoordinated from tough competition. The protection is to prevent physical injury and to avoid the trauma of constant defeat.

Most recreation programs tend to ignore size criteria and structure competition into age levels and male-female separations. The same rationale of protection prevails. The age breakdowns can vary from region to region but most commonly will be found 9—12, 13—14, 15—17, 18—25, 25—40, over-40.

Other refinements are beginning to appear with better understanding of the expanding psychological and physical potentials of the young and old. Competitive sport activity is replacing the low-organized game program for

6—8 year olds, and the over-65's are given consideration as well. There is also a greater effort to define narrower age bands, under-30's, 30—40, 50—60, even to one age year, i.e., 12-year-olds. As program expands in our culture, the growth will allow greater focusing on shorter span age activities.

Obviously such fixed aspects can not really equalize competitive play in a dynamic society. Such rigid guidelines rapidly diminish in effectiveness as adulthood comes to the attention of programmers. Man's experiences prepare him through learning and opportunities to play at various levels of skill and knowledge.

Skill and knowledge readiness can be measured but in itself represents an obligation of time and effort. In many cases, it becomes a functional, motivating program in itself. People are interested in seeing where they stand in comparison to others, which the cooperative effort of team play often does not provide.

Measurement and classification provide fulfillment for certain individuals that the competitive game experience does not. A major program device is the skills day which has been structured in its most sophisticated form in the pass-punt-kick extravaganzas which follow nation-wide rules distributed by its commercial sponsor. When employed primarily as a method of classifying participants for equal competitive team play rather than determining winner types, the skills contest reaches its zenith.

Closely coupled to the skills contest is the sports clinic which encompasses the measurement of skills as well as activities designed for learning and improvement. The clinic often uses the remedial approach to upgrade deficiencies found in participants to create well-rounded teams for league play. When local intramural programming, which stresses play for all rather than stars, is organized there may be a wide disparity between abilities. Play designed for all comers may make the game satisfying only for the highly skilled.

Skills contests and clinics need not be undertaken only in the planning stages of league play. They serve well to repair leagues in midseason if the breakdown is due to serious differences in playing ability.

At the adult level, under the pressures of time, it is seldom appropriate to run measurement activities merely for classifying purposes. Adults want to get on with the game. Youth moves in this direction also. We are all impatient to do the real thing rather than practice or qualify for it.

Sports programmers who keep good records maintain files on highly rated individual players. The most extreme example is the softball pitcher who can dominate play so that his team mates and opponents rarely become actively involved. The strike-out artist can create a great ballpark tableau in which he obtains fulfillment while others merely stand and watch. The records on the aces develop out of actual league play. Many agencies join in associations to pool knowledge covering ratings on individuals and teams.

We have covered the concept of seeding under organizational patterns of play. It is the way we use ratings, not how they are determined, that keeps the best players and teams in action. For purposes of rating teams, the tournament form of play is often used prior to regular season play. Even a pilot or sample first round of a league can be executed to aid the programmer in equalizing competition for official play that counts toward a championship.

Even with a shortage of teams, first class (A) and second class (B) teams can be scheduled into one league where standings are only affected in A vs. A games, and B vs. B games. A plays a B as a non-counting practice or bye. It is possible but difficult to assess a handicap for A team.

The Handicap

Programmers have their finest hour in the skewed competition crisis. To aid competitive play in reaching its fullest potential the idea of *handicapping* slips into high gear. Handicapping is merely a device which gives points to the weak or obstructs the full skill of the superior player.

In team play the concept of handicapping is not as widespread or as effective as with the individual or dual type of activity. The more players involved the greater the unpredictability of outcome.

Golf is one of the prime examples of handicapping, probably because it is easy to determine and apply on an on-going basis. A player merely registers at any course which has par rating, par being the number of strokes a champion would take to cover the eighteen holes established by the reigning professional golfers association.

Score cards are turned in by each golfer, signed by himself and a partner. A percentage of his top scores, say 10 out of 25, are used to determine his average score. Par is subtracted from it, and taking 80% of the difference, the handicap is set. For example, a golfer with an average round of 90 on a par 80 course would have a difference of 10, eighty percent of which is 8, his handicap. That handicap can be used in a wide network of courses all over the world regardless of what the par of any course is. It also gives a programmer immediate information to use in scheduling tournament or league play.

Golf also has a variety of devices for setting handicaps even during tournament play. First rounds are often used to set handicaps. Even the best three holes shot or blind bogie set-ups where players do not know which holes they played will be eliminated from the score or used for averaging out a handicap.

Golf is rather the exception in the complexity of handicapping by score. Of the other individual, carry-over sports with large participation bowling has the framework for score handicapping. It should be noted that in golf and bowling the player is allowed a clean attempt at scoring. By this we mean his opponent does not attempt to interfere or obstruct.

Almost any of the "Clean shot" sports — track and field, skiing, shooting, or weight lifting — may utilize a scoring handicap method. Horseshoes, a rare organized happening in modern times, used scoring handicaps in its days of past glory. But score handicapping requires constant attention and full-time organizers. Golf and bowling seem to be the only successful manipulators, perhaps the only ones that can afford the complexity.

What of handicapping that is used when superior-inferior players are not separated into different flights, heats or leagues, the kind of handicapping that places an additional physical burden on the superior player or team? Most artificial obstruction attempts turn play into novelty contests. They are often disappointing to all participants. They change the nature of the whole game by making a stunt out of it.

Nevertheless, there are times when for the sake of safety or merely having an activity this method is employed. Champions can be made to play lefthanded in tennis. Superior teams have to shoot from 25 feet out in basketball or can't block or run with the ball in football. Girls are allowed unlimited handling of a volleyball while an opposing boys team must adhere to the three contacts rule. In wrestling, an inferior opponent can be given a position of advantage on the mat over a superior opponent. In handball, two inferior players can be teamed against a champion.

One of our prime examples that moved from a handicapping concept into a full-blown sport that adapts itself well to inferior ability is slow pitch softball. But this is basically an adaptive method which depends on equipment and abilities rather than handicapping one player against another. The point is that out of the physical handicapping of sports can arise an entirely new form of play.

Extreme caution must be taken whenever this physical handicapping involves equipment. Tennis players have been handicapped by having them wear floppy, view-obstructing hats, baggy clothes to trip on, or carrying umbrellas or weights. To purists, such programming insults the true game and, more importantly, exposes players to possible injury. Whenever you change the game from existing rules and accepted practices you tempt mishap and ill feeling from dedicated enthusiasts. The inner circle of programmers refer to this form of handicapping as the "blind bull fighting syndrome."

The job of the programmer is not just to throw out the ball and stand back. The goal of perfect play, total participant fulfillment, is a demanding, creative, scientific, and perceptive challenge, not the least of which is the constant need to equalize competition.

112

CAPSULE HISTORIES

A programmer's enthusiasm about scheduling specific sports is directly proportionate to his knowledge of their exciting backgrounds. A major qualification of professional programmers should be a sense of sports history in order to understand the importance of each sport.

This section will neither be exhaustive nor encyclopedic about sports' lore. The capsule histories are intended to spark initiative for further study and reflection on the current roles of some major sports.

Baseball enjoys the stamp of being typically American. About 12,000,000 Americans are probably *actively* involved in baseball and another 12,000,000 regulars watch it. A world series game can occupy half the United States on a good day.

Baseball probably originated with the English cricket which was brought to colonial America. But 1839 was the date publicists in the 1930's dreamed up to credit Coopertown and Abner Doubleday as its founders to boost sagging big league promotion. Baseball's rules and playing field were established in 1845 and have remained relatively stable ever since. In fact a number of historians identify Alexander Cartwright who created the rules and field, as the founder. As baseball evolved from cricket it took on names such as "town ball" and the "New York game."

Baseball has been the most important means for bringing highly organized competitive play into the lower age ranks of children. While it still draws great numbers of young participants and older spectators, it shares preeminance with several other sports.

Softball came into being around 1900 as an adaptation of baseball to the inside of a firehouse in Minneapolis. It went outdoors soon afterwards and was a slowed-down game which involved more people than the more demanding baseball.

Softball is often a pitcher's game, the play controlled by his speed and curves. An offshoot itself, baseball nurtured other offshoots such as lob ball and slowpitch with bigger balls, more hitting. But softball failed to sustain its former popularity in competitive play, while baseball has come back to replace it.

Football is really the new king sport. Like baseball, it's a spinoff from an older sport, soccer, and the English adaptation of soccer, rugby. Everywhere except in the United States, people think of soccer or rugby as *football*.

Football is a more natural mass sport to which a transition may be made from children's games. Goal games are the core of early play patterns, and football is merely a big, grown-up version of most of them.

Rugby was (and is) a pretty brutal, hazardous game, so much so that Harvard banned it in 1860. American football was born in 1869 between Rutgers and Princeton. Its form is hardly recognizable with the modern game. Rule changes have been constant and radical since the beginning. About 1913 the real change in appearance took place with Notre Dame's Rockne-Dorais invention of the forward pass.

113

Tackle football is the core game, probably the most demanding bodily contact experience in sports. It has a team violence that comes closest to war, man's primitive survival activity. But there are offshoots of the tackle form in touch and flag, modified versions that remove some hazards and permit play with a minimum of protective equipment.

Americans probably accept football today as the best sports expression of their nature. The season stretches longer than ever and there is a mushrooming growth of year-round programming.

Basketball has an extremely inspirational history. It shows that with any given problem a new recreation activity can probably be invented to solve it. Scholars credit the Mayans as the originators whose wall inscriptions show a vertical hoop game.

But James Naismith at the YMCA training school in Massachusetts never saw the Mayan inscriptions. In 1891 the YMCA, after 40 years of growth, was having trouble keeping members active during winter since the popular competitive athletics were designed for the outdoors.

Naismith noted that the common denominator of the popular outdoor sports was a ball. As an indoor sport roughness would have to be eliminated as well as running with the ball or kicking it. The goal was the real key, a curved one rather than upright to cut out driving the ball at it. High up, too, to keep the defensive team from ganging around it. The 1891 goals were peach baskets.

Basketball is easy to get off the ground because large platoons of players aren't necessary. But at one time the rules called for nine players to a team.

More spectators watch basketball than any other sport in the United

States. Several countries, such as the Philippines, have adopted it as their number-one major sport. It is a sport which has had no fundamental deviations from its basic form. All age levels may play the same type of game as the professionals.

Tennis owes its American adoption to a woman who brought the racquet and balls back from a party in Bermuda in 1874, and women who pushed its development here.

But tennis is a real antique. The Egyptians and the Greeks were doing it — on horseback. Twelfth century France was busy with handball, but finally made up racquets when women complained of the ball stinging their hands. So tennis itself, old as it is, is a spinoff too.

Somebody at one time found the courts indoors filled and moved outside and played over a hedge which became a net. In America lawn tennis was the mode of development and, because women were pushing it and playing, men tended to look on the game as effeminate, a stigma whose traces still exist.

Tennis is moving strongly back into an extremely popular position today. It is our number-one major outdoor individual or dual sport, relatively inexpensive, and an excellent opportunity for mixed participation.

Bowling is tennis's indoor counterpart. But it is probably better rated as the top family sport of them all.

Ancient drawings show a form of bowling in which rounded stones were rolled at objects. But the rolling of balls at pins as part of a religious ceremony originated in 4th century Germany. Italian Boccie and the Dutch lawn bowls were original forms without the pins.

The Dutch probably introduced nine pin bowling in New York about 1650. But play by the masses, especially families, didn't come until the early 1900's, and uniform rules arrived about 1895.

Bowling suffers a mixed image in America today, the facilities ranging from hangouts to luxurious palaces. Somewhere in between is the settling point with the middle class the continuing participants. It has great social overtones, but does not carry very high potential as a physical activity.

The big five sports set the pattern for all sports as we see them capsulized. What should be noted is the openness to change and the actual changes that are an important basis for the success of sports in recreation programming. The game has always adjusted to the players — as it should be. Rigid forms and patterns need to bow to participant needs regardless of how it changes the original form or offends the purists.

The following chart suggests the need fulfillment of the big five in contrast to other popular sports:

CURRENT STATUS AND TRENDS

It's very easy to get out of breath trying to keep up with the yo-yo nature of sports. The success in programming any activity is based on keeping up with the enormous fluctuation of interest in a world of constant change.

The media has a lot to do with how we think. Our minds are electronically controlled by television. It is the powerful nerve center of the

Activity	Dominance	Physical Activity	Creativity	New Experience	Social Interaction	Security and Belonging	Relaxation	Mental Activity	Recognition	Service to Others
Football	Low	High	Low	Medium	Medium	High	Low	Medium	Low	Low
Basketball	Low	High	Low	Medium	Medium	High	Low	Medium	Low	Low
Baseball	Low	High	Low	Medium	Medium	High	Low	Medium	Low	Low
Track	Medium	High	Low	Medium	Medium	Medium	Low	Low	Medium	Low
Bowling	Medium	Medium	Low	Medium	High	Medium	Medium	Low	Low	Low
Ice Hockey	Low	High	Low	Medium	Medium	High	Low	Medium	Medium	Low
Golf	Medium	Medium	Low	Medium	High	Low	Medium	Medium	Medium	Low
Tennis	Medium	High	Low	Medium	High	Low	Medium	Medium	Medium	Low
Boxing	Medium	High	Low	Medium	Low	Low	Low	Medium	Medium	Low
Horseshoes	Medium	Medium	Low	Medium	Low	Low	High	Low	Low	Low

SPORTS PROGRAM ACTIVITY NEED FULFILLMENT POTENTIAL RATING SCALE visual communications used to make us think and behave in conflicting ways.

Because sports lends itself so well to the instant transmittal of images, it has become a vicarious way of life for many, often more important than jobs or families. Phantom sports usually seen only by dedicated afficionados become popular and may eventually boast of players as well known as stars in the great days of Hollywood. The new sports begin to occupy the whole week instead of merely the day off.

But the competition is fierce, and a giant popularity escalator seems to be constantly at work. An off-beat sport, such as soccer or lacrosse, begins with a few dedicated followers who speak the language and play on adapted fields. Then suddenly a small ripple of interest swells into a wave of mass enthusiasm, up the escalator goes the sport, something new and different for the many to make as habitual as hot dogs and beer. But there is a saturation point for all popularity growth. The congestion of players and fans finally overwhelms available facilities, routine sets in, and an elite corps of enthusiasts leave to discover a new or forgotten sports interest. Why, we ask the sports participant who seeks identity over affection?

"It's a matter of being unique. When the half-wit neighbor, his idiot kid, and the typist at the office start talking game strategy, the whole interest cheapens."

On the other hand, the enthusiast-participant who wants to be in the mainstream life style responds to being part of the big crowd.

"It's good to feel a part of something that everybody is interested in — the parking lot attendant, my partner, my children. It's on television, in the newspapers. I belong to something everybody thinks is important."

Sports undoubtedly have been the Americans' substitute for the old pioneer survival adventure. But there are no new physical frontiers in which to move when staleness and routine begin. Instead, a new kind of sport moves into the attention arena or the existing sports colossal is overhauled and given new glamor and excitement. The oscillation of popularity is a universal aspect of human behavior we can predict.

Professionalism

We now move from the fresh, sweet smell of the day-off amateur taking his fling to the paid, polished, exhibitionist athlete. Professional sports are choreographed productions in modern society, a product of the spectators' unquenchable thirst for greater excitement. Participation is less for the game than for a performance by careerists who are paid extraordinarily high salaries.

While interest remains relatively constant for schools, it soars with the professional plateaus of each sport. The increasing vicariousness of leisure has made sports big business. Full-time, year-round production is the dominant trend.

The positive side of professionalism is that a facade of amateurism purity has been advocated but abused. America stands almost alone in maintaining a kind of volunteer play nature to its sports as a recreation. The professionalism wave has pushed a kind of revolution by the amateur athlete who wants to compete on an equal basis with athletes elsewhere and/or in other educational and leisure pursuits which are subsidized in various ways. For example, a young film maker or budding chemist can get a grant to aid his most effective application to the effort. Why not the amateur athlete?

The new aura of respect and dignity afforded professional sports has made the amateur less heroic and significant.

Professionalism is big business. An intricate web of farm systems is developing in all sports. Little League Baseball — a miniature but almost exact replica of professional baseball — sets the pace. Pop Warner Football has upgraded the entering high school athlete to the point that he begins with extremely advanced skills.

The dominant trend in sports is to create at very low age levels highly structured sports programs imitating the professionals. This abrupt initiation to highly organized play is the opposite of the earlier system of lead-in games, to low-organized sports, to the more structured participation. But where we have homogenized the nature of the sport for all ages there are many instances of backlash. The intensity of the structured program has caused many young players to drop out of sports for several seasons. In some cases the next age plateau offers less excitement and glamor. The stress to emulate the professionals constantly frustrates participants because the contrast is so great between their own abilities and the professionals'.

Professionalism will continue to grow and direct the interest and organization of sports. Only the competent recreation programmer can turn this into a stimulus to reinforce interest in participating. He should not set impossible goals.

Loss of Risk

Adventure and new experiences continue to diminish. Liability laws, which place the emphasis on the safety of participants, have all but driven most of the exciting risks from sports.

There is undue stress on safety procedures. We have allowed safety rails to be placed around sports experiences, fencing out adventure and excitement. Equipment is continually being designed to soften and protect, while rules are invented to eliminate injury. In some ways, because the spectators are far removed from danger they seem to want violent, hazardous conflict or unseemly behavior. This never-satisfied lust for brutality in order to maintain interest has bred the hate-hurt-kill attitude of players and coaches.

We also have prevented the individual, through physical or legal restraints, from taking on the elements at certain times and in threatening places. For example, we often cancel team games in inclement weather, keep skiers off treacherous slopes, and cut down bodily contact permitted in the major sports.

Laissez-faire Life Style

The counter-cultures refuse to be computerized, dehumanized, and scheduled. Where professionalism takes sports play too seriously, the spontaneous, spur-of-the-moment participant tends to treat all such experiences as dispensable trivia, superficial amusement.

"Don't tie me down, man," asserts the casual, non-conformist rebel to the orderliness of structured life style. "It's just a game isn't it? If I show up I'm there and then it's my thing to do, I'm in control. My feelings tell me to be there and do it. No schedule is going to tell me."

The break with the old order always brings on chaos. If sports just happen weird forms appear, misshaped by ground rules made up as you go along. There is no exhilaration from anticipation. And a lot of the magic of the planned-to-fulfill joy in expressing one's potential within some literal and figurative boundaries is missing. Recollections have little depth to rest upon.

But the laissez-faire participants retain the advantage of flexibility and the ability to take things with a sense of abandon and freedom. Girls and boys can play football together, with a rolled-up sweater, twenty to a team, if that's where it's at — and if the score isn't kept too seriously, there are no losers.

While we have described laissez-faire program participation in the extreme, the sandlot, pick-up kind of play, there are lesser degrees of under-organized sports activities. Under-organization doesn't guarantee freedom and self-actualization; instead it can frustrate everyone involved. It's possible for a good programmer to organize carefully the most informal, casual, spontaneous experience simply by being prepared, seeing that the right cross section of people drift into the arena at the right time and that the resources are handy. Freedom is really a chance to select alternatives, not to have none at all.

118

Technology Guides

Technology is mechanizing sports. Climate-controlled playing arenas — plastic bubbles — take the elements away as unpredictable agents of change. New kinds of playing tools arise: foam rubber instead of sandpaper table tennis paddles; steel tennis racquets, super springy running shoes, motorized skis, extra-flexible glass vaulting poles, special kicking shoes, golf balls with chemically treated cores, fluorescent tennis balls — all bring new dimensions to traditional sports, almost to the point of radically changing the nature of the activity. And then there are all the new wheel sports.

Someday, the electric bat in baseball may not be a ridiculous thought. Ask the classical guitarists. There is always resistance, especially by old record holders, but ultimately the new device wins out and a sport takes on a new glow and the goals are extended outward by the new development.

Loss of Nature

We see the continual and inevitable disappearance of nature. We are simply going to use it all up. After all, who are we saving it for — man might not even be around later on. Some say he's only a link, and a better form of life will ultimately replace him.

As nature disappears, we creatively try to fill the void with artificial environments that offer playing fields and gaming areas as substitutes. The golf course is a fantastic invention of modern man, holding vast green spaces, structured and manicured though they be. They exist, a compromise between wilderness and parking lot, rationalized because man learned to make a sport out of hitting little balls in a hole with a stick.

We are clever at creating plastic ski slopes, breeding domestic trout in cement ponds for fishing, and building fibre glass over rubbish mountains to climb or bobsled. We groom parks to replace forests for hikers.

We have been preparing for a long time to meet nature's doomsday. Our major sports — football, basketball, baseball, tennis — are contrived physical skill and knowledge outlets. They have nothing to do with man's survival against the elements. We have replaced the beasts of the forest and the threats of the elements with manufactured obstacles and friendly human opponents.

We are very skillful at substituting. And we have surprised ourselves with the discovery that the created sport can exceed nature in providing fulfillment. It just may be we are on the verge of another era for invention of new sports. These new sports are likely to be heavily laden with great mental challenges, a marriage between chess and football.

Travel and Play

People are on the road, on the sea, and in the air. Going places. Holiday in another place, change of pace, escape, hibernation. Travel is going to take most people into climates and places extremely conducive to various kinds of sports — especially the carry-over-lifetime sports, the individual ones.

If the weather is right, sports offered at the resort are going to introduce many uninitiated people to the joys of participation.

Resorts will upgrade recreation personnel and emphasize their sports activity programs as an important device for developing repeat business. Once the native charm has been absorbed and the sightseeing exhausted, tourists will settle down to learning something new or getting back to an old sports interest.

The vacation away from home lets a person concentrate his energies, thoughts, and time on a sport. There is no better opportunity at any time in life to get deeply involved in a short time with a satisfying sports commitment.

The Younger, The Older and The Women

We've come a long way toward recognizing that stereotyping age groups is erroneous. We no longer just pass out blocks to three-year-olds. There exists a potential and a readiness with them that means we can effectively organize sports for the nursery gang. How desirable this is remains to be seen.

At the other end of the pole sits the retired, discharged citizen; the aged. The aged are becoming younger and younger because of new retirement rules. The best definition of an aged person is one who has passed forty and has total leisure. Participation in the structured programs of society isn't easy for the over-the-hill group. Their sports have to be selected and modified to some degree but not to the extent to which we have traditionally condemned the aged.

We come up with 67-year-olds all the time running in marathons, pro-football players in their 40's still excelling, 80-year-old skiers. There should be a greater openness in programming the 40-and-up people, no holds barred. Who wants to die in bed?

The same goes for women. They've pushed themselves onto the same plateau with men. There are few sacred-cow sports left — only boxing and handball, maybe. But they're into football and driving race cars. If the trend continues there may be no sport left a pure male domain.

The women groups talk about batting averages and punt-return statistics instead of clothes and wigs, even without men present. They're becoming bigger sports fans than the men. A healthy thing, too. Couples will be able to explore new areas of sports experiences together. Through exposure to the opportunity, there's no important reason why women can't compete on a mixed, open basis.

Rule Changes and Import Sports

We need to stress again the need to find new sports interests. Rule changes and adjustment of sports to meet demands for more action and better controls seems likely.

The other way is the revival of antique sports, like jousting, and importing foreign sports activities to pick up the growing hordes of sports enthusiasts.

120

Inter-interest Clubs

Club membership will grow as the means for perpetuating sports interests, following the recreation ways of England and European countries. But multi-interest clubs — fly and ski, golf and tennis — will probably be the new form of maintaining participation without limiting people to one narrow interest.

Clubs will increasingly utilize professional services to aid them in building broader areas of advanced participation, devising progression programs, staging special events, and planning highly competitive contests.

Lifetime Sports in Schools

Schools will continue to profess the need for carry-over lifetime sports, but will continue with the major team sports. One reason — and a good one — is that the big team sports take on the purpose and thrill of life itself, not a preparation for a delayed life. They are a life style, not the mere preparation for one.

There seems to be no way out of the problem. Professional recreation programmers will have to wait on the sidelines until the students graduate or drop out, and then ride to the rescue. It will take something powerful to follow the Friday night football production — and it is a production, worthy of filled bleachers.

The media continually thrusts splendid physical specimens and rundown meatballs in front of us to emulate or avoid. Persuaded people will be driven to active sports participation by the very commercials that support the programs that are designed to keep them passively watching television.

Programmers can expect in the future to be pressured to schedule sports that emphasize fitness and health. The professionals must be able to talk intelligently about what each experience contributes along these lines. One amazing development is the full-blown programmed activity that prepares one to participate in a sport. Dry land ski schools, especially the conditioning classes for veteran skiers, are a good example of this. There are places in which the preparation is a more highly programmed experience than the activity itself.

SPORTS PROGRAMMING EQUIPMENT AND FACILITIES — ADAPTATION

Sports derive much of their character from the facilities and equipment employed, probably to a much greater extent than any other major programming area.

Since sports activity is merely an assimilation of basic physical skills such as running, jumping, throwing, hitting, catching, lifting, and balancing, it is through the arena of play and the tools used that a differentiating identity is best established.

121

Take baseball, derived from cricket, its field, equipment, and uniform are unmistaken. The strung tennis racquet, the low net, the unwalled court clearly differentiate it from the smaller racquet and the four walls of squash. Then there is handball with its gloved hand and four walls. Is tennis a closer relative of squash than handball? Can players easily transfer skills and knowledge from squash to tennis or handball?

Part of the usefulness and pleasure derived from programming comes from making the most out of existing facilities and equipment. An effective analysis of the population to be served may yield a need-fulfilling sports plan, but if Irish hurling is a primary desire then a puny ten-acre recreation center studded with apparatus won't accommodate the giant playing field required. The compact little sport of table tennis is demoralizing in an outdoor area in a windy city. Tackle football without protective gear can be a bloody mess.

We have learned to mold our program to the facilities and hope that we can be good enough promoters to draw participants from an impossible first love to a less desired one that matches facilities and equipment.

Some programmers have been more creative, however. They have learned to adapt both facilities and equipment to serve their participants' readiness to play a particular sport. It's amazing how many intense and highly competitive table tennis tournaments have taken place on a dining table in the mess hall with books stacked for a net and hardback book covers used for paddles.

The above is unusual, but we have the traditional half-court game in basketball. There's the zoned short field in boys' football, where first downs arise from passing into a zone rather than making ten yards. Goal ball, a form of basketball, uses a basket on a pole in the center of a small congested space in a cramped urban ghetto.

Girls play volley tennis when the strength isn't there to push a volleyball over the high net. A regulation tennis court is all that's needed. Exciting badminton may be played over a rope stretched between two trees.

Track relays can be run in a shuttle, back and forth on a straight runway if a full 440 oval isn't available. Indoor shot putters use a leather-covered pellet shot to save the floors. Basketball for the shorties has employed a lower basket and smaller ball. Kids' baseball has shortened baselines and four square is another way of squeezing volleyball down into a smaller package, different yet similar.

Whether we design smaller or larger balls, compact or redesign playing areas, the intention is not to downgrade or eliminate the traditional nature of any established sport. We can get too pompous about violating purity of form. Some people get offended when they check the level of a billiards table or object to the insufficiency of the candlepower over the ping pong table. There are Philadelphia lawyers everywhere with tape measures and rule books talking about official dimensions and tournament play conditions. They intimidate the best of us.

Sometimes postponement, cancellation, or simple avoidance is the best path for the programmer. But don't be afraid to take a few chances. Not only do most people go along and, once involved, forget exacting demands about conditions but often a whole new sport evolves. If you examine the history of sports' origins you will discover that flukes are the order of the day.

So play ball, even if you haven't got one; fake it, be creative and inventive, adaptive and modifying. The *mail* must get through, the *show* must go on, and a good programmer can get everybody playing even in a *vacuum*.

A SPECIAL LOOK AT AQUATICS

We noted in the discussion of sports in general that certain apparently physical activities, such as vehicle sports and hunting, deviate from the physical challenge concept. Because of technological innovations man places less physical effort into his play experiences. Vehicles and hunting tools take over much of the effort once required.

Aquatics seems to be a reflection of all the other sports. It fills man's need to be physically active. It is possible that man first immersed himself for health reasons, to bathe in mineral waters.

There is a great natural resistance to movement in water caused by the density of water itself. Thus a man using his own power to move himself or his craft through it experiences a great physical challenge. Water contact itself seems to have a salubrious effect. Water also has a cushioning effect which aids the avoidance of hard bodily contact, the hard blows and collisions found in many land sports. Water also, because of its adjusting effect, gives way against man's effort, affording a margin of safety not possible in the rigid hard earth of land activities. Because of these considerations, most aquatic experiences provide a very high potential to fulfill a physical need.

Most aquatics tend to be programmed for individual involvement. Swimming, surfing, water skiing, skin diving, and life saving are team efforts only secondarily. The individual can perform the skill in most aquatics without the need of team participation. While water sports provide a more individualized recreation involvement, they also have a high potential toward fulfilling dominance and recognition needs. Since many of the water areas are subject to unpredictable conditions, creating surprise experiences and challenges, most water sports also rate high in fulfilling the need for new experience. Skin and scuba diving are excellent examples of sports with high new experience potential since they basically explore the unknown. There is also the new experience that competition may generate artificially.

There are two team water sports. One is yachting, and the other is water polo. The first is a racing contest, but the complexity of the crafts used and the complications of the water arena require a number of functions that could not be carried out by one individual. Water polo is more of a game situation, with a necessary network of different playing roles to be filled in order to experience the fullest challenge. Practice before games and the camaraderie after combined with the formality of the official game experience, provide moderately high social interaction.

Swimming teams are a major programming activity in aquatics everywhere. But because most competitive play consists of individual contests the team aspect is merely an organizational convenience to hold groups together. In fact, most teams become swim clubs, encompassing physical and social interests in order to obtain the greatest possible sustained involvement. There is a moderately-high structured sense of social interaction and belonging. The individual must still compete at any given moment by himself.

One value that is frequently debated is that aquatics, because of water's therapeutically soothing effect, basically provides relaxation. Opponents point out that not only is the stress of competition as great as in any sport, but there is also the ever-present hazard of drowning. Whatever is decided must be done situationally. Each specific experience will have to be rated.

To summarize, aquatics provides the greatest potential for providing unique physical challenges in an environment that is in itself a new experience.

As we separate aquatics from the major category of sports programming, we are, nevertheless, being repetitive in defining the nature of the activities involved. In many ways aquatics is a microcosm of all sports placed in the water.

And yet there are unique aspects that defy the simple solution of saying "see sports for explanation." With water we introduce several new skills beyond running, throwing, and jumping. Floating and propelling oneself through the water are distinctly different human skills that must be handled separately. It might be appropriate to move some of the aquatic experiences to other categories, e.g., fishing to wilderness sports or boating to vehicle sports since it is basically a transportation activity. But water is the glue we have chosen to use, and while we include certain activities here, they might also show up elsewhere because they are many-sided.

Another aspect to consider is the amount of program in aquatics that is involved in swimming motivated by self-preservation and lifesaving motivated by service to others. There are no parallels in the general sports field to these developments.

There are several classifications that we might make with aquatics. First, there are those activities programmed in the swimming pool and those in open water. This is a *facilities* classification in the same manner as splitting sports into track, field, gym, or court. Aquatics in open water, such as yachting, is obviously not for pools. Surfing and water skiing probably could be carried on in some abbreviated way in pools, but we should not confuse our classifications, which are as follows:

Pool Aquatics	Open Water Aquatics
Recreational Swimming	Recreational Swimming
Swim Instruction	Marathon Swimming
Competitive Swimming	Skin and Scuba Diving
Synchronized Swimming	Water Skiing
Water Polo	Surfing — Body & Board
Skin and Scuba Diving	Sailing, Boating, and Rowing
Board Diving	Fishing
Lifesaving	

It is not our intention to imply that an activity is exclusively one classification; rather the traditional orientation and effectiveness is indicated.

Another classification approach is to divide activities between those *human-oriented* and those *equipment-oriented*. This criterion is based on the distribution whether the activity can be executed without equipment. The advantages of knowing which activities can be programmed with nothing more than the people themselves permits low budget aquatics programs. This classification is as follows:

Human Oriented	Equipment Oriented
Swimming	Skin and Scuba Diving
Synchronized Swimming	Water Skiing
Water Polo (needs ball)	Boating
Lifesaving	Surfing
Board Diving	Fishing

The safety focus is an aspect that divides aquatics into two classifications. Its counterpart is game focus which emphasizes a much higher degree of play. Safety tends to deal with either self-preservation or service to others, swimming or lifesaving, with both resting in the no man's land between survival motivation and play response.

This classification can simplify efforts in matching program to people's needs. It is as follows:

Safety Focus	Play Focus
Swim Classes	Recreational and Competitive Swimming
Lifesaving	Synchronized Swimming
Boating Safety	Water Polo
Skin and Scuba Classes	Boating/Sailing

Rowing
Fishing
Surfing
Water Skiing
Skin and Scuba Diving

Aquatics may also be separated into those activities that concern *mobility*, i.e., propelling oneself in the water, and the more complex experiences that emphasize creative expression, exploration, or game play. Activities may be classified as follows:

Mobility Emphasis	Technical Emphasis
Swimming	Lifesaving
Boating/Sailing	Water Polo
Rowing	Fishing
	Surfing
	Synchronized Swimming

Combination

Water Skiing (expression)
Skin and Scuba Diving (exploration)

The last classification system is the one used most commonly for general sports programming. It is the individual, dual, and team categories that we have discussed with sports. One designation does not prevent an activity from being structured for the other two designations as well. If individuals are grouped for convenience, if it is not necessary for others to be present in order to execute the skills or experience the fulfillments, then the activity may be considered individual.

Individual

Swimming
Surfing
Fishing
Sailing

Dual

Lifesaving
Skin and Scuba Diving
Water Skiing

Team

Yachting
Water Polo
Synchronized Swimming
Rowing

It is important not to be trapped by any classification in programming. Classification systems should serve to aid understanding how specific activities affect people and in what structure they can best fulfill the most people.

Swimming Swimming wasn't invented as an artificial game skill. Someone fell in the water and groped his way to safety. Or maybe he watched an animal do it. When he had time to think about it he decided that his groping could be pulled together and used for more than escape — it was a means of transporting oneself.

Swimming as recreation developed in the YMCAs, country clubs, and Red Cross training programs before the competitive programs fully emerged. The swimming pool was a key factor behind the growth.

Swimming traditionally was learned by the middle class in waterfront programs at lake camps in days when swimming pools were available only to the wealthy.

Age-group swimming, an intense AAU-sanctioned youth program rivaling Little League Baseball, emerged as young swimmers developed in backyard pools and grouped under professional coaches at YMCAs, recreation centers, country clubs, and the commercial swim clubs.

The Red Cross merit badge programs in swimming and lifesaving spread and became an established institution. Beginning swim classes have become major volume programs for all recreation agencies with water facilities, clearly one of if not *the* major structured summer recreation activity in our age.

Water Polo The boys took their football into the water in England in the late 19th century. They mixed violence with swimming and came up with water polo.

As a full-fledged aquatic sport, the only team water activity of a real game nature, water polo has remained a minor recreational activity. The explanation for this is not entirely clear, but some reasons show up. First, there is the factor of poor audience appeal since the most exciting visual grace of the game is hidden away underwater. Officiating is difficult because of poor visibility with unseen rule violations leaving the activity open to chaos. Another factor is the makeshift playing conditions that must be set up in pools with shallow areas that are basically designed for multi-purpose use.

A number of other sports have been adapted to swimming pools, such as basketball, baseball, handball, and volleyball, but none have caught on beyond the stunt stage. Even water polo is not always regarded as a serious team sport.

Yachting (Sailing) Oliver Cromwell probably started yachting as the aristocrats' favorite aquatic sports activity. After Cromwell beheaded his father, Charles II fled to Holland where he encountered the small Dutch sailing ships used to chase pirates. He wanted one, built it, and when he returned to England, began yachting as a sport in the 17th century.

It is probably unfair to imply that yachting is restricted to the affluent classes. It's true, however, that yachting and polo are almost the last domain in sports for the man who has everything. Despite J. P. Morgan's famous comment, "If you have to ask what it costs to run a yacht, you can't afford one," the middle class has moved in strongly. Yachting is really another form of sailing involving a craft which requires a complex crew. Yachting is team sailing carried to its zenith.

It is possible to feel very much in control, dominant, and challenged by new experiences caused by unpredictable elements, whatever the form of boating pursued. It is the sense of activity and physical movement that draws many into boating, with sailing making the most demands covering the most people. It is one of the few machines that we can control rather than be controlled by it.

Water Skiing Unlike boating, water skiing is an aquatics invention of modern times. Its origins are unclear. Some believe that it is an adaptation of snow skiing to water. Others credit early forms of surfing and point out that water skiing was preceded by the aqua-plane, dragging a type of surfboard behind a boat. Boaters believe that water skiing was the logical development of an accessory for power boats, something to do with a boat besides going from one shore to another.

The current tendency is to find a close association between snow skiing or boating with this aquatics activity, and for obviously different reasons. There are formally sanctioned tournaments involving slalom, jumping, and tricks, but no racing. Competitively we have one of those physical activities that lacks both game or racing challenge, instead depending on individually expressed form to be judged. Board or platform diving is a parallel in the pool aquatics program.

It probably won't rise to major competitive proportions because of its novelty status due to the large areas required for the individual performer, its infringement on other aquatic interests, and the limited dimensions involved in the experience.

127

Skin and Scuba Diving People everywhere have been exploring under water since Biblical times. But it was all done very primitively, using goggles and holding the breath.

Diving, or underwater exploration as it is called in order to avoid confusion with people jumping off boards into pools, has two forms that create two separate aquatics! Skindiving, i.e., free diving, and snorkeling, i.e., diving holding the breath, are one form. It is the most physically demanding and places the burden of performance on the individual. It has no game aspect to it unless contrived.

But the development of Scuba, a self-contained underwater breathing apparatus developed by Cousteau during the war, made underwater exploration a beginning in the 50's. Skindiving had a daredevil, youthful aura to it, but scuba captured a broader age group, many who trusted the magic of the bubble machines over their own skills and fitness.

While aquatics has a general safety overlay, scuba diving plunged the participants into a complex and extraordinary jungle of hazards involving physics, physiology, and dangerous marine life. The equipment was technical, the experience scientifically complex. It turned many off and, for the same reasons, turned others on.

Because of the many complexities and unusual hazards in a strange environment programming moved in the manner of lifesaving, essentially providing a hierarchy of instructional experiences. Basically, this pattern continues. The novelty of going underwater to see strange sights sustains a constant flow of novices.

Activity	Dominance	Physical Activity	Creativity	New Experience	Social Interaction	Security and Belonging	Relaxation	Mental Activity	Recognition	Service to Others
Recreational Swimming	L	M	L	L	M	L	M	L	L	L
Swim Instruction	L	M	L	M	M	M	L	M	L	L
Competitive Swimming	M	M	L	M	M	M	L	L	H	L
Synchronized Swimming	L	M	L	L	M	H	M	L	M	M
Water Polo	L	H	L	M	M	H	L	L	M	L
Skin & Scuba Diving	M	M	L	H	L	L	M	L	L	L
Board Diving	M	M	L	L	L	M	L	L	H	L
Lifesaving	H	M	L	L	L	L	L	M	L	H
Water Skiing	M	M	L	L	L	L	L	L	M	L
Surfing	M	H	L	M	L	L	M	L	M	L
Sailing	M	M	L	M	M	L	M	L	M	L
Fishing	M	L	L	M	L	L	H	L	L	L

H – High Potential; M – Medium; L – Low.

AQUATICS NEED FULFILLMENT POTENTIAL RATING SCALE

Exploration replaces the competition motivation. Underwater hunting holds some for a while, but photography has become the dominant interest for advanced participants. Since performances are unseen, as in water polo, divers are eager to bring back their experiences and have them recognized. The camera does this and, of course, adds more scientific and technological dimensions to the sport.

Skin and scuba diving eventually may suffer the fate of all wilderness sports, i.e., extinction and replacement in controlled play areas. *Surfing* parallels this capsule history of diving, and it too is dependent on rugged natural features. In contrast to diving's preference for calm, clear waters, it needs waves and turbulent seas.

The chart on page 128 analyzes various aquatics need fulfilling potentials.

Chapter 7

SOCIAL PROGRAMMING

THEORY OF SOCIAL RECREATION

There are many beautiful quotations that have become cliches in our time. We all know that no man is an island unto himself, and a long time ago Cicero said that man could not have any pleasure in discovering all the beauties of the universe unless he has a partner with whom he might share his joys.

The late, late prison movie on television has made it clear there is no punishment greater than solitary. Stick a man off by himself and he atrophies, goes mad, becomes a vegetable. That's how the brain-washers in recent wars turned men into pliable robots.

Robinson Crusoe was on a fantasy trip with his goats and parrots until he found footprints in the sand and turned Friday into a companion, albeit a subservient one. We're attempting to construct the foundation here for the acceptance of the idea that an individual alone, cut off from interaction with others, loses much of his humanity.

The proposal runs into some strong opposition. With the population explosion there's a lot of pressure for privacy and social space. Thoreau's Walden, representing the idea of going away from oppressive controls, has become a desperate dream. In the urban crunch, traffic jams on the freeway and waiting in lines for life's necessities, many people dream about being set adrift alone in a rowboat on the high seas.

But what the recreation programmer must do is balance things. Neither solitude nor constant involvement with masses of people creates the fullest potential for good feelings. Somewhere in between hiding in a corner and being swept along in a crowd lies social interaction.

People need people. That says it pretty well. We must provide the right people in the proper doses. Social recreation programming sets this as its primary goal.

There is a need for other people, a gregarious impulse to be satisfied. Man pursues his mission on earth when he develops his identity by relating to other people — in a direct not vicarious way.

In other people we find reflections of ourselves, clues that help us in our search for worth and identity. The reflections aren't always positive, of course, and we take the chance that our self esteem can be lowered by any contact. Social recreation should be designed to make all contacts reinforcing experiences if possible, or at least eliminate the possibility of damaging anyone's psyche.

But it isn't only for measurement that we have relationships with others. Social situations should provide growth opportunities, new ideas, and behavior models. One should be able to discover from others new ways to improve his life style. Of course, the social experience may serve as a complete, serious, and vital segment of a life style in itself. The great social recreation activity may be the best human experience anyone has.

The theory of social recreation is derived from knowledge of the human need of people to have contact with other people. Social recreation is based on activities that bring people together in congenial, cooperative, and intimate participation in a common interest. They come to play with people, not against them. Cooperation rather than competition is the essence.

The social situation at its best is a relaxed one where the stress to excel is minimal. The common bond interest is really secondary to being with *desirable companions*. It is an atmosphere that yields invigorating vibrations.

If skill or knowledge are important, the social values slip away. If participants come into the situation concerned with achieving skill or knowledge goals individually as their motivation, the social interaction can be strained and damaging to all participants. As in card games or special interest clubs concentration on improving individual skills usually increases unless regulated by good programming. The pursuit of mastery tends to carry individuals out of the group or socially-oriented area of interest participation.

Obviously skill levels change and common interest fragments as participants begin to specialize. Both are inevitable and the programmer must move to restructure the social nature of the activity.

There is also some difficulty for the programmer in making intimacy a result for the social recreation experience. Is putting one person with another person the ultimate in intimacy? Yes it is *if* the two people carry on direct intercourse of all senses — taking, holding, touching, and listening, among other things. There is a difference between two mute people sitting in separate chairs intently watching week-end football games and a lap-sitting couple, gazing into each other's eyes and exchanging ideas about their lives. Intimacy has a qualitative dimension as well as a quantitative.

One has contact in a mob but usually not much intimacy. Sitting in the bleachers at the super bowl with 103,000 other people doesn't guarantee social recreation. Usually the situation takes on enhanced social value if one is part of a smaller group that is sitting together at that game. But the best possible social results would be the small group, say eight people, stopping for coffee around a table in a warm, congenial atmosphere on the way to or from the game. Fine social values have their best facilitation if the structure of the group social situation allows each member to interact face to face with each other member for an exchange of feelings.

No measurements are universally established for gauging the extent of intercourse or the minimum or maximum numbers of participants. Our social situations are very diverse, and we are left with situational judgments. We've been elated at small family parties and exhilarated at big 150-people open-house parties.

The dependence by one person on another means disaster if one withdraws from the situation. The preference in the theory of social recreation is to spread the risk but not to the point where the essence of the crowd so dilutes the social contact potential as to leave most participants adrift in a sea of loneliness again.

ROLE OF SOCIAL RECREATION

There is socialization in about all recreational activities. It occurs whenever people come together with mutual interests.

Boxers may tear away at each other, but because it is boxing and not a street fight, the contestants cooperate and agree on certain rules in order to have any activity at all. We may not care whether people even notice the presence of others in a jewelry class where highly skilled creativity is demanded. But because contact is unavoidable, interference possible, and sharing probable, eventual cooperation becomes a necessary facet of the experience.

133

Social recreation derives one role from the need to generate cooperation rather than antagonism, alienation, or conflict. We stage social experiences within or in conjunction with an activity in order to create fellowship and the feeling of camaraderie that facilitates friendly relations. If either cooperative team work or diminishing of hostilities are needed, social recreation program may achieve it.

Nothing eases the strained feelings of strangers in close quarters as well as social programming which takes away that strangeness, that fear of the unknown, that feeling that people might ridicule or harm you. The deliberately programmed social experience, a set of mixer games or a full-blown party, serves to chisel away the walls between people.

One role is to produce an activity that is designed to create socialization that in turn enables other activities to function better. A tennis club with people bickering, complaining, or losing interest gives itself a booster shot by staging a dinner dance that permits people to know one another as individuals rather than as tennis players with whom they fight for courts and rankings. Social recreation serves such a function.

Beyond being a supportive device, social recreation has a second and more important role. *It is a program arena in and of itself.* Parties, picnics, dances, and games are often put together for no other reason than to get people together with people. That's where the excitement and action is. We are all really fascinated with other people for an assortment of reasons. People-watching is a universal pastime. We can't keep our eyes off them.

The reasons have already been partially suggested. Other people represent the yardsticks which we use to keep score on ourselves. We see how we stack up by comparing ourselves to them. But then there is the entertainment aspect of watching the unpredictableness of minds and bodies that remind us of ourselves but are entirely different. Contemplating a tree or a babbling brook may be relaxing but watching people, the most amusing moving objects on this earth, is captivating and stimulating entertainment.

Those people-clustering scenes that intrigue us most as spectators are those in which we also seek to involve ourselves. Programmers perceive this drive to be together and program ingenious activities. They have invented charitable causes or revived forgotten dates to honor through some reunion or gathering. It is hard in the logical, rational productive society to just say let's have a party or a carnival for the hell of it. We must justify them by saying "because we bought a new house, or got promoted, or a special visitor is in town."

The picnic is good for company or family morale, the carnival to raise money for uniforms, the fair to unite the community — all kinds of reasons influenced by the work ethic. Recreation programmers recognize that people are embarrassed to expose themselves by admitting that they need social contact.

Most people have trouble when they are in groups because of the fears we have previously noted. We need the subterfuge of being attentive to some project or involvement in order to find some ease in the presence of others with whom we desire to relate. Social recreation activities must be disguised as activities with which we are already familiar, e.g., sports, arts and crafts, dance, drama, or special events. They differ because of their role intent — to provide companionship that is pleasure-giving. It is also a relief from the depressing emptiness and loneliness that lurks close to our surface, emerging at times to discourage our positive acceptance feelings.

134

The social recreation activity recognizes that privacy and solitude are positive drives intermittently directing the behavior of participants. For this reason, because recreation is an involvement for the sake of an activity, it allows participation without binding emotional commitments. One doesn't have to sign up for a long hitch or make elaborate preparations — withdrawal from interaction is easy. It is much easier to feel alone and to be ignored by people than to become involved with them. Social recreation activity provides an easy reversal of positions after a choice is made. You can't beat that kind of psychological mobility with any other of the available people contact areas.

VALUES OF SOCIAL RECREATION

We've hopefully made our case for social recreation's value as the best opportunity for interaction and response. The very title of it clearly labels its top echelon value.

Of our ten basic needs, for which of the remaining nine does social recreation have a high potential in fulfilling? Merely being in contact with people may be so strong a value, such an intense need fulfillment, that to consider the others may appear somewhat redundant.

We will approach it from a different perspective. In a word association test "party" would command an impressive popularity in responding to "social recreation" as the stimulus term. If we overlay "party" with each of our basic needs, we will see how its fulfillment potential ranks with each.

1. *Dominance.* This receives a low rating. A party doesn't have anything but token leader roles for any participants. There are occasional exceptions if someone knows a particular game or stunt and is singled out to demonstrate and direct it. But we're dealing with the common and overall evaluation of potential here. There is not much opportunity to control the elements of one's participation, let alone control other people.

2. *Physical activity.* Parties receive a low here also, although vigorous dancing and games make up a sizable portion of many parties. Overall, the physical is a side effect.

3. *Mental activity* gets a low rating for the same basic reason as physical activity.

4. *Service to others.* This is low, too, because people are basically self-serving in normal participation roles. Leaders' helpers might have a fulfillment outlet but that's a small fragment of the population again.

5. *Creativity.* It does not have much of a chance in the party situation. The challenge isn't there for participants, and the plan is set to avoid innovation.

6. *Relaxation.* This is counter to stress and involves rest and escape from the normal routine situation. It deserves at least a medium potential rating. Certainly if we accept the concept that social programming implies a structuring of a free and unpressured experience, then the intent seems to justify a fairly good rating. A high rating is withheld because, in practice, perhaps because of ineffective planning, social situations do create risk by placing individuals in the vulnerable position of being accepted or rejected. Bad placement or an unforeseen event can leave participants in a state of tension and anxiety.

7. *New experience.* This receives a medium rating for parties. The great bulk of social experiences in recreation involve repeat contacts with people one already knows in other spheres of life. Men who do business together get together for drinks, ball games, or a card party. Clubs are sustained on repeat attendance. In those cases, however, where first time contacts predominate, the possibilities of new experience radiate from the new people themselves.

But even assuming the overall view is that people tend to repeat social contact with old friends, people change and are unpredictable, which brings new experiences and adventure. This unpredictability is enhanced by the fact that social program often involves non-routine activities and challenges. Unfamiliarity means that there is a relative equality with performance skills since no one is supposed to have consciously prepared to participate. Unexpected individuals may succeed, causing new attitudes to spring up as people see each other in new perspectives. Putting people together in most social recreation activities deserves a strong medium rating.

8. *Security and Belonging.* A party doesn't come off as well as a club involved in a multi-club scavenger hunt. While an overall analysis of social activities might deserve a high potential rating, the party receives a strong medium rating. A party is one of the more superficial gatherings of social recreation — a reigning one because social programming depends on limited

commitment. It is a very tricky judgment, and more trained observation needs to be directed to this aspect before a definite conclusion can be reached.

9. *Recognition.* This is another difficult need fulfillment potential to rate. To be part of a group experience means a substantial amount of conformity. This would hardly seem a conducive avenue to recognition opportunity.

But if recognition is to mean identification as a unique person, then being part of a group gathered for a special reason gives some distinction. It may be you are one out of society's "four hundred" invited to the Governor's Ball — the invitation being recognition of established status in itself. Social recognition becomes a possibility for many who are unsuccessful in the more highly structured work and leisure areas of their lives.

Recognition potential receives a very strong medium in our rating of a party.

In summary, social programming is built around the core of social interaction. Its name describes its main value. Additionally, we credit social recreation with providing strong medium potential to fulfill security, recognition, and new experience needs.

136 PLANNING PRINCIPLES

Social programming subscribes to all the general planning principles we have previously presented. Several should be emphasized because they are especially important to social recreation. These are, however, simply guides to help devise specific actions to reach objectives and goals.

1. *It should be planned for both sexes.* Stag lines and old-maid corners still abound at co-ed activities throughout recreation. Social activities in which one sex is bound to feel inferior or to be spectators for the activity of the other creates separatism that violates the basic purpose of social programming.

2. *It should encourage family recreation.* "The family that plays together, stays together" used to be a rallying cry for community recreation everywhere. The primary group influence of the family disintegrated as youth "got wheels and split." Affluency, technology, earlier maturation, and disenchantment with the older generation were some of the social factors that were blamed.

The family unit of father, mother, and children is still dominant in our society, but there have been a growing mass of other forms of family living established in our culture over the past few decades.

Whatever family forms we ultimately accept, it seems important that we program them to help hold them together. From a very selfish standpoint, our chores are eased when we can count on stable units for programming.

3. *It should be planned for interaction among all ethnic groups and cultures.* Social activities, because of their casualness and congeniality, are the best possible places to confront people with the fact that there are

decidedly different life styles based on elaborate cultures a few blocks either way from them. The unknown aura that breeds strangeness, that produces fear and hate, can be dispelled rapidly in a series of exposures through social recreation activities.

4. *It should encourage cooperative behavior.* We have been elaborating on this feature rather extensively, so there is no need to elaborate on it further.

5. *It should provide for the total group and equal opportunity for everyone in it.* If the social situation is to meet some ideal then it can't leave anyone on the sideline, either by neglect or by plan. A picnic is a good example of how we schedule passive events such as a pie-eating contest for teenagers, a checkers contest for the grandpas, and a tug of war for everybody.

6. *It should provide opportunities at varying levels of participant proficiency and adjust to individual differences.* If we are going to operate a relaxed, non-threatening experience where as many as possible experience success, then we have to keep the highly skilled segregated from the unskilled by programming separate games, races, contests, or stunts. Differences go beyond the proficiency aspect, covering things like shyness and aggressiveness, two opposite traits that may require some quick program adjustment so that neither type of participant is disenchanted.

These are six important ones. There's no guarantee that following these six principles is going to give you great results in all social recreation programs. They will take you a long way, however.

137

LEADERSHIP

With the creation of a leadership function, there must be a reconciliation of participants' goals, the leader's personal and professional goals, and the agency's goals and policies.

Putting these somewhat diverse goals together is not easy. The agency and the leader usually have similar aspirations, but the participants create problems. What the agency sees as misbehavior and the participants see as a goal may be identical.

While all the general characteristics of leadership apply to social recreation, there are several that should be stressed.

1. *A leader ought to like people.* It's difficult for a program leader to make social activities work simply on the basis of repertoire and methods. He'll come close, but somehow the very essence of social interaction will elude him and participants will sense an impatient attitude.

A leader does not have to like everybody. The choice is very often not his, but he has a right to withdraw from any situation in which he feels an overwhelming amount of alienation between himself and participants. Individual participants will often adjust if it's a clash of personalities, but if they continue to disrupt other participants' enjoyment, such misfits should be gracefully released from participation.

2. *Empathy and sympathy are great attributes for the social recreation leader.* He has to be sensitive to the feelings and attitudes of others. A lot of socio-drama unfolds in social recreation, and the leader has to be able to read it to make the activity work for each individual. Be loving and never embarrass anyone. Never have fun at the expense of others.

3. *In one time social experiences, a leader has to lean toward an authoritarian style.* There isn't much opportunity to create leadership from the group because of the short time span, so direction is given. We advocate guidance over direction when the time stress is relieved and for repeat experiences. Democratic leadership is the best course of action for predictable success.

4. *The leader in the social recreation situation has to operate in a loose style.* To demand skill perfection is an evil practice of self-indulging, hard-line coaches in rigid class and game activities. With social objectives the leader must have the attitude that whatever the activity the level of proficiency is secondary to the development of friendships. Individuals are more important than the activity.

5. *A good leader cultivates assertive leadership from the group.* He turns the reins over to participants with dominant inclinations by involving them in responsible functions. He picks and trains them in advance, if possible.

6. *A good leader stays in the background.* Gifted participants should assume the foreground so that people later will wonder whether the programmer was even there.

7. *Be prepared.* Over-prepared so that if something bombs there is a ready substitute. This means flexibility, too. The leader should adapt to unforeseeable conditions, moods, and reactions without visible signs of distress.

But the plan, written and perhaps rehearsed by a trial run, should be obvious. It eliminates fumbling delays and inspires followers to cooperate with a leader who seems to know what he's doing.

8. *The leader should be a competent communicator.* He has to be heard and seen above the "roar of the crowd." Preparation leads to self-confidence, which in turn permits an explanation that everyone can understand. Getting attention can be achieved by gimmicks but is more predictable when achieved by a confident manner, a presence, an assured, unemotional and enthusiastic presentation.

In some ways this leadership principle seems to refute the preferred state of tarrying in the background.

There are social activities that can be so well planned that they unfold automatically. In some cases, programming only involves providing the place and accessories, like food and decoration, setting up and permitting the interaction to unfold unstructured.

ORGANIZATIONAL PATTERNS

There used to be asylums where the insane were dumped. Many of these asylums were just big barns in which people behaved so strangely and badly that attendants called them snake pits.

There are many snake pit happenings taking place today in social recreation programming. We are very primitive in how we put people together with other people.

Part of the problem is the *failure to selectively match the right combinations of persons.* Obviously, in captive participant situations such as remote military bases, prisons, or hospitals, there isn't much leeway in choosing the kind of people to make an activity work. But ask any successful party giver who does have the freedom to invite who shall participate.

"I've done parties that had to serve a whole industry or the entire membership of a club, where every kind of temperament and hang-up get mixed together. You just have problems with a hodge-podge participation.

"Why, I've had construction workers, hair stylists, prostitutes, and babes in arms bouncing around one party. You'd better have a lot of magic and flexibility and even then a lot of people can have a miserable experience.

"Once in a while you get lucky and the odd mix makes for an unpredictable success, something you couldn't have planned. But the best party is one where you assign the players, invite the combination of people who are almost guaranteed to interact with great zest and enjoyment."

The point seems to be that a programmer's job is more than half done when he has the power to choose the participants. Of course, there are occasions where an activity is designed by the programmer to serve a group of people regardless of predictable conflict or disinterest. But such programs are of a private nature, exclusively made to give the participants a sense of status. That, of course, means others are made to feel unwanted. Exclusiveness is a delicate manipulation and tends to go against the grain of the free-and-open-to-all image of recreation.

Let's consider some other organizational influences in the breakdown of people get-togethers.

139

Group Size

We have already suggested that social interaction takes place best in small group special interest activities, especially those built into a pattern of experiences for people already bound together by membership in a club.

The following facilitate social interaction: intimacy allowing face to face contact; focus of common interest; and an adhesive bond created by membership loyalty. The magic happens most frequently with blocks of eight to twenty people.

There is conflicting thought on this:

"The more the merrier. Of course it's a cliche, but you get too much air space between people. They'll clique off, couple off, withdraw, and the mixing goes to pieces. The number depends on the physical space involved and to some degree on the nature of the activity."

"That's right. If a craft class is put on with a primary intention of creating fellowship, you still have the secondary objectives of actually making something. Crowding in a small space can blow the whole thing by interfering with the craft activity that's being used to focus attention and dispel nervousness."

"That's true also with the atmosphere of the space involved, not just the volume. I mean a group picnicking in a serene fern glen is going to lose the quality of the place just by exceeding its physical capacity. It's a lot different from a cocktail party where people need to lean up against people, use the congestion and accidental pushing to escape from boors, keep moving around to meet as many people as possible."

No one seems to have an infallible yardstick on this issue and, at this point, it is up to the programmer's judgment. The basic guideline might be that the size of the group should not exceed the maximum anticipated. That maximum should be established on the basis of the leader being able to control effectively and relate to the involved participants.

Group Cohesion

Cohesion is just one word covering the process of people being drawn together, the glue that holds them in united interest and effort.

To give an activity some support from the beginning, we trade on established cohesion or artificially create it. Clubs, the family unit, or the place of employment already pull individuals together. The belonging they feel usually means that many inhibitions are already put aside and the participants go right into the more significant experiences. More chances can be taken with self-absorbing, secondary common interest involvements without fear of the socialization process being broken down by it.

There are other cohesive patterns that can be built into the social activity itself. Common ones are the formation of planning and preparation committees, the task forces of deputy hosts to carry out specific actions at the gathering, and the volunteer leader corps that serves as an extension of the professional programmer.

It does more than just create a basis of homogeneity. There is that old go-boil-some-water concept of manufactured involvement at work in these created patterns. When people are needed, have contributing roles, something pre-arranged to do at a social activity, resistance and inhibitions are put aside.

But involvement as one of our important organizational patterns doesn't have to be prearranged. It can and should be utilized as the leader notes waning interests or hostilities in an individual. "Here, keep score" or "you ring the starting bell" are simple devices to recruit cooperation from participants who are drifting away from interaction.

Sex and Age

We have generalized about age groups and sexes. An effective program takes into consideration both the unbounded energy and limited interest span of youngsters and the physical limitations of the elderly. The skill level, health, and physical condition of participants are important in planning activities to match its chronological, physical, mental, and emotional factors.

One guideline should be that the younger the participants the greater the structure to control the bubbling energy and to time the attack on boredom.

As for the sex or sexes thing, the only safe rule is to strive for an equal number of both sexes, a balance, wherever possible. We may be idealistically inclined to treat everyone as individuals but a biological urge has to be reckoned with.

Mixing the sexes is part of the socialization process leading to mating. It is mating which is the fulcrum for much social interaction. If participants are married, mixing the sexes becomes less important and in the case of established couples may even be hazardous. A programmer shouldn't be a divorce broker.

Focus of Interest and Stress

All organizational patterns in social activities should avoid creating stress.

If participants are required by an activity to concentrate on skills or mental challenges, they become self-absorbed. This, of course, can interfere with socialization. Achievement should be a byproduct of people getting along with each other. If emphasis is placed on superior performance in the secondary common interest of an activity, frustration, tension, confusion, and damaged self-esteem results.

Another stress arises from bad social manners. Show-off hosts, name-dropping guests, performing leaders, and pushy participants can twist a social experience into a nightmare for many.

Nowhere in recreation does stress create such emotional traumas as in the social situation. Since acceptance and response are key life expectations for participants, their denial is explosive. Leaders and hosts have a responsibility to program social experiences that do not elevate some egos at the expense of others.

Culture and Local Custom

Some stress and chaos may result if the programmer has not anticipated cultural mixing. A common disaster area is in social dancing involving bodily contact. For some religious and nationality groups touching or mixing the sexes is taboo.

Words mean different things to various cultures, and humor, the great relaxant for many social experiences, is a delicate emotion that can hurt or disgust people from different backgrounds. The practical joke can convulse the crowd but tear apart an insecure victim. One must know from what cultural background his participants come in order to avoid offending their beliefs and customs.

Basic Formats

Considering these influences, for effective social interaction the basic organizational patterns for activities must be geared to one of the two different sets of participants with which we began the discussion. The first is the gathering of strangers and the second the assembling of people with established relationships.

The program activity for strangers demands a pattern that is best described as a mixer. A mixer is a low-keyed, uncomplicated, nobody-can-fail-at-it opening activity. It takes on different forms, such as a grand march pairing off or ladies' choice at a social dance; or name bingo at a party; or the auctioning of box suppers at a community bazaar; or the color teams' approach at a play day (see sports); or the tug-o-war at a picnic. The purpose is to mix the people by creating a basically non-challenging, no special-skill-required, cooperative experience. If competition exists, it is superficial, easy-going, and friendly, with neither ribbons nor awards.

The mixer gently pushes people together with a common cause or interest, such as solving a puzzle as a couple or team. The mixer does not have to be restricted to an opening role. If the interaction freezes and people fail to move beyond their initial contacts, the programmer can begin a mixer at that point to begin the mingling again.

With confident, self-assured people, simple introductions may suffice to trigger interaction. But for most there is a need to momentarily hide in the folds of some active involvement to direct the critical attention of others away from them. The recreation mixer provides the security with which the inhibited can loosen up and prepare themselves for unstructured, spontaneous interaction.

142

Social Lubricants. Not enough can be said in favor of atmosphere as an enabling device in socialization. Gaiety, the holiday spirit, or colorful surroundings do much to spark things. No one would condemn any effort to create superior atmosphere.

A problem does exist if the atmosphere is chemically rather than physically created. Booze and drugs are important social lubricants. Whenever we set up a physical environment to create a spirit of camaraderie, everyone is affected equally and at the same time. With chemical social lubricants, individuals are turned on and off at different times to varying degrees.

This is not a book to moralize about demon rum and drugs — whatever works to fulfill needs deserves consideration. But reliance on chemical stimulants to enhance a party, picnic, or gathering is an admission by a programmer that his activities cannot carry themselves.

The result of using drugs or alcohol may be a form of play or pleasure, but chemicals spell fantasy and escape, an internalization of feeling and interpretation of experiences. There is a withdrawal from others in most cases, a breakdown in socialization, as the drinker or drug user concentrates on his own feelings and senses. Nothing says this better than the caricatured morning-after party-goer who comments, "I must have had one helluva good time last night if I feel this lousy today." If reminiscences are accepted as the necessary third of the trilogy that constitutes the completely satisfying recreation experience — anticipation, participation, reminiscences — then chemical social lubricants often cheat people out of it.

Food may be a more acceptable lubricant. Can you imagine a party or picnic without it? It is a sense-pleaser rather than a mind-bender. Good food sets up a good psychological mood, a readiness to accept other people. But food is also a major common denominator in life since we all eat food and talk about it like experts.

You can hold a drumstick or a canape with the same hand involvement you get holding a drink. Of course you can't sip or puff but you can nibble with some grace and extend the use of food as a bit of action to ease the nervousness which occurs when people have to relate to others. Food can be a whole activity in itself, not just a mixing or socializing tool, such as the pot-luck, banquet, or service club luncheon.

The social lubricants are not any less necessary for those participants with established relationships. People who see each other often have common grounds upon which to interact, but they also may have used each other up as audiences. Familiarity can generate boredom, or annoyance. Lubricants are often used to fill the void instead of having the programmer revitalize meaningful interaction.

A programmer has to know the nature of his people, what they're ready for, capable of, and how they react to each other. As one hostess put it, "The secret is being able to recognize the doers and the watchers. Put the doers to work entertaining the watchers. Simple as that."

Another said to mate your participants and let them circulate as a team, using their relationship for security but interacting with strangers for new experiences, adventure, and stimulation.

Another programmer commented, "All of our big hurts come from other people, rejection, ridicule, scorn — but on the other hand, all of our major elations are enforced or enhanced by other people. A social activity is a gamble for everybody. It often doesn't work, causing withdrawal inclinations in those who have low risk-taking capacities."

143

The risks are enormous with social events comprised of strangers. In social activities with people in established relationships the risks arise from the failure to provide challenging new activities. Since theoretically everyone is incapable of being surprised by long-term acquaintants, it is through the use of surprising, untried activities that these people can find new dimensions and renew interest in each other.

Sustaining Interest The successful programmer follows some basic and universal guidelines in organizing any social event. (1) Start with an interest grabber, an old familiar guaranteed success activity. If it's a campfire sing, rush to a roaring start with a familiar favorite that leaves them wanting more. (2) From the familiar move to simple new experiences, building to more complex and difficult ones. (3) Use food and other lubricants to pick up lagging interest, slow down an over-paced program, or cover the fallout after an activity in the program that went sour. Use a pause in activity to renew flagging group spirit and to think out briefly the balance of your plan. (4) Have more activities planned and more materials available, e.g., food, than you think you'll need — just in case. (5) Let the participants dominate the situation — not the leader. (6) Have a climaxing activity on the program that unites them and leaves them "wanting to do it all again, soon."

A last word on the organizational patterns of social programming: People exchanging ideas and feelings, identifying each other as individuals, and desiring to be together again under similar circumstances happens more often and easier under the staging of a programmer.

Everyone is still interested in everyone else. That news shouldn't startle anyone.

People do need other people and like to be around them. But selectivity enters the picture. Today, the farmer's daughter is no longer an easy mark for the first slicker that comes along, nor is anyone forced to get along with their neighbors in order not to be lonely.

America has become totally mobile, rich and poor; anyone can move around any time he wants and seek out a new arena of people. Nobody has to wait for someone to pass his way.

Unfortunately, this feast of people which provides most people with multiple contacts each day has spawned carelessness. Friendships had some depth and strength when people had lots of space between them and had to make do with infrequent visits.

Modern rootlessness and the ability to buy substitutes for genuine encounters have left us quantitatively enriched and qualitatively impoverished. Many relationships are not cherished any longer because replacements seem so available.

Many authorities think it's a stage we're going through. A comparative study of culture indicates that the shallowness of today's social interaction is more a product of the doomsday attitude than simply increasing population. This is especially visible among affluent, educated youth.

There is a feeling that each day has to be lived as if no tomorrow were in sight. It may be a reaction to watching the older generation's "work as if you're going to live forever" credo and end up with a world gone out of control.

Today's social casualness may be the result of the many surface changes going on throughout society. Human beings have changed very little. Regardless of how thinly or broadly we spread our contacts with others few can stand alone. We are torn between wanting companionship and avoiding being pressed by the needs of others. We cry out when the crowd pushes, and we cry out when the crowd has left us. A very delicate balance controls our social behavior.

Our pure social experiences have been the most stable of all recreation program: the classic party, the eternal picnic, the coffee break, and the visits with friends.

The Superficiality Trend In recent years the Good Samaritan has become extinct in our society. Some call it the Genouese syndrome, after the incident in which a young girl was attacked while people watched from nearby windows as if viewing soap opera on television — and did nothing to help. We have become such viewers of fake life — sports, movies, and television — that there is great difficulty separating reality from fantasy.

And we are afraid. If we get involved with other's needs will we end up victims. . . ? We are afraid of each other. We throw up walls of superficial contact and it shows in our recreation experiences.

There are also some paradoxical trends that suggest the possibilities of two opposite extremes.

First, some newer recreation forms have great potential for creating social interaction, especially along the lines of the traditional family. Television in its new forms brings big-time entertainment into the home on demand, possibly eliminating the need to seek this type of amusement away from one's primary group. The twister on this is that the individual members in the family may begin conflicts over choice of programs or isolate themselves in cubicles to watch individual TV sets. Another paradox is that TV exposure actually stimulates interests in activities outside the home, and family members may leave in pursuit of these interests.

The recreational vehicle, the living space on wheels, seems to be an assimilating device for family togetherness. But its compact living style violates personal living space needs and most people are unable to adjust to it. The trailer and camper boom should and often does represent a special interest focus for new social groupings, but it also isolates people. The question is how convenient camping may become before it becomes simply the repetition of routine living in another place. If confronting nature with one's resources and cooperating with others for survival is the essence of camping, then conveniences can negate the experience. If people don't need others meaningfully — not just superficially admiring each other's rig — then the socializing potential of the camper developments must be questioned. Motor bikes are individual recreational vehicles, and yet they have gained strong support from authorities advocating them as a good way to keep the family together on a common interest. Snowmobiles are parallel development. Vehicles have become the common denominator toy in our society over the past years.

They are not subtle as toys and their use contributes to the noise and destruction of the environment. They serve individuals more than groups and often serve as irritants to non-participants. In their use, they seem to lack force for social interaction, and at best only serve a programmer as a focusing interest to bring people together.

Travel has opened opportunities for social programmers. New blood in an area helps stimulate program activity by giving residents a chance to show off and visitors a chance to become involved without the group having expectations based on past behavior. It's a fresh chance situation. But travel as a recreation form also places people as strangers in alien cultures. The barriers to social interaction are therefore multiplied.

Programmers have remedied this flaw by developing the tour in which compatible social groupings are moved intact into new environments. The danger in this is similar to conveniences in camping because programmers may so over-structure the tour group and its itinerary that the social interaction might as well have been attempted back home. Interaction with new people in different cultures is slowly eliminated by the tour.

We are dealing with a delicate balance in programming. In the social arena recent innovations have a high potential for fulfilling the need for response, but programmers can easily over-manipulate them, causing withdrawal and isolation. Only constant vigilance by the programmer can harvest good results from the paradox.

When describing extreme impressions, discussions on fragmentation caused by individual pursuits often causes confusion. The individual involves himself less with his primary family group and more with shallow interest-oriented groups which are easily entered and easily left. The confusion arises in trying to explain the new living development taking place in planned communities, condominiums, and communes. There seems to be a conflict in trends.

This approach to living in permanent relationships means less general participation in public life but more intense contact with small groups with similar life styles. The home, car, and office are capsules, islands physically containing a subculture. These social groupings are created to obtain privacy, a withdrawal from the disjointed involvements outside the capsule. These life styles, originally based on a desire for intimacy, require conformity to a certain life style for acceptance.

CAPSULE CLASSICS

The Party It is the indoor counterpart of the picnic. It also stresses food and drink, but the games are often replaced by social dancing for adolescents and young adults, reverting back to passive sophisticated games, like cards, with older adults. But don't count on it, and don't deliberately plan a party that way.

Parties, unlike picnics, tend to be built around a special need or celebration. A picnic happens because it's just fun, but parties generally seem to need a justification with a theme or occasion. Parties occur with greater frequency in programming than picnics, partly because weather conditions for picnics are less predictable.

While we have characterized parties with food and games or dancing, the secondary ingredients of conversation and music have a lot to do with the effectiveness of the socialization. Music is merely mood-setting background unless, because of the conversational inabilities of those at the party, it must substitute for the sound of voices and serve as the unifying force for bringing people together. In recent times a greater reliance has been placed on music to pick up for the "lost art" of talking to each other. If conversations are taking place, music should fade way into the background.

The great party programmer Elsa Maxwell sees music as a better loosener than anything that comes out of a bottle. But she accepts the stimulation of alcohol for those who need it and limit their intake. "People are not gay when drunk," she says, "nor have imagination, nor can there be any real conversation with a drunk."

It's all in the planning since the party serves the purpose the programmer gives it. It may well be the number-one people mixer, regardless of what other purposes it seeks to fulfill. It is not likely to be a good party, however, unless the participants are selected carefully for balance. The smaller the group at the party, the more discriminating should be the selection process. But don't confuse selection with homogenizing the participants. On the contrary, it is the mix of age, sexes, types, and interests that create the best surprises at a party.

Surprise makes each party different. Break the rules; avoid rulebook behavior. Dare to experiment. Inside each person is an adventuresome child

146

waiting for someone to make play acceptable behavior. That's why simple childhood games work at parties, for all ages. Do the unexpected, such as having each guest bring a favorite food or behave like his favorite movie star. Hire a phrenologist to tell people's personalities from the bumps on their heads.

The Dinner   This, the breakfast, or the luncheon permits in-depth interaction with people across the table and to the sides due to their immobility.

The dinner has much more protocol than either the picnic or party. It makes eating a ritual, prolonging the process as a means for deep conversation.

Eating, a survival need, is used to justify getting together — "one has to eat anyway, so why not here?" We suggested that the party often has themes to make it seem "necessary," but the dinner goes it a bit stronger. If we were to rate the dinner on our need scale, the following would be our scorecard: physical activity, low; mental activity, medium; creativity, low; service to others, low; security, low; new experience, medium; relaxation, medium; social interaction, high; and dominance, low.

The recreation programmer employs the dinner concept as a socializing activity in many related forms; the box social, the pot luck, the progressive dinner, the tea, the coffee break, the bar-b-que, the fondue get-together, the old taffy pull, or the pop corn or fudge happening. Their common denominator is food which is the magnetic center with conversation fringing the outskirts.

147

The Social Dance   This is the next major classic activity that traditionally has been programmed to socialize. Dance in its pure form is a body language for creative self-expression, but when it serves the same role as food or games in bringing people together, it takes on a different nature. There is activity and physical contact, with music a motivating force rather than mood background.

In the social dance the programmer intends to mix and mate participants. It is neither a dance class nor a performance. The old teen dance represents the perennial programming mentality of people responsible for that difficult age group. It continues to follow a mercurial pattern of great success to great failure almost overnight. Dance styles have gone through radical transformations. Uniformity and coupling gave way to individual expression and multi-interaction with many group members during a dance. Whatever the style, however, dancing is the magnetic center for interaction between strangers and friends, with a strong overlay of mating propensities.

The square dance, a dance that anyone can do, is distinctly more social than cultural. The limited self-expression involved is far overshadowed by the undemanding skills required, thereby allowing a broad participation. It has been a prime upper-adult activity and is the best example of a physical skill activity that can carry heavy socialization — touching and talking during the dancing — without resorting to food or alcoholic beverages.

The Club   This is considered by many programmers to be the best developer of social competence (which may also be recreation's best objective) in our repertoire of activities. Now let's get it straight that *The* Club is not *a* club.

The club approach is one of the best organizational patterns to bond people together on a semi-permanent basis. As an organizational pattern a club is a shortcut to programming, for groups of people clustered around some interest are in ready reserve to support a league, class, or special event in their interest area. A club makes it unnecessary to solicit individuals to launch an activity.

A club emerges out of established interests but *the* club is a social construction — a pure model — whose primary motive is to create a cohesive force among a selected population. The Club may be founded on the basis of age, e.g., a teenage club, senior citizens club, or boys club. In such cases interests and participation come after the club's formation, as a result of it rather than a cause of it. In industrial recreation large employees' clubs exist to provide a framework for gaining special deals or discounts by providing the necessary participants for large-scale services and activities. The pure club concept allows for experimental programs, too.

Probably the simplest difference between the special interest and social interest club is that people with a special interest, e.g., square dancing or rock hounding, have their interest as their reason for joining.

The Social club is a multi-faceted convenience for a programmer. The YMCA has been most successful with the multi-interest club, using it as a dependable base for launching vast programs in sports, arts and crafts, and snow trips, among other things.

While we have isolated two concepts of social programming by use of the club, there are many hybrid versions in a constant state of evolution. An Alcoholics Anonymous club of multi-interests after a few years ends up being a pinochle club; a mountaineering club may end up doing more bowling and partying than climbing mountains and eventually emerge as a general interest social club.

Clubs are a unique socializing force, whether used as organizational patterns or as pure activity forms in themselves. They are responsible for developing a sense of give-and-take in people, a motivation for cooperation, an attitude of citizenship responsibilities, and a spirit of order and system into which activity is fitted. On the other hand, the club participant must be ready to submerge the self as he conforms to the group.

Clubs are high providers in social interaction and security/belonging.

The Play Day The play day, community sports night, or sports open house is sport's contribution to an activity primarily designed for social interaction. In all cases the emphasis is taken off skill, winning, awards, and competition. The various sports activity units are selected to allow varying ages, sexes, and abilities to merge into a fun situation of unpressured interaction.

Part of the effectiveness of this device is the opportunity to break up habitual cliques and winning combinations that are made up of individuals clinging together in order to stay on top. It will expand their horizon of contacts.

The play day program is high in physical activity, relaxation-escape, and social interaction.

Encounter Groups These are a relatively new social recreation phenomenon.

Other names covering the concept are T-groups, psychodrama, sensitivity training, emotional learning, and group therapy. By the names it would seem we are dealing with a special kind of problem person in need of therapy or a unique educational process. Some have designated it as an inexpensive form of analysis for the public.

Whatever its original intention or lasting results, for large numbers of people it has become a way of life, a continuous process of getting one's head straight and developing self-esteem. What happens is honest, open conversation, conflicts and hostility, and confrontations with emotional realities.

Some have found the encounter group a place to mate and meet people — a socializing crossroads — with a self-improvement purpose to justify the participation. It has become a mass recreation participation, perhaps reviving the art of conversation, possibly because the subject matter is so personal, but it is an emotional time bomb with potential danger in the hands of amateurs.

It remains to be seen if recreation programmers will be able to complete a safe and worthwhile adaptation. It is claimed by drama programmers too, and may be better suited there.

The Campfire This is one of outdoor recreation's joyous occasions. With the fire as the magnet, people are unified and hypnotised into a sense of oneness. With skits, fun dramatics, stunts, and simple little songs, one has the old-time family parlor fun that existed before everyone became entertainment consumers.

A campfire at night is a potent experience. With the huddling together, the body contact, the elements, the cold, the night shadows. You can get away with almost any activity, even the corniest recreation idea, and the group will stay in solid form. It even works in the daytime but to a much lesser degree. A great socializer, and with the pressure of expectations off, people can invent spur-of-the-moment contributions and behave without inhibitions before an easily amused audience held captive by the flames.

149

The campfire is high on social interaction, creativity, belonging, and relaxation. Let's hope in its pure form it doesn't disappear along with the rest of the natural outdoor environment.

The Entertainment This causes a real hesitation here in our writing, mainly because we are oriented toward active participation. But entertainments are staged not only for performers to express themselves but also as socializing activities for audiences. Many go to entertainment events primarily because of their cultural significance, but the interaction among small groups dressing up, conversing, and sharing a cultural experience is also significant. In addition to small group or couple interaction, intermingling with a crowd pursuing a common interest creates a certain vitality.

The Class This also is an organizational pattern like the club. Probably more so because the instructional class must arise out of an interest and specific need.

It deserves a special social consideration because in practice many special interest class participants extend their relationships beyond the class situation into other social spheres of interest, some evolving into clubs. Indeed, some programmers use the class scheduling as a subterfuge to bring people together for more involved social interaction.

GAMES AS SOCIALIZING PROGRAM CLASSICS

Life is full of simple activities that Recreation has traditionally labelled "games." According to the environment in which they are found, they are further identified as "low-organized games," "playground games," and "children's games." None of these describe fairly one of leisure's and play's most important phenomena.

It is not easy to spot when what seems to be aimless, time-killing play shapes up into a controlled pattern of behaviors directed at a goal. Challenges are identified, specific action is channeled by rules and what emerges is one of recreation's first, simple units of experience — the basic game.

There are action games, quiet games, and table games. In some cases the active ones are the lead up to organized sports, permitting youths to ready their muscles, endurance, and coordination for the exacting demands made by quality sports. So physical needs are often served, and games are sometimes placed in the sports programming arena under many listings.

Games can also often provide a cultural programming base, too. The individual can express himself or establish an identity in some of the more advanced forms of games, e.g., the card game of bridge. And with bridge we open wide the spectrum of usage of games far beyond children's preparation for other things. They can act as a fulfilling activity device in themselves for people of all ages.

What seems most logical if we employ our key needs concept of evaluating participation is that games contribute more to the socialization process than the physical or cultural areas. The game arises out of the need of two or more people to put order in their chaotic play. The rules of the game prevent destructive conflicts and establish a uniform contract and language by which participants can both cooperate and compete without the situation being turned into a serious survival clash.

The basic game is a tool by which introverts and extroverts may interact socially, a liaison device upon which their interests can be focused and the common denominator for their coming together.

Take, for example, the open-space game of Red Rover, an exciting, physical, any-number-can-play team activity of the chase-and-capture variety. It is a spontaneous happening that can be initiated anywhere there's room to run a little in all directions. Any objects can be used as goals and boundaries, no uniforms or special equipment are required, yet there is the sweating exuberance and effort which is found in highly organized athletic contests.

Games are programmed to bring people together in a non-pressured fashion. In their basic forms they are building blocks of experiences that do not take meaningful shape unless brought together into broader participation, such as activities or special events. These blocks are easy to work with and serve the programmer well as he constructs fulfilling occasions that emphasize socialization.

150

Games do not remain simple. The progressive nature of people causes them to demand more complex and sophisticated forms of games as they become more experienced. This is not entirely different from the progression patterns found in any of the other outlets of the play spirit — people have to move from novice status to mastery or else switch their play involvements so they can start as beginners in something different. Games are pure elements of play and are constructed mainly from simple one-dimensional challenges, but they can be made more complex with added rules and more mental and physical challenges.

For example, an individual can't play "I Spy" against himself since it consists of hiding an object and searching for it. He can play against his own past record in a card game like solitaire or a table game like carroms — but opponents enhance even these exceptions, make the play experience expand into the fulfillment of multiple needs. Double solitaire is terrifically stimulating, far and beyond the single game. Bridge is a refined game in which heads of state engage with the same dedication they give diplomatic affairs. Bridge is a towering game compared to a simple two-handed high card game.

Another aspect to be considered, and one we know little about, is the need to create stakes in a game experience in order to stimulate or maintain interest. People bet on outcomes to spice up repetitive play activity. Stakes seem to be inversely proportionate to the complexity of the game. With complexity in games, there is also the danger of diminishing social experience. Everyone can jump into the simple game and probably succeed every so often, and fear of failure doesn't inhibit them. But complex games, like chess or bridge, drive the individual into himself and he concentrates on mental endeavors rather than socialization. Complexity then makes games a tool for purposes other than socialization — mainly as devices for physical and mental challenge. It is up to the programmer to use games to best serve the needs of the participants.

We have referred to the three-staged, most productive play experience as one that provides the participant with a chance to anticipate (prepare, practice, look forward to), to participate (the actual doing), and to reflect (the recall of the joys of an experience). We should add another stage that helps participants fully gain from an experience, that is being appreciated. It is one of the major motivations in the social interaction process, and games as our simple basic program building units thrive on it.

Chapter 8

CULTURAL PROGRAMMING

The big four of cultural programming are arts and crafts, dance, music and drama. Organized recreation has not been bold in producing any of them.

There occasionally exist some exceptional cultural activities in remote and unexpected places. A great church choir in one place, an outstanding little theatre and a masters' crafts workshop in another. Why they exist must be explained by an investigation of each situation by programmers who understand cultural programming.

What is cultural programming? We define the cultural experience in terms of how it serves participants. It is the prime area for individual, creative self expression. Although sports, social program, and special events may involve creativity, cultural programming is designed to give the individual participant an outlet for the personal expression of his ideas and feelings.

It is individually oriented in contrast to the group orientation of social programming. It is structured for communications in contrast to the emphasis on physical activity in sports.

Much of what we define as cultural programming is often described as the fine arts or performing arts. Man has developed writing abilities and ways of using his voice and body to please the senses. He is often compelled by inner needs to express his feelings, ideas, and experiences to others. Perhaps he wants to reflect upon them or see how others react. He has found that dance, drama, music, and crafts are unique means to tell his story effectively.

The values and roles of the four art forms are not often understood by the public. They are subtle ways of expressing complex ideas and feelings. Recreation, with its traditional concern with the experience for its own sake, has not been as comfortable with cultural programming as with other program areas.

Programmers of what we call the "New Recreation" will have to be more daring and innovative. They will have to experiment with old and new cultural experiences to meet the needs of all rather than only the talented few.

Culture as a refined concept of life is not the private domain of an elite. There is not *one* level of achievement in it. The recreational participant should not feel he is violating some standard if he attempts to be expressive and creative through one of these four art forms.

Cultural programming, man's best channel for projecting the human spirit and perpetuating ideas, is a complex activity resource that most programmers have approached uncertainly and superficially.

THEORIES OF ARTS AND CRAFTS

There's a little bit of me all over the house. An unplugged drain, a painted bedroom, the doorbell that works again, a wood carving entitled "Man Emerging" by the telephone, and a mosaic made of glass and semi-precious stones in the hallway.

The drain and the doorbell were repair jobs which required a certain kind of craftsmanship, saved money and provided a sense of self-sufficiency. The bedroom was all right as it was, but a new color made those moments of life spent there seem a little different and gave a certain amount of the same satisfaction created by the repair jobs. All three were part of urban man's survival life style. They could have been done by painters and repairmen, but they were executed by the individual to maintain a feeling of control over the environment.

The carving and the mosaic which I did are different. They are not necessities. Neither basic comfort nor control over the environment were affected by them. But of the five tasks they are the two that represent my unique identity. They are the only ones that might be of interest to visitors. They provide a visual impact that uplifts or depresses others, including myself. They contribute to the beauty of the environment.

What needs motivate us to work with our minds, imagination, and hands to shape materials into new things? Is it to please an audience who will provide recognition, or are arts and crafts the arena for a very personal need to express the latent creativity in each person? Or is the brushing, mixing, squeezing or carving simply pleasing our tactile senses?

In programming we make the choice of how arts and crafts will serve the individual. They can fulfill any of the ten dominant recreation needs to some degree. But traditionally the art experience has been utilized as the most predictable process for the fulfillment of identity needs through creativity. For our purposes it is best to think of arts as a higher level of crafts, somewhere up the ladder of progression in skill. Why people engage in the activity may again be our best clue. They plunge into crafts to create something for themselves, test their creative potential. Art seems to be a more calculated involvement to succeed, produce a finished object that will enhance the environment, perhaps prevail over the work of others in an exhibition. Historically crafts have arisen out of utilitarian needs in society — fine furniture, utensils, clothes — whereas art has produced the refinements and ornamentations for a flat world.

For those who explain differences by examples, art has been oil painting and crafts have been papier mache. Economists might find art in expensive materials and crafts in scrap.

ROLE AND VALUES OF ARTS AND CRAFTS

One of the most positive values of arts and crafts is that making things puts your hand back on the steering wheel of your life. We need the feeling that we could make it on a desert island without vending machines or shipments from Hong Kong. It's a chance to spit in the eye of the machine. Regardless of how unwanted the finished item really is, it provides a sense of self-sufficiency and resourcefulness.

When we shape and mold in an arts and crafts project, we put our personality into it. We call it self expression. Society is often guilty of trivializing us, deluding us into thinking that holding someone's coat in a fight, or adding an egg to a cake mix is a contribution. Crafts permit you to leave little bits of yourself all over the place for everybody to see.

Every project isn't a blue-ribbon winner. Many leaky ceramic vases end up buried with the garbage, crude kites get stomped on, or lovely pictures for mother are stored in the attic trunk. All the misshapen craft horrors of our daughter were dutifully shipped to the Museum of Kunj (until our daughter learned to spell backwards and made us account for everything thereafter). Even the craftsman knows when something misses. But all is not lost. Out of difficulty and failure comes a deep appreciation for the real masterpieces of others. Only someone who has entered the arts and crafts arena and felt the pangs of endeavor can meaningfully pay hundreds of dollars for a handcrafted carving that is also available for $1.98 in molded plastic. He understands craftsmanship.

Creativity is one of our universal needs closely linked to establishing our identity. Each of us asks if he is merely reflecting the world around him, consuming but not creating. If you add one positive small dot that somehow benefits, inspires, or pleases another, then that dot represents creativity. Arts and crafts as a process is self-indulging; it becomes creative when something is produced that positively adds some dimension, small as it may be, to society. Creativity is often defined as originality. Originality is the rare gift to do something that has never been done before. A person can be creative and do imitative work; the original person invents deviations from the known and expected. Because of the individual effort that can be tolerated by arts and crafts, creativity and its purest form, originality, are especially encouraged and cultivated.

There's another kind of appreciation possible through crafts. Involvement in crafts sensitizes the craftsman to the feel of raw, natural materials. A sculptor can touch good wood and feel like purring. This can't be built into the program, it just happens. There are vibrations from melting glass, watching clay turn colors in heat, or folding paper into an admiral's hat. Don't be disappointed, however, if this value doesn't emerge. The primary values are the development of self-sufficiency, a chance to function individually through self-expression, the understanding of craftsmanship and appreciation of beauty, the sensitivity to the feel of raw materials, and the finding of a receptive outlet for personal creative potential.

On our need fulfillment potential scale, crafts in general receives high ratings in creativity and mental activity. It has a medium high potential for achieving new experience, relaxation-escape, and dominance-mastery (over tools and materials).

ARTS AND CRAFTS — CAPSULE CLASSICS AND CLASSIFICATION

There's as much a reason for placing crafts into classifications as there is for separating vegetables in the garden. It aids communication by enabling leaders and program planners to discuss preparations and improvement without confusion.

Magic titles such as "woodworking" and "mosaics" also entice participants who look down on arts and crafts as kiddy fun or unmanly. The broad classification title helps the acceptance of whittling under the more impressive designation of woodworking. Decorating a box with bits of glass may be referred to as the ancient artisan craft of mosaics. People tend to think in terms of specific projects, rejecting really enjoyable craft experiences before trying them because they don't understand that a project is a step in a broader category that includes prestigious advanced projects as well.

How should we list the various crafts activities of a program for the participants? Identifying the material used lacks excitement. Wood, paper, clay, glass, fabric, and metal seem like the blunt guidelines of a purchasing agent. There are distinctive words that describe the process rather than the material used. The following are some capsule classic craft classifications:

Ceramics and Pottery — The two labels appear interchangeable. But to be a potter seems more rugged, antiestablishment; a ceramicist seems to have more refinement, is less functional, and more aesthetic. In this craft the clay is kneaded, spun on a wheel, pounded into shapes, mostly pots, cooked, and glazed.

Sketching and Drawing — Everyone doodles a little. Most people feel uneasy with this art area. If you can draw a horse that doesn't look like a cow there's a chance.

Sewing or Needlecraft — Knitting and stitchery belong here. Making clothes is an important aspect.

Painting — It's hard to find someone who hasn't felt the urge to paint. Palm Springs' drug stores have counters of beginning oil sets for people seduced by the sunsets. This is difficult to succeed in, and overwhelming when one realizes that a painting by a master sells for millions.

Jewelry Making — There's a lot of interest in jewelry, but people find this one of the real skill-demanding areas. You can't get away with mediocre work. Lapidary, the cutting and polishing of stone, falls here and includes a vast number of participants.

Leatherwork — One of the biblical crafts revived by young back-to-the-earth people. Leather was the original craft material. There is not much you can't make out of it.

Weaving — This craft has high status but serves as a cottage industry in many emerging countries. As a recreation, it takes time and patience and lots of space for a class in advanced stages.

Printing — This takes all forms, from operating a printing press to carving a potato stamp. Silk screen printing, tie dying, batiking, and lithography have been high participation areas lately.

Woodworking and Woodcarving — Carpentry can be fun. Making furniture or refinishing an antique piece are status activities. Relief carving and sculpture carving permit high personal expression.

Papercraft — Cut it, fold it, glue it, crumple it, and glop it together. Paper is cheap and handy. Collage is a type of painting with paper cut-outs and is always popular.

Mosaics — You can copy or be creative. The process is to take bits and pieces of stone, glass, and seeds and put them together like a jig saw puzzle.

Sculpture — You just chip away pieces of stone, wood, and soap.

Along with these broad designations covering numerous projects are some major craft activities that could be covered by one of these classifications but are effective on their own. They manufacture participant interest without promotion. For example:

Puppetry, which is primarily a paper craft, gets into sewing, is involved in drama but remains one of the most versatile and popular making-things experiences ever programmed.

157

Papier-mache overlaps puppetry, serving as one of the primary materials used to construct puppet heads, but it also is used in molding, modeling, and sculpting three-dimensional figures as well as providing decorative covers for boxes and containers.

Gyotaku or fish printing is obviously a printing process and yet painting can enter into the more advanced work. But then painting, printing, and drawing could be included in graphic arts. *Gyotaku* is one of those exotic deviations in crafts that can take over a whole crafts program for a season or two.

Model building is probably one of the many half-breed items that involve mixed media, i.e., a variety of materials, and several processes. Putting together a dune buggy or a soap box racer or a miniature airplane are like that. The fascination with miniatures over many centuries has made models in kit form an extremely popular form of crafts, perhaps the number one mass craft that has held interest over a long period of time.

Candlemaking has been around the recreation scene for a long time. A great holiday craft, especially at Christmas, the back-to-basics youth thrust has vastly increased its popularity.

Tie-dyeing is an old craft recently revived. Batik is a more advanced and demanding printing process.

Classification Systems

These are simply ways of organizing and in themselves add little to generating interest and involvement in crafts. But the leader/planner needs to structure his thinking into systems to be sure he considers all possibilities and can project his crafts program into the future with a sequential and continuous flow of crafts related to each other and other parts of the program according to stages and degrees of difficulty.

For this purpose, we present here a new system of classifying crafts, but encompassing the old ways in which crafts have been viewed. It is based upon the way arts and crafts serve participants. While each craft project can easily be programmed to serve most or all of the following service areas, each one has a greater potential for specific motivations because of its basic use history and because of the nature of the process it uses.

They are listed here on a descending scale of their service toward fulfilling needs of participants.

Expressive Crafts They communicate feelings. They are personal interpretations that tell how one feels through the items made. Painting is a potent viewing screen for the emotions. The shapes, colors, size, and emphasis of objects in the painting all deliver messages.

Image Crafts Often blending with expressive crafts, image crafts explain how a person sees himself and how he wants others to see him. The self-image is indicated by deviations from orthodox craft processes and finished product guides. The completed project as a whole represents the total person, his bizarre uniqueness or his conforming imitation. This is me, it says, this is my statement about myself; I want this project to represent me to whomever sees it. Sculpture as a three-dimensional medium does this through the material used, the size and shape it takes, and its subject matter.

Kinetic Crafts The feel of our hands shaping materials is a tactile, sensual experience at its best and at least a sense of power and control over materials. We work with our hands because it feels good.

Segment Crafts Arts and crafts are often integrated with other recreation program areas, creating scenery for dramas, pinatas for special events, printed wrapping paper for holiday gifts, clothes for puppets, murals for the 4th of July, or posters boosting a Saturday ball game. The craftsman likes to contribute to something bigger than himself or the craft project.

Instrumental Crafts Making the instrument needed for a recreation activity has been one of the most highly motivated craft involvements: constructing a can stove for a cookout, making instruments for the rhythm band, building the planes for radio-controlled flying, constructing kites for the kite contest, or shaping paper masks for the Halloween parade. The lure of future use involves many participants in craft activity.

Utilitarian Crafts Utilitarian crafts are quite often the inspiration for originality and invention. They are closely related to instrumental crafts but arise out of a practical survival need. An item is needed but unavailable. Lint on suits may inspire different types of lint lappers made from coat-hangers and cardboard tubes; the periodical search for string once triggered the making of the monkey-faced coconut shell string dispenser. The dresser clump of wallet, credit cards, keys, ring, and watch started a wave of dresser caddies. Often the commercial firms have already manufactured a similar product, but there's nothing like the one-of-a-kind pride of the handcrafted item. Listen for clues like "wish there was something to . . . " or "why don't they invent . . . "

Decorative Crafts   Decorative crafts are low-grade esthetic crafts. They have a temporary nature, adding a touch to other things rather than being things complete in themselves. They include Christmas tree ornaments, mosaic designs on box covers, and holiday candles. All projects intended to be ornamental but not enduring are in this category.

Gift Crafts   These are motivated by a love of others, a drive to please. We all like to say "I made this just for you." Mantles all over the world feature lop-sided, dog-eared, enigmatic clay, wood, and paper objects from the crafts. This is often a hardship area for the chosen one: who wants to wear a size-18 knitted sock or pull down a Van Gogh so a first attempt lithograph can go up in the living room?

Sale Crafts   When crafts are made for profit then the ugly spectre of work appears. It's a big controversy today with artists and craftsmen everywhere. The self-expressing artist wants the freedom to spill out his mood and please himself. Nonsense, say others, ultimately there must be an audience for no one can be satisfied with making something and then discarding it without having it measured by the opinions of others. There is no answer for this, but there does seem to be a thrill in having someone want to purchase it. If we have to keep score in crafts for some participants, money is a very tangible system. But it is a circus balancing act between work and play when profit becomes part of the motivation.

159

Learning Crafts   We're split on this category. The opposition says there's learning in all crafts. The loyalists say, of course, there's learning in every human experience, but the point is that the basis for doing this craft is to develop an understanding of other cultures, peoples, substances, geography, environment and other theme areas. These might be important in establishing a German week on a playground, a pioneer or Indian atmosphere at camp, or appreciation of George Washington's birthday. Learning crafts are related to Segment Crafts.
     A relief map of the Hawaiian Islands is a good craft project, but if we're trying to improve a recreation environment in a ghetto by pretending we're Polynesian natives, the map or leis really put us in touch. Try jewelry making, and see if new insights on Navaho silversmithing doesn't evolve.
     The participants don't have to know about the learning; the leader has it as a behavioral objective in his own mind. The craft project has got to carry itself without any boring lectures or forced teaching — that's what makes it recreation and not formal education.

Time-filling Crafts   This category is better known as chewing-gum crafts. This is a low on powerful recreation crafts programs but not uncommon. Crafts too often end up as a means to fill required rest time after lunch or something to do instead of fidgeting. When crafts are the answer to "Oh hum, what's to do," they are being prostituted. But if it's the only way to get someone to try crafts then do it, but do it well. Unleash your best one-shot project and hope for a convert.

Classifying the crafts is important to the good organizer. Through it he can set up a well-balanced, smoothly-paced, adequately-prepared arts and crafts program. If he wants to understand what's happening as a result of his effort, he must also apply an examining classifications system that analyzes the motivations of the participants in relation to the aim of the arts and crafts experience.

ARTS AND CRAFTS — PLANNING

Participants in arts and crafts are generally creative, resourceful, and aesthetic. Is it that we plan to attract those types, or are the participants molded by the activity? Obviously we can plan for both possibilities but such manipulation not only slights the insecure and the sports-directed people, but it also keeps arts and crafts from achieving a larger and stronger role in program.

It is important to refine our male-female stereotypes to regard wood carving as a tough man's craft in contrast to feminine textile painting. Neither has to be so narrowly constructed, of course, but a planner should be aware of whom his participants will be and if their attitudes about specific crafts are affected by experience and general public attitude. An ambivalent craft like jewelry can be directed toward either sex. A good planner will keep this in mind when planning mixed sexes craft activities or dealing with any all-male or all-female program. The craft that matches the participants' image of themselves is the best starting point.

The level of competency, often based on previous experience, is quite vital in arts and crafts. There are no minor roles, set painting, or back row choruses in which to hide the low skilled participants. As craft experiences narrow the focus and advance in complexity, the levels of skill should be evenly balanced for greatest effectiveness in program. The planner can determine some of this by verbal or written survey, or a classification of skill levels can be set up at a pre-program workshop.

Progressive projection is a universal program stimulator, but in crafts the reliance is based upon the materials used and the complexity of the projects undertaken rather than the challenge of other participants. No one interferes with an individual's achievement, nor is it dependent upon cooperative effort. The man stands alone with his materials and moves at his own pace through a hierarchy of increasingly more complicated and demanding projects that require more refined, creative, and dexterous application of mind and hands.

Plan the nature of the recognition and reinforcement in advance. False praise can be thwarting, criticism traumatizing, and lack of response debilitating. You may draw participants into the planning by letting them establish the type of response they desire from the leader.

For beginners, plan a range of alternatives in the initial arts and crafts experiences. The wrong project — too tough, too easy, or too messy — can create resistance against participating again. A variety of possibilities will let the individual move from a failure area to one with the opportunity for success.

Everybody needs the feeling of having accomplished something at every session. Plan to complete at least one whole step or stage in the project unless it is a one-session project.

Schedule crafts for a low energy time, when the jumping, running, and hopping tendencies have run down. That is, unless you're running one of the big muscle crafts like stone carving, pot throwing, or carpentry. Most crafts are sit-down-and-concentrate experiences, in which physical expression comes through the hands.

Planners should have experience in the craft themselves. Do a mock-up or walk-through to be sure that "even a monkey can do it" is an accurate reassurance to the hesitant. You can use your trial-run project as the visual sample.

Your budget is especially important in arts and crafts. If you can't afford exotic materials, such as suede or oil paints, then adjust your plan to utilize substitute materials, e.g., plaster carving instead of marble. The participants themselves are often investors in the crafts program, making it self-supporting to an extent. Since materials are for individual use the assessment is usually simple, but it is not as easy if special tools and equipment are needed for all. Most planners don't trust the participants to procure their own materials. They prepare for this by having supplies on hand for sale to those who forget or are unable to obtain them. A good planner would probably know via the telephone if everybody was going to be prepared or not.

161

Arts and crafts are often messy. If messes are individually identifiable, the clean-up stage of a session is just a matter of reminding each participant to take care of his own station. In overlapping messes it may be more effective and less damaging to facilities and tools to have special assistants assigned to take on such duties. Don't deprive those who need to feel needed the opportunity to slick up the area after an arts and crafts class. Do not stand alone and bitter after a crafts session, bearing the burden of cleaning up like a martyr. Clean-up is part of the arts and crafts process, an integral part, and it should be programmed to serve the participants by providing fun and fulfillment. It's a challenge to every planner. Clean-up patterns are scheduled into the activity since nothing vanishes faster than people after a crafts class, leaving their mess behind them.

Facilities

You can conduct arts and crafts in the men's room on a card table, in the ball closet, or even squatting on the asphalt. Adaptability to place is one of the attractive aspects of this activity. There are no greens to manicure, floors to polish, or acoustics to worry about. A surface to work on is its only demand.

This doesn't mean that arts and crafts do not deserve a special well-equipped facility. Environment refines an activity, gives a gloss to it, controls the group, and generates respect for the activity. The more appropriate the environment, the more effective will be the craft experience. A bad facility is an obstacle but not a deterrent.

Ideally the multi-roomed crafts center is the opulent, ultimate dream of every crafts-oriented recreation profession: an art studio for painting classes, a ceramics workshop, a children's all-kinds-of-crafts room, a storage vault, an outdoor patio, and an exhibition hall. The dream has come true for some of the larger operations in organized recreation. College recreation is a good example of special rooms for individual crafts in the emerging campus recreation centers. A room full of weaving looms is not an unusual discovery. Private communities and walled-city condominiums often boast specialized crafts rooms from lapidary to sewing as selling features. Most of the big municipal recreation departments run arts and crafts out of a complex crafts center centrally located, where advanced skills are pursued and crafts ideas are developed and disseminated to branch parks and play grounds.

But a card table in the corner will do in case you're not ready for a big league arts and crafts.

Motivation

Persuading people to participate in arts and crafts is accomplished by following the general principles of promoting program. There are several procedures, however, that deserve deeper consideration for this activity area.

Our major concern is with the use of the inspirational masterpiece. It is a delicate instrument which may create interest and ignite first attempts, or it may cause irreparable disappointment. The trip through the Indian section of a museum to arouse craft interest may expose the shallowness of "a basket is a basket is a basket" outlook on life. A fine Indian basket is eye-pleasing and extremely practical, and collectors pay thousands of dollars for the work of certain vanished tribes. There's something about seeing the best there is that makes even the uninitiated feel that anything is possible. Perhaps there's a sense of guilt, too, a feeling that if another human being can do something so excellent that they too can produce something of merit in crafts. For the talented, the masterpiece dangles like a carrot in front of them.

But the masterpiece used as a standard of achievement by the leader who projects his own high tastes may stifle enthusiasm. The example of the finished product, an item completed by the leader or former participant, has some dangerous aspects along the same lines. More of a guiding goal-creating direction for those who have trouble visualizing how a craft project will look, the example is less inspiring than the masterpiece and, of course, should not serve as an exacting measuring stick. Pictures of examples are good for creating interest, especially slides of completed projects. In some cases they inspire without creating the burden of trying to match exactly the real object. Our recommendation is perhaps a combination of all, with several finished samples, flaws and all, including the leader's.

Because we are dealing with different need profiles, some participants will build confidence by imitating, and others will be challenged to exceed the completed examples. Arts and crafts exhibitions (no awards, no measurement) is a good way to motivate new interest and challenge the veterans by exposure to other styles and ideas. The contest with competition and awards, imposes standards and values and, while generally discouraged in organized recreation's arts and crafts activities today, must be considered as serving those who need to be judged in all that they do.

The example in arts and crafts is a much more primary motivational device than in other recreational activities. Handle with care. Being absolute about anything is questionable; it is best to imply that this is one of the items or styles that many experienced people think has merit.

In arts and crafts, the modern, practical mind often says, "But what do I want to make a basket for? I don't need one. Yeah, it's really pretty but . . . " To answer this with the same inarticulate and mysteriously spiritual "because it's there" of the mountain climber will not work. A good motivator may have to keep his charges surging forward by finding practical outlets for the finished craft project. The esthetic justification may arise later and maintain the commitment to arts and crafts, but a leader shouldn't feel he's betraying culture if he points out a craft will make a good gift for Mother's Day, or if he ties the craft into an impending shingle boat race or lines up a bazaar that needs things to sell for charity. Imitating or sustaining interest in crafts is not unlike selling soap, a used car, or a trip to Hawaii.

Organized Patterns

Let's focus on the dominant needs potential again. How do crafts serve the participant? The group process or individual application? The structured class or the drop-in craft center?

Arts and crafts may be a uniquely functional activity with each participant doing entirely unrelated things in the same room, from making a leather wallet to weaving a basket, to printing personal business cards. No one is needed to help anyone else. The solitary aspect, along with the great opportunity for creative expression, is a major value in recreational arts and crafts program. In fact, creativity seems to be directly proportionate to the degree of solitude. Ultimately it is the artist or craftsman alone who creates the masterpiece and savors fully the sense of fulfillment. This isolated self-sufficiency and self-initiated effort is perhaps the ultimate goal of all arts and crafts programs.

Sometimes organized recreation has had to bring arts and crafts in the back door by creating a group situation through clubs, camps, or teams and introduce a group craft project. The first project which gives the beginner initial exposure to crafts should be exciting and rewarding. It doesn't matter if it's imitative, following numbered squares or adding water to a mix. It's the first step in the creative process. Learning requires formal, orderly trails with the group following hand in hand, responding together under confident leadership until they understand the process. Then the individuals may step out and go as far as their creativity and talent will carry them, perhaps moving into more advanced groups and ultimately to their own self-imposed goals. The recreation craft class is a table covered to absorb the spills and spatter, surrounded by a dozen or so pairs of nervous hands. Twelve is a good number for which to prepare in the average indoor small-room crafts situation. Half the number tends to have less dramatic interaction, seems to diminish in importance; half as many again dilutes the intimacy of the experience and fragments the group into cliques.

The class pattern is valid through advanced participation as long as new things are to be learned that benefit by group discussion and require cooperative behavior, such as skill handling an intricate tool such as a kiln. The formality of the class and the mutual concerns of the group insure the social benefits that primarily motivate some of the participants.

The workshop pattern allows the casual, informal, and individual pacing of participation and selection of craft as well as the specific item. It is scheduled in order that group feeling still exists, but participants may jump stages, and are not required to follow any sequence in processing a project. They may even move from one project to another. The essence is selective freedom and more personal contact can be managed with the leader who serves more as a reactor than as an instructor.

The drop-in center requires a special place that is always waiting when the urge hits the craftsman. It has greatest value only after the participant has had class or workshop exposure to develop a sense of craft selection and familiarity with the media and tools. The leader should have estimated the craftsman's potential and abilities. Projects are stored in lockers or on shelves in this situation so that multi-session projects can be conveniently resumed at any time.

164

Current Status and Trends

Arts and crafts has competed with dance over the years for the coveted number-two position in organized recreation program. Its growth has been arrested by naive over-protectiveness of its participants. Somehow the arts and crafts effort has become the lonely road to nowhere in programming because of two commandments: (1) that the finished project shall not be judged or measured, and (2) that the craftsmen shall not compete against each other.

In an effort not to thwart budding creativity, the professional leader today tends to recognize everything as acceptable work in order to reinforce the sensitive creative psyche. Not to be judged or measured against a standard is unrealistic, however.

The arts and crafts leader following this existing practice keeps arts and crafts from challenging the vast popularity of sports, dance, or drama. Sports thrive on competition and much dance and drama is geared toward performance before a critical audience.

The merit of this participant protection pattern is that it avoids discouraging the novice in the sensitive introductory stages when the unknown and failure are feared. It also avoids the star system, the tendency of many recreation leaders to work only with the best. The star system has been unconsciously supported by supervisors and administrators who react more positively toward championship coaches than conscientious leaders who work with the barely talented with less flamboyant results.

Arts and crafts exists in current programming because it is traditionally expected, because it helps fill out the cultural lag created by an over-emphasis on sports and because making things is universally appealing. Advanced arts and crafts form about half of most organized crafts programs but are generally designed for adult-level involvement.

Arts and crafts uniquely permit the individual to continue apart from organized programs. A person can do stages of crafts projects at home, which allows the retention of high interest and expedites progress for participants. The paradox of this is that the individual can function apart from the organized program in his home providing he has the materials, tools, and confidence. Expensive, specialized equipment, such as rock polishers, sewing machines, and kilns, have been the fly paper to keep a number of crafts programs active after the participants had advanced to the stage of initiating and sustaining their own involvement.

Poverty and ugliness are often joint tenants. Ugliness is what identifies a ghetto or slum at first glance — the dirt, the shabbiness, the ever-present lack of beauty. The most successful projects following poverty-belt uprisings have been various types of arts and crafts programs. A carving, painting, flower bed, new curtains have emerged from the programs. Whether it's a new sense of appreciation for beauty, a sense that atrophies in the slums, or simply the objects being created from the activity, or both, the development is one step up and out of perpetual depression for the poor.

The youth culture that has achieved a recent identity is a return to pioneer crafts. Some of it erupts from anguish over the plastic suffocation of the natural environment. Many young people are seeking a simpler life style.

Another move backward that has brought arts and crafts forward is the collecting of nostalgic crafts. Antique collectors have been a small band of wealthy art appreciators for many generations. It is only recently that the newly affluent middle class and the youth culture have become actively involved in the collecting boom. Flea markets, swap meets, and high-grade antique shows cover the landscape in profusion these days. The old rule of pre-1830 to distinguish an antique has slipped away because even an object with a vintage of ten years represents an era of craftsmanship we shall never see again. Selectivity has arisen out of an indiscriminate gathering of everything and anything dated and identified with the past. Specialized collections and refined ability to recognize craftsmanship have arisen. This has inspired a rebirth of ancient crafts, a resourceful decision to make objects no longer available or too expensive to possess. Antique collecting seems to be a good lead-in to arts and crafts.

There will probably be more specialization in arts and crafts too. The increasingly difficult challenge of establishing our individual identities leads us to concentrate our talents where we will produce a distinctive result. Glass blowing, which has been organized recently into workshops and classes, is a sample of this. Some of this involvement will be directed toward impermanent arts and crafts. Sand castles at the beach have become a serious art form. Earth sculpture takes place in the desert, and mowed designs in wheat fields.

Along with this concept, goes the problem of material scarcity. With nature's disappearance the materials of nature are in short supply. Scrap materials are becoming rare collector's items with the escalation of crafts interests by more organizations and people. If we can't discover materials in the wilderness or on the scrap pile, and if it isn't financially feasible to market the raw materials for crafts consumption, then economics dictate that an industry be formed to meet the market need. There will be more and more kit crafts, sometimes unfairly called dumbbell crafts, with more levels of challenge built into them. (Kits are last step crafts in which the participant is permitted to do the finishing step that completes the project.) There is no waste with kits, so many more objects can be projected out of a given amount of raw material. Kits promise success and save time. Modern man responds well to such advantages. The kit manufacturers feel they are building the degree of creativity that people want into the kits. It is an introductory approach to arts and crafts, and when a person is ready to advance, the raw materials or a more complex kit are available. Leather craft, model-making, and decoupage are the most popular areas in recent kit sales.

More competition is coming into style despite conscientious efforts to make success an individual evaluation. The rising number of arts and crafts shows with cash purchase awards and other symbolic acknowledgments is a phase of programming that effectively serves the confident and the talented and, of course, the spectators. Watch for competition to be handled effectively and advantageously in arts and crafts as we develop more professional leadership in organized recreation.

166

DANCE

Theories of Dance Dance is spontaneous expression, but it is also the primordial urge to move in rhythm. The cradle's rocking motion is desired by infants, and man continues to move in rhythm and his body in a pattern to match his moods.

Each of us is capable of internalizing a private drumbeat, plugging it into our emotions, and accompanying our rhythmic body movements with our whistling, humming, or singing. The origin of these repeated movements we call dance still remain unknown to science, and the phenomenon is still one of our mysteries of life.

Dance is physical movement. Is the urge and basic mechanism, then, different from that which sports serve? The physical activity of a skilled athlete is often compared to the ballet forms of dance. But physical movement in sports is directed toward defeating an opponent or record, while dance movement is more dedicated to conveying feelings and ideas, communicating with others while the movements are occurring. Communication is its goal.

An athlete might respond to the above analysis by saying, "In sports there is a physical, material challenge to overcome. There's a goal post and a guy standing in the way. Your physical effort isn't as directed to artistic technique as it is to succeeding, no matter how you look. Dance doesn't really have the game atmosphere to it. Dance seems like it can't exist without music . . . it's a response to music. A kinesthetic response, just as an athlete has to respond to an opponent or a record."

Take free exercise in gymnastics or board diving in aquatics, put music to it and drop the competitive pattern, and they would be a lot like dance.

An artist would reply, "We have very few ways of expressing our identity. It is not possible to have an individual identity when one follows prescribed behavior. Creating things is the best way of expressing ourselves as individuals. Making things is very good, of course, but the creative act itself isn't really shared with others as it is when we use our voices or bodies in movement. In the free forms of dance this kind of individualized self-expression has its best opportunity to unfold."

An anthropologist would say, "Dance is a communication through physical movement, but it exists as a cultural heritage in man's evolution. What's important is with whom the dancer is trying to communicate. The origin of dance is in religion. Man used rhythmic movement to placate, thank, or coerce the gods. It became ritual or sacred dance and was passed on from generation to generation. Finally, some of it took on a secular theme and was performed for entertainment, amusement, or the physical fulfillment it provided."

A geographer would argue, "Dance adapts itself to the environment of a people. The movements emulate the local animals, the climate, or the topography. The Flamenco of Spain or the ground-stomping dance of American Indians reveal a devotion to the land. The Polynesians do a lot of undulating and swaying like the ocean waves they live with each day."

A psychologist would reply, "Dance is a release mechanism, a way of subtly and indirectly expressing oneself without the consequences of direct verbal communication. The Flamenco dancer stamps out his hatred and the hula hands convey love. Circle dancing has a great psychological security overtone. It is circular and repetitive and everybody faces inward toward each other with a sense of belonging. Line dancing is more of a theatrical performance with the dancers facing and displaying their skill to an audience, exposing themselves, so to speak, to the exhilaration of recognition or hazards of criticism."

We believe that the theoretical base for dance lies in a cultural pattern allowing creative self-expression. Dance seems to depend on music, with music serving as the stimulus for kinesthetic response, the sensation of movement of parts of the body perceived through nerve end organs. And while music seems a necessary partner to dance, drama often plays a role of interdependence. To separate the latter two in Japan is impossible, for dance is placed into drama to accentuate peak moments.

There may be some difficulty in accepting the overall function of dance as a self-expression outlet when one examines dance in its exacting classical forms. Classic ballet is a fine art built of ancient traditional styles and techniques, disciplines to specific standards, and intelligently integrated to music. Classic ballet with its almost codified and geometric movements may be beyond the sphere of self-expression for its vigorous standards permit no individual interpretation. But some will argue that the achievement of classic standards is also an individual expression creating a personal identity.

A reaction to the disciplined, practiced techniques of ballet has been the spontaneous, creative modern dance movement. Rather than the lighter-than-air-effortless facade given to the leapings of ballet, modern dance is very psychologically oriented, labelling some of its concerns as cerebral motivations and body ego.

Most dance activity in recreation can be analyzed and classified by its affinity to ballet or creative dance, i.e., whether its basic objective to provide expression by achievement of traditional standards or through personal responsive interpretations.

Dance can be a wonderful activity for all seasons. That is, depending upon how it is employed by a programmer, it can match need fulfillments with almost every other area of program activity.

Physical activity in dance can equal the most vigorous sport participation. It is versatile exercise, and participants who are consistent and exertive are blessed with measurable results. Firm up, lose weight, gain grace, control the body — these are the come-ons of the commercial dance studio, but they are legitimate.

Creativity is primarily limited to the interpretive form of dance which is often labelled modern dance but traces its origin back to the Greeks and beyond. Interpretation, that is, fitting movements to ideas in the mind's eye, is a very inventive opportunity. Ballet is restrictive, codified; folk is directed, memorized. But all forms provide a degree of self-expression even if it is only the sequential shuffling of exacting movements, which has some element of creating one's own routine.

Social Interaction is given its best opportunity to thrive in the simple standardized movements of folk dancing under which square, round, and social dancing are classified. Since success comes easily to almost everyone in this area of dance, participants are allowed to concentrate on each other rather than playing to an audience or striving to meet regimented skill specifications.

The general air of informality is conducive to socialization, and it is found and encouraged as an inherent characteristic of folk and social dancing. (The terms "folk" and "social" in the context of dancing can be synonymous, the difference lying with the intent of the programmer to provide either an historical basis for identifying oneself or getting people together.) Even in the highly technical dance forms, of which ballet and ceremonial are the extreme examples, there is a periphery of informality around the concentrated effort toward perfection. There are the locker rooms, hallway, and rest period exchanges that allow participants to establish their individual personalities. This is also as true of interpretive dance as it is with all recreation activities that allow people with common purposes to converse in periods unrelated to the direct pursuit of that common purpose.

When dance is set up to provide socialization, it works very well. The reason seems to lie in the physical and emotional exuberance of the experience, where involvement tends to divert one's self-consciousness from what seems to be the critical eye of others. It is possible to hide behind the dancing until one feels confident to relate to others more directly and personally.

Appreciation of beauty is a sort of abstract dimension that the philosophers assign to the arts, in which dancing enjoys an exalted position. The word "aesthetics" is often used to describe the concept.

We believe that beauty is in the eye of the beholder, what is ugly to one is beautiful to another. If what aesthetics means in dance is that watching a body turn and twist in controlled designs pleases your eye, then dance has aesthetics as one of its values. We find sports closely related, for our eye is suitably pleased by the movements of the fine athlete. Dance, however, creates the movements as an end in themselves to please the eye, while sports movements are accidentally beautiful for the intention is to win.

Recognition and understanding of one's cultural heritage also occur through dance. Dance and gestures were among the first means by which man communicated significant notions of his ideals, and life styles have been documented by folk dance patterns handed from generation to generation.

Incorporation of dance into an eclectic program event, a folk festival, for example, allows dance to gain utilitarian stature. Participants can feel a functional purpose when their dance activity is used to enhance an activity or event that has a larger purpose and broader audience than the dance activity itself. Dance provides a lively visual flavor and action — a movement of people that often generates the spirit and interests of both active and passive participants in an otherwise sedate and uneventful occasion.

Relaxation and escape are effectively processed through many of the dance activity forms. Dance, with its origins in religion, provides fantasizing opportunities. One can pretend when he dances to things other than what he is. The child's first dance experience might well be the imitation of an elephant walking to the water hole. With fantasy man escapes from routine and himself.

Physical relaxation is generally a respite from normal physical routine. The sedentary desk clerk finds that dance — movement, leaping, and stretching — is his way to relax.

Service to others takes place with a medium fulfillment level when dance is performed before an audience. Under our general need analysis we give credit to audience entertainment as a means for a performer to serve others.

Rhythm and coordination are enhanced as mental and physical entities through dance activity. One's participation in other activities, such as music or sports, are improved in these two areas of motor ability.

The opportunity for adventure and new experience is generated out of new movements, steps, and styles in all dance areas. There is a continuous bombardment of fads in the social dancing area. One of the milestone innovations of the last two decades was rock which split the couple concept asunder. The resulting individualized self-expressing spin-off is still the dominant pattern for the young, who provide the majority of participants for dance programming.

Dance can serve many functions and consequently possesses a variety of

169

values. But it has its greatest potential as a physical vehicle for individual self-expression. It also serves as a means for permitting people to relate to each other in group situations.

Role of Dance in Recreation

Dance has had to carry a heavy load in recreation programming. It has served women and girls as sports have served men and boys.

No stone tablets have ever been found that insist that's the way things must be. Our enlightened era, with its elevated status for women, promises to erase the social differentiations and taboos that have created "men only" and "women only" concepts in programming. Nevertheless, organized recreation relentlessly schedules its bulk physical fulfillment activities along the sports line for men. Dance is the major token offering to the female.

It is assumed that men in general are blood-thirsty competitors, very physical and animal, and constantly in need of muscular outlets in which opponents are to be defeated with concern for neither the appearance nor aesthetics. But sports properly conducted are good for everyone — and so is dance.

Dance in its most common pattern in recreation doesn't involve points, scores, opponents, or winning. There are no losers, nor does anyone take something from others. It is simply that each person expresses as best they can what they think or feel. It is very physical, and it is the only performing art that is often found in the physical education curriculum of schools. But the physical movement with fitness and grace is a secondary concern.

Dance is much more expressive than sports, even if recreation puts the fitness aspect first as a motivating device. Dance is good for everyone who has creative needs, male or female. Unfortunately, organized recreation is highly conservative, born insecure about its legitimate role, so its tendency has been to reinforce traditional mores by programming according to the overlays of the past.

Rare exceptions exist throughout recreation programs in all the various environmental services areas. The schools have been the most innovative. Young male athletes have been drafted into creative dance programs or ballet by disguising the experience as body dynamics, physical movement, or athletic conditioning. Probably the success of such devices depends on whether the environment is such that the male participant doesn't feel he has trespassed into the ladies' lounge.

Recreation has done its best job with children, especially at the younger ages in which they have not been socialized thoroughly into sex roles. Most dancing in recreation consists of instructional classes, the introductory plateau of participation. The classes are highly structured — beginner, intermediate, advanced, and master — and culminate in recitals before a small audience of parents and relatives.

Dance has used the special event rather than the competitive game to motivate participation. Most audience-oriented special events have some place for the performance of dance as either a focal point or background. Another manufactured role for dance places it in a double role as far as our classification of recreation participation areas. It is used as a physical experience to bridge social gaps. If people fail to relate or interact, the physical contact and movements of dance often resolve the strain. Dance has been used as a reason for getting people together, and it certainly gives one something to do with his hands, feet, and body if communicating on a purely verbal level is awkward.

The role of dance in recreation follows this pattern:

1. It is used to compensate women and girls for the massive programming in male sports.
2. It promotes participation on the practical bases of fitness and grace, but may eventually fulfill the participants' needs for form, beauty, and personal expression.
3. It is second to arts and crafts in terms of numbers and hours scheduled for cultural program. Most dance is programmed as a highly structured instructional program with the classes culminating in performances before small, involved audiences, or performing in decorative or functional ways in special entertainments.
4. It also is used by recreation to provide a communication bridge between people in various social recreation programs, from parties to comprehensive social dance.

Planning and Leadership

Dance follows closely on the heels of arts and crafts and music in being identified as feminine in contrast to other program activities. On a recent male/female word association test it ranked as the most female-oriented of fifteen recreation activities. The trouble with such measurements of public opinion is that the appraisal is too generalized. Social and folk dancing require both sexes. If the appraisers understood this, dance would move toward the middle of a male/female continuum.

Traditionally, we're stuck with a public that imagines dance as an activity for nubile young women pirouetting or tapping about on their toes. The influence of the media certainly conveys a strong feminine image toward dance.

We may accept this generalization and let our cultural dance programs help balance the overweighted male sports program. If the programmer believes, however, that the radical male/female dichotomy is eroding then he should feel free to schedule cultural dance activities for both sexes.

A second consideration in planning dance should be balancing the program. As we have noted, dance is a utility activity field, used to plug gaps in participant fulfillment. A good example is the provision of vigorous physical outlets in confined areas, often the case in institutions like hospitals, prisons, or schools. Dance provides the same physical exertion that sports and games provide with larger space. It also carries interest better than a regimen of calisthenics.

Dance can also fill social needs where other activity outlets aren't possible. It can be elevated to an art form covering creativity needs. The key is versatility, and the full potential of dance in balancing program has yet to be exploited.

Another dance concern has to do with standards by which participants can measure themselves. Unlike the casual do-your-own-thing philosophy often found in crafts, the perfectionism in music, or the personality projections in dramatics, dance allows a multi-layered progress system. The essence of it, with some exception, for example the extreme of ballet, is the subjective criteria imposed.

Dance has many forms controlled by programmers called dancing masters. These leaders reinforce participant dedication by a ranking system frequently associated with sports activity. The dancing masters measure specifically described skills, either a total dance, like the tango, or a basic movement, like an arabesque. Since standard specifications do not exist, such as a record in the 50-yard dash, expert judgment is applied. We have seen this in aquatics with springboard diving and in gymnastics. Judgments, which are by nature subjective, are made by leaders and programmers.

Dance provides the programmer a chance to plan attentive participation by controlling the ranking charts that guide and motivate the serious enthusiasts of dance. Commercial ballroom dancing has effectively employed the gold-silver-bronze medal system to keep 'em coming back for more. The various systems we suggested are derived from the latitude dance programmers have in defining achievement.

Dance activity needs periodic culminating performance outlets. There can be disagreement on this planning principle. Purists often say, "Fine arts — crafts, music, or dance — are personal things and one experiences his skill as self-fulfillment, enjoying the act or process without the desire for external approval. This is true self-expression, an individual discovering his own powers to accomplish beauty and form."

It's the ideal self concept that allows a person to be completely inner-directed uninfluenced by outside forces. Realistically, our social orientations always keep us somewhat dependent on others to help shape our values and opinions of ourselves.

The culminating performance outlet is the way the planner highlights the time and effort of his participants. He's saying, "Ok, this is where you are with your practice, learning and experimenting. Now let's see how you can put it together so that it has meaning beyond yourself. Let's road test it."

Such finales to dance activity are not necessarily culminating in the sense that they bring an end to participation. "Culminating" is a word which has been part of traditional recreation jargon for a long time. It actually means bringing something to its highest, finest point. With dance, culmination is used as a means to structure the participant's dance experiences, to rank him to guide future efforts, and to use dance for fulfillment beyond self-expressive communication, such as recognition, cooperation, interaction, and service to others.

Plan cooperation rather than competition to encourage the most effective participant fulfillment. When dance is used to emphasize an individual's creative expression more is gained if everyone wins to some degree. Co-operation leads to achievements of a different dimension than the individual dancer can accomplish alone. The feeling of group achievement is shared success with each individual taking away a sense of achievement. Although competition is used in dance programming, it is usually of a group-versus-group nature, and even then it differs from sports insofar as the outcome of the game overshadows the quality of performance.

There is a fine line here. Dance could easily be pushed into the same rat race as highly competitive sports, but by tradition and practice dance has served as a cooperative expressive effort.

Dance programming should utilize all available community resources. Dance activity has never been an easy activity for involving the broad population. Somehow, when it goes beyond the introductory stages, only a few participants remain who are quite talented and leap to the mastery stage. Why this has been so is open to speculation, but we'll hazard a pragmatic guess. Recreation generalists have always felt a lack of confidence with the fine arts in the cultural programming area and have tended to pick their specialist leaders from the ranks of professional talent. Consequently champions want to breed champions. They manipulate beginners activity as a means to an ultimate end, the spawning of more professionals in their own elite image. That is not entirely bad, and some very fine programs have resulted from the intense push upward. But it does not have the balanced coverage for many levels of competency that the good program should have.

The answer may be in making the generalist more confident and placing the professional in the upper skill echelon. This is being done in some places, but the pattern often takes the form of referral to the specialized commercial dance studio or center. This is a good way for handling it by recreation agencies which seek to cover the full vertical and horizontal ranges of specific populations.

The programmer has the chance to maintain firm control on the dance program without relegating power to a specialist. He can use television and the movies as instant references for inspiring interest, measuring achievement against professional standards, and learning new techniques.

Organized Patterns

The activity pattern that predominates is the instructional class. The introductory dance class may be an umbrella covering all forms of simple rhythmic movement to hula, Spanish, folk, square, tap, or ballet. More often the class is scheduled as a specialty class covering one type. The specialty pattern is usually dictated by the availability of an enthusiastic instructor. If the essence of dance activity is to achieve rhythmic movement that helps express the individual's temperament, then a complex instructional program on the hula should not be underrated.

Most dance instruction is open-ended insofar as one never finishes learning and practicing. There is always another plateau of knowledge or skill to be learned. Programmers have structured the dance classes elaborately into multi-layered levels of classes: beginners, novices, intermediates, advanced, masters, and post-masters.

But since plateaus are reached, programmers must sustain interest. Consequently we build into the dance class a time in which achievement is recognized or measured. Competition is not normally a successful motivating device with activities of self-expression. Recitals, however, do not pit participants against each other, but attempt to give each individual an audience for a demonstration of skills.

The performance dance recital is not an ultimate goal but primarily a device to reinforce the involvement in the class structure. To develop a different pattern, placing the emphasis on the performance or creating a contest between opponents, removes dance from its role as an art form.

Dance is also patterned into an integrated or incorporated approach in which it is part of a conglomerate recreation activity. The conglomerate is usually of special event proportions designed to put dance and music and crafts and other elements together to enhance each other. The purpose is to bring new meaning to each interest area through combination. It is possible to generate enthusiasm for dance by inventing the conglomerate first and creating a need for dancing, e.g., a folk festival or ballroom dance.

Exercise is the basis for a number of dance activities that are patterned to continue without progressive learning or periodical performances. The fulfillment emphasis is basically on health and fitness and as such aligns itself as closely to sports as culture. But the exercise aspect which can develop into a pleasurable experience, is made more appealing to the expressive person because of its cultural overtones.

Social dance has its emphasis in the interaction between people, but it can also be programmed as a special event if the scope and infrequency of scheduling require it. Social dance can be manipulated by the programmer to stress any or all the need fulfillment areas of socialization, inspiration, and creativity.

The workshop or camp pattern is another successful short term, concentrated, one-shot activity used most effectively with advanced dance participants. Total concentration on the dance permits broad cultural experiences that incorporate food and music (and ethnic customs in the folk dancing arena). Folk and square dance clubs have also been effective in sustaining interest on a long term basis and providing progression systems that create dance life styles.

The universal patterns of organization are all possible in programming dance. The learning patterns are the most effective because they stay closer to the art concept of dance. The competitive performance format probably deserves more experimentation if a broader appeal is to be sought.

Current Status and Trends

Dance has not traveled far from its past. The forms that it takes are adjustments but not revolutions. We still dance for the same emotional reasons even if the ritual has become token, no longer a signal for gods but for pleasure.

The dissatisfactions of youths in any era have always found outlets in man's basic two forms of communication, expressive movement and rhythmic sounds.

We have witnessed music fads blend with the dance fads of youth in a struggle for identity. Rhythm and blues, rock and roll, and hard rock weren't new forms at all, they were hybrid carry-overs from other times. The dances they spawned, probably starting with the Twist, have a desperation about them seeking identity and attention.

But the individual dance art form has not been significantly touched by it — ballet, tap, folk, acrobatic, and square are really unchanged. Here and there the music of the day is recognized and appropriate experimentation attempted but the main core remains the established classic. It is in couples social dancing where mating, the expression of feelings, and preening before others take place, that the fads have been more affecting. The possessiveness and intimacy of past forms of dancing have given way to a broader interacting social dance style.

Youth have led the way, for they are the eternal experimenters. The social dancing they support reflects their current life style. If multi-contacts, numerous partners, a wide open brotherhood-of-man attitude is in vogue then the dance will follow that form, even if it evolves in a circle to primitive swaying in large groups to sounds that trigger their various emotions.

The cycles have changed in the past, and they will again. There are signs of a need to relate and care deeply about one person. Dance as a social tool for achieving such ends must move back to a more romantic coupling pattern. What may be lost in physical activity may be compensated by more intense expression toward the other person, a communication of greater depth and quality.

The classic dance forms will hold their own in the future, although social dancing will continue to follow the circle pattern. More male participation is possible in all forms of dance as society stops defining behavior in male and female stereotypes. Programmers will be able to move more males into the dance experience by masquerading it in sports terms and window dressing. For example, body-building and fitness values can clear away the male inhibitions. The increase of performing opportunities and a change in their nature, e.g., the enactment of the Civil War through choreography, or telling stories through dance will broaden the appeal.

175

Our society is deluged by instant media, every home is a visual theatre every night, and dance occupies a reasonable portion of that exposure. The mere exposure to professional dancing stimulates a large segment of the public. At some point the spectators will tire of merely watching and alert programmers can provide participation experiences in dance, adjusted to serve all individuals and their various needs.

CAPSULE CLASSICS

Folk Dance Festival

Folk dancing is potentially the ultimate expression of a culture. The opportunity for individual self-expression is present because there are various styles and interpretations.

But "cultural" applied to a people or a society has to do with their unique ideas and characteristics. The folk dance is a way of describing to each generation how their ancestors felt, lived, worked, loved, played, and dressed. It provides the opportunity for people to costume themselves and imagine through dance their folk heritage and manners. Folk dances and songs throughout history are the way common people express their joy for life.

The folk dance activity with any group can be general or specific. If the majority of a dance group are descended from Greeks or Mexicans they will feel a greater inspiration because of an authentic bond. But origins and ancestral ties do not prevent a group from choosing a specific folk dance for whatever reason.

The idea of the Folk Dance Festival is to create an international flavor with colorful pageantry and festivity. The Festival is show-off time for the class or club built around folk dancing. Its pattern is very much like the non-competitive play day of sports. It is a large cooperative gathering in which each group may perform. The attending groups, knowledgeable and appreciative, constitute the best of all audiences.

Modern Dance Workshop

The emphasis here is on the improvisational. Spontaneity comes off well in the workshop, which by its nature is an experimental place, a place where new learning and inspiration take place because each participant puts aside regular class practice in order to try something new.

The inspirational aspect usually comes from master modern dancers brought in to share ideas and illustrate their styles and innovative concepts. Participants see master performances and can try to incorporate a new technique or a whole body movement in their own routines.

But routine is a bad word in this context, for modern interpretive dance in its pure form calls for expression of the feeling of the moment rather than rehearsed behavior. Take, for example, the simple device of using a balloon to control the body movements. The pursuit of the bouncing, floating balloon cause the turns, twists, and stretches to be guided through reflex movement rather than mentally arranged movement.

This dance activity rates high in creativity, new experience, and physical activity, with a medium fulfillment potential in dominance and social interaction.

Square Dance Club

As we have noted elsewhere, the club is the best approach for indefinitely continuing any activity. It has been most successful in dance programming with the square dance.

The square dance is, of course, a fragment of the broader arena of folk dancing. In America, however, because there are so many participants, it deserves separate recognition. It is considered American despite the fact, like many of our folk ways, it has its roots in other countries.

Square dancing is probably the simplest form of group dancing there is. It's rather hard for anyone to fail at the basic dances. The participant has the directions called out to him by a record or a live caller. Until one moves into intricate weavings and changing of partners, an automatic pilot can be set and one's personal talents can be turned to socially relating.

Square dancing has always been most effective with adults and especially with senior citizens. It is possible to be attached to one partner, the basic couple, and yet to intermingle a great deal with others without jealousy or emotional upset. It's a good system which allows touching many people, but which unmistakably recognizes the permanent relationship of one couple. Most married couples are not mate-shopping, and square dancing allows relating without wooing overtones. The costuming is asexual but enhances the festive atmosphere, which is a big part of the square dance.

It works with other ages, too, but the programmer will find that the club works best for older adults. It is good to have one's main leisure interest integrated with established friendships. It saves time, provides a sense of belonging, social interaction, physical activity, and relaxation. The routineness of the club is combated through interaction with other clubs in large festivals and roundups where competition is often used to put an edge on such participation.

The Teen Dance

The teen dance is the social recreation used in cultural programming for the pre-adult youth.

It has been our most successful approach to coed activity for this age group. Whether it is a simple record or cassette hop or a light show and live band affair, it is a happening that draws them . . . even poorly done.

The teen dance is the justification for young males and females to convene without the embarrassment of open pursuit and possible rejection. It's a great test run to dance with someone; check their breath, coordination, morals, and personality without making any commitment beyond the mechanics of dancing.

Unfortunately the teen dance has been in inevitable decline, even the best organized ones. Why should something so good decline after a run of a year or so? Here are the speculations:

Youths are tremendously fickle, and they drop their fads and in-places like disposable no-return bottles. It may be because newness means attention and identity. In any event, they will inevitably drop a regularly scheduled dance series after a given period.

There's been some spoiling, too. In our modern age, in which electronic media has given youth high expectations about any activity or event, the teen dance needs elaborate light productions and live bands. The teenager is the most likely to fear that he is missing something bigger and better elsewhere if he commits himself to one place or experience. He doesn't seem capable or willing to make do.

Each teen dance has a limited life span if programmed as a regular activity rather than a special event. If the programmer accepts the situation and adjusts his schedule to match the rhythm of interest he will control its success. He can reorganize other teen dances for the entering new teens.

Baton and Drill Team

One spin-off of dance activity is the widely popular baton twirling. Certainly it is related to dance because of its rhythmic movements, but the emphasis is on an implement, the baton, which creates a wider involvement of the upper body.

The drill team is more of a group experience than baton twirling, which demands a personal concentration. But the two are not incompatible; on the contrary, the ideal programming is probably a combination of the two. The drill team is a rhythmic marching team experience, and parallels effectively for girls in the pre-teens and lower teen level sports provided for boys of the same age.

The baton is an instructional class operation because of its focus on individual talent, whereas the drill team is performance-oriented. But the baton twirlers, although they have special competitions, are also motivated by participating in the marching performances of drill teams.

While the baton, because of the space and hazards involved in throwing it, limits the numbers that can pursue it, drill teams often employ other implements to add to the movements. Flags, drums, and bugles are common additions. A lot of experimentation is still going on in this area, and the relationship to pure dance is still a matter of controversy.

Baton twirling is highly rated for physical activity, relaxation, recognition, and service to others. Drill team is high on fulfilling the needs of physical activity, social interaction, and belonging security.

Ballroom Dancing

Ballroom dancing classes work well for all ages, but it has been a popular recreation mainstay for adults trying to enhance their social lives and perfect their dancing skills. Most classes are heavily laced with actual performance activity, and for this reason advanced participants may join the classes for outlet opportunity. There is a large social overlay in this one.

Ballet and Tap Dancing

Ballet and tap are good as a combination class or individually. Both have a technical regimen to be followed, certain classic maneuvers. Purists denounce tying the two together. But it works for kids and has been popular. Modern dance classes have joined ballet and tap in importance. Its success lies with its open-endedness permitting the non-specialist leader to conduct classes and activities. It does have standards of movement, and ultimate refinement and advancement must come through a specialist.

Rhythmic Movement

Rhythmic movements or rhythms is the little people's introduction to dance and, of course, music. The combination is inevitable and necessary. Children can participate in rhythmic experiences as if playing games. It is informal, unpressured, and interpretative. "Let's all walk like deer or elephants" has been the fun starting point for many budding dedicated dance enthusiasts. If

you want to identify the star performers early, try them on their interpretation of a runaway centipede to the accompaniment of a cassette version
of the "William Tell Overture."

MUSIC

Even tone deaf souls among us can hum a little . . . or whistle. And we all
seem inclined to do so every once in a while when the mood strikes us, which
is the key: the mood of a person.

Music is a way of expressing mood through sound. It builds on its own
energy, too, for it also creates mood or expands it. There are some heavy
pronouncements about art for art's sake, that music is an aesthetic flavor
added to life, and that is reason enough to program it. But that's too mystical
and traditional. We prefer to think of music as a cultural language, another
arena in which the individual can express his identity and abilities or unite
with others to say something cooperatively.

In music we've found a use for sounds for which we don't have a useful
purpose, but which please us. If "plink, plunk, bong, and toot" or complex
combinations of them please our ears, then we need them to offset the noise
we so often hear or the doomsday silence that occasionally falls upon us.

The sounds that make up music are not the ones that we use for
utilitarian purposes. They are sounds that go directly to the emotional
keyboard of the individual rather than the problem-solving computer of the
mind. People feel music rather than think it.

If there is a pure concept of music for the programmer to use as a
foundation for planning activities, it must rest with its sensory effects. Our
ears "feel good" when music happens, at least some of the music, for music is
subject to relative tastes.

It is one of those secrets of life that doesn't get clearer when belabored.
Music is simply sounds that stir our emotions, please us, or upset us, whether
we are making them or listening to them. That is its basic function, although
we may use it in a variety of ways, e.g., as background for a special event, as a
vehicle for storytelling, or as the emotional motivator for dance.

179

Values of Music

Music must serve man beyond being sounds that "soothe the savage beast."
People do more than simply relax to music. They march to war or talk to
their gods with music. They court with music, teach facts with it, and
document events with it. They build folk hero reputations with it and protest
with it. They unload it in jungle form and sell soap or arouse sexual appetites.
Aching gaps of loneliness are plugged by it. The drug culture communicates
with it. The young fantasizes with it, and the aged reminisce with it. Holidays
receive vitality from Christmas Carols in December and "Yankee Doodle
Dandy" on the Fourth of July.

An invigorator, arouser, and revitalizer, it is more than a soothing agent.

It is a life force that can be injected into any experience to magnify existing elements or create a separate influence of its own.

This then is the large, all-encompassing value of music for the recreation programmer — *the ability to set mood in those who receive music as listeners and, more importantly, to allow those who perform or create music to express their moods and ideas.*

There are some refinements of this broad value, perhaps even different specific values, that should be stressed in the context of recreation programming.

Music controls behavior The programmer can use it to slow down over-zealous play, freeze rough-housing, or end lethargy. The last mile of a long hike is executed vigorously if the leader can get the group to sing a trail song. Or any program that has been full of high-pitched activity can be slowed down by suggesting that the end has come with a low-keyed traditional kind of "Auld Lang Syne" sign-off. Music has kept many crises from becoming disasters, converting riots into dance happenings, and fire panics into orderly exits.

Music requires cooperation and develops group unity Music is a group experience. There is the audience on one hand, and, more importantly, there are the harmonizing participants. The sounds must harmonize to meet traditional standards or please the ears.

180 *Music is a background tool for many other types of program activity* We've already made a point of this, but music above all other aspects of program provides this benefit. What would social dance, synchronized swimming, a major football game, or a party be without music?

Music is a therapeutic device If music controls behavior, it has the power to provide therapy for the emotionally disturbed. Although the scientific validity of the effects of music for those in hospitals and institutions is still unknown, its acceptance as a major programming element in therapeutic recreation is universal.

Music is aesthetic It is not related necessarily to material results, behavioral objectives, or need fulfillments. It makes the environment more than simply a bleak basin on the way to the grave.

As for need fulfillment potential, music ranks high in relaxation, creativity, social interaction, and medium in security, belonging, and service to others.

Role of Music in Recreation

Music's role is very small in the overall recreation picture. To make music an activity to stand alone, as more than a support element for other program areas, requires close scrutiny of existing programs.

What's the reason for this sparse listing? Programmers have had this to say in explanation:

"Maybe because music is such a personal thing. People can pursue it, listen, play, or sing *in private* without being judged. They entertain themselves."

"Music is available — in packages today, so people don't have to get involved in it to create it. It's everywhere now, whereas once music only existed if people got together and manufactured a home brew."

"Music is pretty technical, like math. Even mistakes in art get credit. Dance at most skill levels is fairly tolerant as is drama. Screw-up in a music activity and you really feel like a bungler. Most of the active things you do in music make rather precise demands."

"You get fads going through. The rock concerts were big as far as a listener's special event goes. Guitar has been eternally popular. The jam sessions where musicians just get together and improvise with their instruments have been successful. But nothing really sustains."

"It depends on whether you have a real specialist on your staff. Then you're stuck with that specialty. Maybe he plays the piano and can accompany singing. Or he can play 'Oh, Susannah' on a harmonica for starters and can keep one lesson ahead of a group. Most generalist programmers stay clear of music as the domain of the outside expert. They hold music in awe and are afraid to try anything in music activity because the standards they imagine are too demanding."

"Most recreation leaders who have had an all-ages program give rhythm band instruments a fling. They're really basic, keeping time with accompaniment, the piano, and being able to start and stop together. It's a rather primitive form of music, but it's a first step. But that's the only step the leaders are brave enough to take."

The general consensus has been to launch music activities when someone arrives on the scene with expertise. No other activity areas so disturb the generalist programmer. But, fortunately, there are a few isolated exceptions, such as a community orchestra, a barbershop quartet, and sometimes even opera geared to a recreational participation level.

These isolated cases mean it can be done, so why aren't we trying them elsewhere? Probably because courageous leaders aren't around. Most leaders seem to feel that it is better to avoid what appears difficult and emphasize those areas in which they feel comfortable, like sports.

Music is a major aid to other activities, but it fails to occupy today any major role in recreation programming as a separate experience.

181

Planning and Leadership

There is a temptation with music in recreation to use it as a programming spill-over for the unathletic. We conjure up the picture of the weird kid in the neighborhood toting his violin case to practice every afternoon. After all, what's the good of playing the violin? It's something one doesn't take to camp or have much use for when grown up.

Americans are terrible stereotypers. Because we are, music has suffered from a poor image. Programmers haven't felt any real pressure to accommodate this strange minority interest. Yet music is a very dominant force in all life styles. It refines the jungle in which we live and, if health and happiness are legitimate goals for the recreation experience, then music does as much as any other activity for the human spirit.

It is a desirable goal for music to play a larger part in program to provide a many-faceted leisure life style for all. Several of our general planning principles deserve special stress with music.

Programming should serve all interests There is a substantial minority population dedicated to music as a consuming interest. It has emerged recently for many pre-adults as a more meaningful participation than sports. In it they have found a less regimented way of self-expression and, in the creation of new forms, have made music their contribution to society. Because this generation is the vanguard of future life styles, all ages are concerned with musical activity.

Use all available resources in a community Although music has a small role in the programs of pure recreation, music is piped to listeners and performance opportunities abound in community life. Certainly radio, TV, and cassettes have given us in recent years a round-the-clock cornucopia of music for listening. Less conspicuous are the private special-interest organizations and commercial establishments that carry on extensive instructional and performing programs that provide active participation. Much of this has been fermented by commercial manufacturers of instruments, such as accordian studios, and, more recently, by foreign companies producing a variety of instruments. Profit has always been significant incentive to begin programs. The schools also have provided a fairly formal opportunity over the years in both choral or instrumental programs, but the carry-over into a prolonged recreational participation beyond the formal training has been quite limited. Recreation agencies need to cooperate with these nuclei of existing activities.

Music programming should provide for all skill levels As a principle this is a noble guideline. In practice it may well be the most brutal obstruction to a greater role in planned program. Weak links in any group singing or instrument activity obstruct the precision necessary to produce a pleasing result. In no other area of recreation program does the failure of one individual so detract from a result. Therefore, the matching of skills creates a monumental task for a programmer who, from the beginning, is working with a relatively narrow segment of a community.

Veteran programmers have suggested that we have established inadequate lead-up patterns in contrast to sports, arts and crafts, and drama. Also, the talents involved are probably as diverse as can be found in any activity area. Limited attempts have always been made through large group programs with choirs, harmonicas, xylophones, and guitars to establish a common mass base, but for unknown reasons the opening experience was the final one for the great majority.

Recreation music leadership should be technically knowledgeable The degree of technical knowledge required for leaders in this activity is much greater than all others. It may be because the meshing of elements and participants' skills is so vital to produce acceptable results, whereas in the other activities the results are tolerable at various levels of achievement.

182

The leader in music can rely less on his people-tricks, his organizational patterns, and motivational devices to hide unfavorable results. The leader really remains a tutor throughout most group music activities, working to improve individuals so that they can carry their part effectively.

Organizational Patterns

Music is easily introduced and beneficial to almost all recreation situations, but it is not easy to launch it on its own as a self-contained program element.

Listening Opportunities

Probably the most prevalent participation in music in all structured program occurs with the staged event. People have always been audiences. The recreation programmer creates the listening opportunity on a group basis because the sharing experience of an audience at a musicale, concert, or music festival creates an emotional dimension beyond the individual's aesthetic appreciation. A beautiful sound is as valued by the ear pressed to a taped cassette recording as it is at a great opera. Sound can take on stirring proportions when it is produced in an impressively staged environment. The programmer should not ignore the provision of solitary listening opportunity by arranging facility use, but his major goal should be live performances before an enthusiastic audience in an arousing atmosphere. The larger group organizational pattern makes possible the procurement of extraordinarily good music, live musicians rather than canned, thereby creating a participation moving away from the passive toward the active, our ultimate objective at all times.

Instructional Classes

While the programmer serves the greatest portion of his community through the listening arena, a minority of gifted and potentially talented performers are organized into instructional classes and performing activities. The class approach is extremely crucial for music since, as we have stressed, music requires a high degree of technical perfection. The class is the starting point for most program we encounter. The music class is effective with simple singing units and simple instruments, such as the harmonica, accordion, recorder, or guitar. The drum and bugle also seem relatively simple. Shift into more complicated ones, like the piano, organ, or violin, and a form of tutoring becomes necessary. The class organizational pattern is appropriate only with simple instruments.

Performance Units

The more familiar pattern for recreation programming is to move to the performing plateau of participation. The programmer structures his activity to serve those who already are trained or skilled enough to meet the demanding requirements of music. The community band is an example of this in which a staff specialist coordinates people who play various instruments.

The performing group pattern is most common with singers and appears to be the most fulfilling. The programmer, unless he is a music specialist who can technically guide the group, becomes a producer who expedites facilities, equipment, and audiences on behalf of the group.

Nowhere else in recreation programming does being an observer constitute a respected art. While social psychologists bemoan passiveness in almost all leisure pursuits, listening to music is encouraged as fulfilling people's needs.

The programmer has a positive foundation upon which to erect his musical activities. Music is a positive force which places man above the animal state. But music's aura of refinement acts both ways as a motivating force. For those who feel the necessity of a refined image, musical activity is easily embraced. But music is often rejected as "sissy," as unmanly involvement for those who feel their masculinity threatened. Women do not experience this anxiety over music. The problem appears to be growing less in modern society, as male/female stereotypes diminish.

The programmer must be aware of the ambiguities of the refinement image. He motivates the anxious ones by introducing them to music through their existing interests. Off-color beer songs in a pub may be low-grade music to a chamber music set, but it may be a starting point for a programmer. Songs around a campfire are not very demanding and therefore offer another starting point for those who are a little frightened of music's technical requirements in its more advanced forms.

Music generally lends itself to all motivational devices suggested under our general chapter on motivation. It can ride the coattails of other activities quite well. Drama often needs it, a sporting event gets its fighting spirit from it, and social and special events find it an indispensable tool. People like useful things and music as a tool for other activities often creates a deeper involvement through such utilitarian exposures.

Listening and publicly singing songs permits everyone to get a taste of music. For those whose expressive needs are deeper, real participation comes through the specialized areas of choirs, bands, orchestras and, at the peak, solo performance before an audience. More emotional than mental or physical, music still depends upon the motivating devices of experts, awards, competitions, and the roar of the crowd to generate its following.

184

Here's what some experienced programmers say about the current status of music activity as a recreational pastime:

Senior supervisor of music, big city department — "There really isn't much going on except for the super talented. We put on big city-wide productions of special events proportions. The same people are used over and over. A lot of them belong to three or four groups and are busy every night with chorus or community orchestra rehearsals. Sometimes all I see our role as is caretakers of rehearsal halls."

Boys club program supervisor — "No, actually we don't have music or dance or drama. Arts and crafts sure, but sports and games are where we're at. Except for guitar. We have four guitars and we get a pretty good showing for the classes."

Church recreation director — "Choir has always been the church's biggest social-recreation drawing card. It's big everywhere, it becomes a whole social life style for the participants, partying together, going on picnics, it's like a club."

Hospital recreation therapist — "Look, I really have a thing for music myself. I play the guitar some, but I can't teach it. I get the people singing with me while I pick and grin. A lot of the new music I'm not up on, so I use a record and just hold the guitar, and it still works. I've got them copying their favorite songs and putting them together in a songbook. I don't know . . . the music, when they're singing or keeping time with rhythm instruments, seems to let them vent their emotions . . . I mean, a lot of them would be screaming or shouting instead."

YMCA building director — "We're big on guitar, mostly the pre-teeners. The guitar has a lot of identity with the youth movement. Nothing else works. Even our campfire singing at camp falls apart unless we've got a really talented leader on staff . . . or a piano player. A piano player can hold a group sing together anywhere, cover up outrageous voices."

Company recreation director — "We've got an opera club, but it's mostly just a bunch of members going together to the opera. That's about it. We procure discount tickets for musical events."

Commercial recreation - accordion studio manager — "Our school never has a bad year, hasn't for 25 years. It's a kids program and the parents will sacrifice food to get junior trained in the accordion. They'll go in hock to buy an elaborate instrument as soon as their kid picks up a tune on a rented one and wows a family gathering. We've got a progressive merit system, you know, an incentive system where we give medals as the accordionist performs at various auditions we stage. No, not many of them carry their accordion interest on over into their adult leisure. I don't know why."

The consensus is that organized recreation has waxed eloquent about music's great role in the balanced recreation program, but in reality there is often little beyond the rhythm band for children. There remains a lot of nostalgia for band concerts in the park, harmonica bands, and community sings. But they succumbed to convenience of listening to records. Here and there we find a revival of an old music activity form, but there is no need for us to make our own entertainment any more.

Music plays a large support role in recreation program but generally does poorly if it tries to carry participant's exclusive interest.

Are there any trends in the future? There are a few, but they appear transitory. Permanent innovations do not seem feasible.

First, there is a growth of instrument manufacturing, especially by foreign companies using cheap labor and producing relatively inexpensive products. With a more affluent public the natural law of availability could generate an upsweep of programming in music. Programmers will have to work with the manufacturers on co-sponsored instructional and performance programs.

Secondly, music not only retains its universal role as a relaxer or arouser for the listening public but it also has taken on larger functions. Always a device for storytelling, it has become one of the most influential emotional means to communicate for younger generations. Its even greater mass appeal presents a readiness platform upon which an imaginative programmer can work as he looks to the future.

Thirdly, the schools, under critical attack, tend to cut the "soft" subjects and programs. Music and general recreation are always logical choices for surgery. If the school cancels music appreciation classes, glee club, and the school band and orchestra, then these might become the domain of organized recreation. But this is not exactly a blessing. Recreation has never had a chance to develop outlets for existing skills and knowledge because it has been so busy teaching. No strength is gained by assuming the abandoned responsibilities of other social services.

Rhythm Band

This is another example of simplistic recreation when found in its basic form — people hitting things together or blowing through horns to make sounds in time with a record or piano accompaniment. But it works!

The pre-schooler has been its major beneficiary. Throughout America little hands have clicked sticks together, brushed sandpaper blocks, and rung bells to the sound of a record or a piano. A lot of it has been sheer chaos, a crude outlet for surplus energy. But it is a starting point. Skilled leaders have been able to make the transition to the next step, i.e., playing folk instruments.

Its fulfillment potential is high on relaxation and medium high on interaction. If we add something about the human spirit to our need scale, call it emotional activity or arousal, then music in this goalless endeavor ranks high.

The Outdoor Concert These are band concerts and folk music concerts in which instruments dominate or share the spotlight with vocal performances. In almost all cases we work with experienced, talented participants.

Although the active performing participation is restricted, the concert is an audience structured activity and the public participates with great sensory involvement through listening.

There is a saturation point in indoor listening to music, but the outdoor environment adds a new dimension to the music as a change of pace. The outdoors mechanically alters the sounds and gives them a uniqueness.

The concert must be ranked on the need scale for two different publics. For listeners, the fulfillment is high for emotional activity and relaxation. For the performers it is high for belonging, service to others, recognition and, in some cases, creativity.

The Chorus It's called "choir" in church recreation and "glee club" in the schools. The barbershop quartets and other small singing ensembles belong under the general category of choral singing.

The common, successful pattern employed in recreation is the mixed chorus. It's an arena in which coed interaction works well. It carries some exacting requirements found in advanced group forms of music activity, but practice and preparation permit loose, informal social interplay.

The blend has been a good one. The group is held together with performance goals but is kept from becoming work-like by the informality surrounding the experience. The good programmer keeps a balance between fun and regimen so that joy accompanies achievement. Most of the leisure expended revolves around the practice periods — not unlike sports.

The Song Fest This is a small group adjustment to the chorus activity. There is a great convenience in putting together only small vocal units such as quartets, trios, and duets. While the chorus depends on a good technical leader, the small groups are self-directed and the programmer involves himself only with obtaining rehearsal facilities and scheduling performances.

It is the competition found in a sing or song festival that motivates the small groups to practice diligently and improve without the constant influence of a professional leader.

The song fest has been a top echelon college level activity and has great appeal to all youth because its challenge is comparable to an athletic contest.

Guitar Class If any instrument has taken on the universal power of being the symbol of a movement, it is the guitar. A basic folk instrument, it has a long history of social protest involvement, the power of being a musical story-telling machine.

Like most informal folk instruments, the guitar doesn't normally make the exacting technical demands of the more advanced string, wind, and percussion instruments. Its chords are good companions to group singing. A guitarist can get by in a lot of situations just faking it, strumming, or even slapping the wood occasionally.

The guitar, above all other folk instruments, has a mass appeal and sustains a high following in the recreation program. But its programming is primarily through the instructional class, and is the single most common musical activity found in recreation's service fields. The guitar, beyond the class, is a self-directed, individual activity. Guitar bands or special performing events have not developed except as rare exceptions, although there is no legitimate obstruction against a good programmer developing performing group activities beyond the learning plateau.

The Orchestra The orchestra is a high-geared, specialized, formal type of programming. It is not unusual for recreation agencies to serve as the sponsoring foundation for community orchestras, but the role is again one of coordinator of peripheral things, e.g., publicity, facilities, funding, and scheduling. The actual elements of program activity generally rest with a highly technical leader who operates autonomously and somewhat beyond an agency's power, although he may in a legal sense be an employee of that agency.

The orchestra is made up of the more complex musical instruments, and the participants are generally quite experienced and talented. Although performance-oriented the technical perfection achieved during rehearsal activity can be as fulfilling for individuals as performing for an audience. This is generally true when we operate at the mastery or championship level. There are bad orchestras, but the orchestra experience demands far more exactness than any of the other musical situations.

The orchestra rates fairly high on dominance at the mastery level through the control of the elements, as well as recognition and service to others. There is a medium degree of social interaction; the belonging need is medium if the participant feels he is necessary for group achievement.

The Marching Band The marching band is a strange activity that has elements of dance, dramatics, and perhaps a little sports in it as well. Music is the unifying core, but the performing aspect is very high. In fact, marching bands travel to find their audiences.

Nothing in music or in the other cultural programs comes as close to organized youth sports. There is team spirit, and the parades in which the bands march are like games. It includes competition, uniforms, equipment, awards, and traveling companionship. The season is whenever the weather permits parades, but in many places that's all year. Some marching bands are able to find a parade every weekend.

The marching band is high in social interaction, recognition, service to others, self-expression, and physical activity.

The Jam Session This is one of the growth activities in recreation programs. It's fairly simple programming in that an agency merely provides a sound-proof room and invites youths with instruments.

In some cases semi-organized combos show up and mix with other groups or individuals. It is like an experimental laboratory in which no special format is followed. The musicians try things together or on their own for their own satisfaction. An audience is not a motivating factor although some jam sessions permit each player to bring one listener.

Ultimately individuals form performance-oriented formal groups or else existing groups discover new performing possibilities. Social facilitation also takes place, much like a talk session in which people open up to the group and discover new possibilities about themselves. It might well be described as a musical encounter group.

It is high on social interaction and creativity.

Community Singing This is an old-timer among recreation program activities. It was always a way for those small in talent to become more than mere listeners.

It doesn't appear frequently any longer, probably because courageous, extroverted leaders are scarce. Singing around the campfire has survived fairly well, probably because darkness creates anonymity and an open fire loosens people up emotionally.

Most of the songs used in community singing — "Home on the Range," "Yankee Doodle Dandy," "The Man on the Flying Trapeze," "Camptown Races" — are almost like chanting, just a step above talking.

Community singing rarely stands by itself, but is used as an opener or loosening up exercise for other activities. Where it does work well there is usually a good piano or guitar accompanist and a leader who has flamboyance, an expressive face, extravagant gestures, and audacity.

It is medium high in social interaction, belonging, and relaxation. It is fairly low in need fulfillment for the individual.

DRAMA

Somewhere away back in time, an exasperated caveman gave up trying to describe his recent dinosaur encounter by grunting. Even gestures weren't enough. He began playing the roles of the people and animals in his story, re-enacting the movements with a few embellishments here and there to give it color.

Man has always been a storyteller. It is the most personal and direct way that he passes on his culture. More personal than the printed word, more direct than the symbolism of dance and music. He needs only his voice and body to create that pure self-expressive art form called drama.

It is self-expressive creativity because it allows man to interpret his environment and feelings to others with techniques and styles that not only communicate but entertain. Unlike dance, music, or literature, it must have an audience to sustain meaningful participation. Man can retire to solitude and talk to himself with music, dance, and crafts, but drama demands others to witness it.

In recreation we deal with structured play. Play, as we have noted in our earlier general theory, is an imitation of life designed to provide momentary fulfillments of needs without serious consequences. Drama, which of all recreation activities is the most literal, direct copy of life, is a very important need provider.

If life is but a stage and we are actors on it, then role-playing may be all there is to it. We are all constantly playing parts in a great drama. What really makes programmed drama in recreation different from the drama of life is the option to walk away from any role. Roles are invented as a prop for the expression of ideas, feelings, and skills through a visual storytelling device interesting enough to make others watch. Through the recreational drama experience, man can try out new personalities and thoughts and relationships in an hour session without survival pressure.

189

Values and Role of Drama

Drama, a performing art form which communicates and preserves culture, consists of two major categories. The first, creative drama, is associated with undirected imaginative play and creativity. The other category is highly structured and traditional, in which man's expressive skills are reinforced and cultivated. This second form is staged drama.

For clear-cut examples of these categories, one should compare the imaginative activity of the children's sandbox to the written, directed, and staged theatrical play.

The first type requires the programmer to manage the environment. This is a general condition for creativity that we have noted in the other cultural programming areas. The more the programmer manipulates behavior and structures it through planned criteria, goals, and processes, the less can the individual express himself creatively.

But individual creative expression in organized recreation is primarily a group process. A lack of organization or planning brings chaos. Individuals need conflict. One man's creativity can thwart another's, and so the programmer controls the situation to provide opportunity equally for all. For example, the child in the sandbox may decide that the entire territory is necessary for his make-believe construction project, or the adult in a psychodrama may try to carry on an unending catharsis, excluding any interplay by other group members.

The two categories differ more in degree than in basic structure. The programmer must provide the setting and manage the environment for creative expression to unfold, but he must also be ready to provide guidelines of overt direction if full opportunity for all participants is jeopardized.

In this creative category the values of drama include a chance to achieve a very personal, original expression without the pressure of rigid standards. It may well provide the greatest creativity in all recreation experience.

Besides fulfilling creativity needs, drama is also valuable as a socializing experience in both categories. The informality of creative drama provides interaction for many individuals and probably a much more authentic projection of personality. The creative process and its expression may be quite individual, but they invite interplay between people.

Understanding others, i.e., empathy, is a positive value gained in both categories. Not only does the interpretation of a role about fictitious character require the analysis of motives and behavior, it also requires relating the role to others and cooperating in a group production. It requires sensitivities toward others.

Appreciation and development of voice and body movements as art forms are other possible achievements of the drama experience in both categories.

There is full opportunity to express all emotions and project hostility and despair under the protective covering of make believe. Drama has been one of the most successful therapies, and the rise of psychodrama represents its powerfulness.

All talents and abilities can be recognized or used in drama. People may participate in drama through such support functions as stage craft, costuming, lighting, script writing and directing which possesses almost as much individual recognition as acting. Although the support concept is true in all recreation, only drama has fully recognized its potential in programming. A variety of talents are needed.

Drama is a great melting pot for a variety of other program areas, such as music, arts and crafts, dance, literary activity, and even aquatics with its water pageants.

Both the creative drama and staged drama can provide physical activity if the choice is made to create an action presentation. They both require a medium degree of mental activity, the first in the imaginative sense and the second in the selection of alternatives from a repertoire of skills and knowledge.

The opportunity for new experience is also present, although genuine risk or adventure — which we have previously identified with this need — are not present. The risk is vicarious, of a fantasy nature. Along the lines of fantasy fulfillment is the opportunity to dominate. The actor is controlling his character, and, by so doing, dominates another "person." Both of these need fulfillments are highly speculative values. If the acting is not seen by the participants as acting, it could generate negative results. It is possible to carry over a destructive character to real life or to avoid real risks because one encounters them imaginatively in drama.

The staged drama rates higher in two values than creative drama.

First, security and belonging are needs met by the cooperative team efforts that are required to present a theatrical production. Being a part of a successful drama undertaking elevates the sense of belonging as much as any team sport. The staged drama experience is group-centered programming which depends more on people working together than any other cultural programs.

The second value for the staged drama that exceeds creative drama is service to others. The concern for an audience is very high with structured drama, and participants are highly motivated to entertain others.

We may conclude by discussing the fantasy aspect of drama. Its unreality provides escape from the routine pressures of life. If escape is a primary motivation in participation then drama rates high for relaxation. But fantasy as it relates to drama is not without its own private pressures. Concern over audience criticism, for example, may make the fulfillment of relaxation needs impossible.

Drama in recreation is the most self-contained activity in cultural programming. Unlike music, dance, or even crafts, drama is rarely integrated with other activities. It has a grand history in world culture but has never developed a middle range of participation. It may be the nature of the interest that there are only amateurs and masters with no intermediate levels. More likely, the type of leader-programmer responsible for recreation drama in the past has not exploited its full role potential.

191

Drama probably runs a third with music — just behind second place dance and first place arts and crafts in terms of programming frequency in the cultural arena. There are exceptions to this generalization, of course. Drama occasionally dominates entire recreation programs. For example, little theatre programs have overshadowed sports and absorbed the biggest share of budgets where driving special interest leadership has emerged.

Drama has an explosive potential that exceeds all other activity arenas that may challenge sports. Because this potential exists programmers should analyze carefully the extent to which they feel drama should be scheduled. They may prod what is apparently a sleeping animal that awakes to become a monster. *Planning should set some limits to maximum growth in the interests of program balance in addition to establishing basic minimum offerings in any interest field.*

Planning, motivation, and leadership are closely related in recreation activities. The interrelationship is intense with drama. Selecting those most influential general planning principles applicable to drama reveals their relation most clearly.

The principle of planning for both sexes in program is probably easier to follow in drama than in the other cultural program areas and in sports. Drama is probably on a par with social programs and special events. Drama has a neutral male-female overlay. There is no strong need to prove masculinity as there is in sports, nor is there any general public impression of femininity as there is in music, dance, and crafts. The neutral image permits easier motivation for either sex, which is a powerful plus for drama.

Another principle met fully by programmed drama is providing passive as well as active forms of recreation. Next to dance, drama has the flexibility to be designed for quiet, thoughtful presentations or wild action plays that provide vigorous activity. This range of mental and physical outlets can be utilized by the drama leader in ordering the drama experience to meet a broad spectrum of individual and group needs. The rare play-reading group is an example of what is basically a passive experience with great value for incapacitated participants. Drama at this level matches the introspective possibilities of crafts, exceeds dance, and demands less technical excellence than music. At the other pole, the action of a play like *Julius Caesar* exceeds the activity fulfillment of crafts, or music, and comes close to that of dance. The planning principles about program being weather sensitive and about making optimum use of available facilities are both met with drama. Dramatic activities can go indoors or outdoors without any real loss of effect, which is true of all cultural programming. Sports, in contrast, are much less adaptable in that the specific activity has to be altered to such an extent that it becomes basically a different experience. The only defect in the indoor-outdoor shift for music and drama is acoustical problems and for dance and drama, viewing convenience. Drama is the best adaptor of them all when it comes to utilizing any available facility. It can use any niche or room or adjust to any large or small space situation.

One can project himself into the escapades of a daring revolutionary or the discovery of radium. The very essence of recreation is that it is programmed human behavior, a necessary balancing service in a crowded society with a spiraling abundance of leisure. Adventure and new experience generally are thought to arise out of the natural happening, the unforeseen, unknown, and unplanned. But the general evolution of mankind and technology dictates that the manufactured situation must replace the natural because the demands exceed the supply of natural happenings. Artificial adventure is what the future holds. Drama, because its essence is make believe, is man's best preparation for surviving in the years ahead.

A program principle that concerns itself with the individual stresses *awareness of individual differences* and provides for those differences. Drama does this more easily than group music and dance, which have more exacting demands, or even crafts, which have informal but traditional standards. With many roles from which to choose, it is convenient for the programmer to fit the participant into the specific role that demonstrates his differences.

You can't go wrong with the theoretical principle when you plan program, but you can miss its full potential if the leader doesn't recognize the spontaneous motivations of a situation, the spur-of-the-moment reactions of people with people, especially in the role-playing world of drama.

The most effective organizational patterns for handling the drama experience in recreation are ranked in order of their frequency and success:

1. The *workshop* with culminating performance, single session, or series.
2. The *workshop* with no performance goal. Self-contained. The goal, if any, is self improvement or therapy, such as the psychodrama of the encounter group or creative drama.

The term "workshop" here combines the concept of the instructional class and the practice session. It implies a greater informality, more experimentation, and greater concern for the individual.

3. The *club pattern* which works its normal magic by institutionalizing interest, creating a more permanent sense of belonging, in the form of the little theatre group or puppet club. Drama is one of the most difficult activities to activate or reactivate. The club's basic structure as socializing mechanism works to hold together a group of people already acquainted. Interest in drama is usually secondary to the social needs and benefits of the club involvement.
4. *The tryouts* is a pattern that we haven't identified elsewhere in program. It is quite significant in the other performing arts. In sports, somewhat parallel patterns are the skills day and, to some degree, the clinic.

Drama has compounded the process of evaluating existing skills and talent into a fully formed activity, too, probably as powerful in its impact on participants as the sports skills day.

193

The casting ritual from stage play to the small group skit can be challenging activity in itself, wrought with all the competitive vitality of the game or contest. Of course, the casting process must still be seen as a programmed step in the direction of rehearsing and then performing for an audience. But the casting experience, with readings and demonstrations, can be programmed as a progressive growth device helping participants fulfill themselves by measuring their talent.

The talent show is of special event dimensions, but it has overtones of drama. It is generally scheduled as a complete experience in itself, but programmers have used it as a form of tryout. A percentage of talent show participants move into little theatre groups or are formed into traveling units to present variety shows.

5. *Traveling units.* Moving facilities such as show wagons, portable stages, and performing groups is a popular pattern. It provides a crack at different audiences and is used to seed the interest in local units without drama activity. Often the pattern is to bring in the sophisticated staging equipment and a polished nucleus of talented participants around which the locals can perform in peripheral but satisfying roles.
6. *Drama tournament* is a good pattern to capitalize on the competitive spirit that is often found in a highly sports-oriented community. It might be the device for capturing the elusive male interest in the cultural program. It can be used within a local unit or on a regional basis. Dual or large group teams can find appropriate story material to use in presenting a short play in the one day or week-long tournament.

There are no rigid boundaries that prevent a programmer from making drama do whatever he wants. It is a very versatile interest area, and since everything about our lives has the design of self-expressive role playing, the programmer shouldn't hesitate to organize patterns that work regardless of tradition.

Current Status, Trends, and the Classics

Recreation is always in the process of trying to launch a sustained drama program for all environments.

"We really should have more dramatics programming," say programmers in hospitals, youth agencies, playgrounds, armed forces bases, and other service areas, "but unless you can put together a committed club pattern structure, say a little theatre group, it seems to fade away."

The programmers who continue to struggle for a continuing drama program believe drama has vast potential. The reason drama has such potential is that unlike other cultural programs that are basically championed by cult-like minorities, drama, packaged in television and theatre films, has a mass following. Furthermore, there are an enormous number of roles in dramatic productions that people continuously observe and in which they are able to project themselves, saying, "Hey, I could play that part, in fact, it's me or what I'd like to be . . . "

Programmers who have constructed a continuing program generally cite the power of performance in retaining involvement and interest. "Not so much the active participants, but the audience. People can handle the spoken word and relate to the actors' behaviors in a story form better than they can to the abstraction of music or dance movement." But these successful programmers have covered this audience concept with a little insurance. In the genuinely lasting drama programs which have become almost institutions, an elaborate, specialized facility has been acquired.

The power of the special facility to generate special interest programming is not particularly unique to drama, but for drama it works exceptionally well. The conversion of multi-purpose rooms to lighted stages and the construction of million dollar theatres are still uncommon, but they are appearing with enough frequency to indicate a significant trend. Drama's survival as either a recurrent or a continuous recreation activity with an impact rivaling arts and crafts, if not sports or social program, is related to the continued expansion of audience-oriented performances and to the procurement of more specialized facilities.

Up to this point, we have focused on the more sophisticated forms that drama takes in recreation. We should not demean the less magnificent efforts in drama, some of which are introductory, some transitional, and some complete in themselves. Take, for example, one of the classic parlor games, charades, and examine its varied uses in all types of programs. It can serve any or all of the three purposes just stated. At a party charades are a complete activity without any carry-over purpose. As part of a children's dramatics program at the beginner level it is a start on role playing, the essence of dramatics. It can also be the best kind of transitional exercise for a little theatre group that needs to assess or encourage new attempts at meeting

194

challenges for participants who have become locked into memorizing and feeding back scripted dialogue.

Creative dramatics will continue to expand. Its unregimented openness, allowing the individual to interpret and express himself, lends itself to the scheduling of self-improvement classes or practice sessions where no emphasis is placed on a culminating performance. It has allowed the generalist leader to conduct program with minimum technical knowledge or skill. It makes no demands for special equipment or facilities as does the more formalized theatrical play.

At the adult level creative drama has been more difficult to sell because the adult requires a more productive goal. The encounter group, which is a kind of creative dramatics experience, has probably served to fill the gap and achieve parallel results.

Puppets are big in a general way throughout recreation programs. Their current status is that of a fine, short-term activity, perhaps too often merely a phase of the crafts program. But it is a classic of recreation programming. Whether used as a transitional drama experience or as an end in itself it has been one of our most reliable activities.

The Drama Workshop is another short-term transitional experiment that has become somewhat permanent everywhere. When neither the permanent staff nor the facilities exist to generate the full-blown youth or community theatre, the workshop approach allows guest specialists to run a limited series of sessions to expose uncommitted participants to the potentials of the drama experience. It is a trial balloon to see what support, interest, and achievement can be developed to justify more permanent and sophisticated programming. What has happened is that the workshop has become an activity unto itself, neither a preparation nor mini-version of theatre, but a complete and rewarding set of experiences. It has the self-improvement flare of the instructional class and the goal orientation of the little theatre group. It helps prevent unfortunate budget and personnel commitments in order to balance program with drama.

In summary, we expect to see a continued trend toward the individually oriented creative drama as the volume short-term programming. There will be a less frequent but more elaborate development of high-powered little theatre centers doing amateur performances that rival the professionals. In fact, we look for a blend of the amateur and professional, with recreation building performances around a professional actor. For example, a number of the civic light opera companies, which are more drama than music, are filling in talking roles with amateur talent around a top lead singing voice.

The trend is toward openness and innovation. The psychodrama of the encounter group is an indication of this but so is the amateur cinematography group where a small group and an 8 mm camera can produce drama on film. Indications are that this may be one of the biggest recreation departures from classic program to be undertaken in the coming decade. To some extent the participant-observer experiences made famous by novelists and film makers in the last few years, in which the artist-participant plays a role in a real life drama, represent a new kind of reality-fantasy recreation that deserves consideration.

Chapter 9

SPECIAL EVENTS

THEORY AND IDENTIFICATION

A good program can lope along in a fairly routine manner without feeling any tension. Everyone appears satisfied with the available recreation way of life.

Loping is fine, but why not gallop every once in a while just for the fun of it? If you can fly you might be able to soar. Reach out for some new potential or dimension of feeling.

That's what special events are all about. They're rip-snorting changes-of-pace, happenings in which flagging spirits are ignited, growing egos are nurtured, craftsmanship rewarded, new things announced, and old things remembered.

Identification

Most people, especially recreation professionals, do a lot of throat-clearing and stammering when it comes to telling you exactly what a special event is. They usually end up giving examples. That's all right, but often someone else's special is another person's rut. Here are some random interviews with people in the field.

How often does a special event happen?

"Not every day, not often, maybe annually, but not necessarily, but annually would be best."

Does it involve a lot of people?

"Everybody. That is, everybody that's eligible. Like a teenage Christmas dance means everybody that's a teenager. There's something for everybody who shows up. Lots of prizes, too. You're out to get a big attendance, especially non-regulars who aren't involved in the regular activities."

Can a special event spontaneously happen?

"Not likely. Oh, it can, of course. A bunch of drop-in musicians can convert a routine sit-around into a ball. But it's an accident. Top special events take extensive preparation. There's more organization and effort required if it's going to be a highlight over the everyday program."

How do you know when to have a special event?

"Depends on the event, what it is. Holidays are good, they're traditional, people are in a festive mood and holidays are a natural break in the regular schedule of activities. But you can spring one any time it's needed."

Needed how?

"To get attention, like when you're starting the summer program. Or to boost lagging interest in an activity or to climax an activity, reinforce the people who have participated, give them a chance to show off skills acquired in the regular program."

Is a special event an experience that participants look back on as a memorable occasion?

"All good program qualifies, but a special event has a greater potential to succeed just by its rarity and magnitude. There are the two other pleasing dimensions of a planned event — the anticipation of a promising experience and, of course, the joy of the actual participation."

198

It seems to me that a really special event would be non-recurring, be of short duration, and have no carryover if uniqueness and infrequency are criteria for qualifying.

"That may be true by some logic, but the principle of second-chance improvement allows a programmer to eliminate the flaws of an initial effort. The second, third, or tenth time may be that point where the resources all mesh, click, ring everybody's bell, perfect through practice. There's no denying, however, that a good thing can get overplayed by a desperate leader trying to milk a success by frequent repetition until what is special becomes regular."

ROLE IN RECREATION

It is difficult to define "special event," but we can examine its role in recreation program. We have given it top echelon status in our thinking, ranking it on par with our other four programming areas. Why is special event programming, which covers any or all subjects, entitled to this consideration?

We don't have a good answer to that. But we do know that the special event is the single most powerful means to impress people that recreation programmers have. Special event programming is used to draw lines around recreation's activities, giving them a beginning and end. The special event summarizes in bold face the elements of recreation program of which we want the whole world to be aware. Of course, that still says we're just making things bigger and more prominent. A baseball tournament at the end of a baseball league is still just more baseball, or a crafts exhibit is still crafts.

The concept of special event programming helps us cover a number of odd experiences that defy easy classification in the four subject areas of programming. Pet shows and on-wheels days are examples. Some of these odd experiences may result from combining sports, cultural, and social activities, so that a whole new species seem to emerge, a giraffe that roars and eats peanuts.

The special event serves recreation by being a very bright light we turn on to catch attention, illuminate what we're doing and to attract everything in its range. Its role is to serve the other program areas, but it also emerges as a separate and distinct set of limbs in the anatomy of recreation programs.

VALUES

We have touched on values with our discussion of role and identification. Special events bring attention to existing activity, climax an activity, and provide recognition for participants and their abilities. They unify different program interest areas, and bring together people in and outside an agency's existing service area and generally lift the spirits of people.

199

Let's tackle these values in moderate depth. Referring to our need fulfillment analysis once again, the special event is high in potential for new experience, for it is new by reason of its being special. Additionally, it denotes larger groupings than usual. Increased numbers provide a broader opportunity — if the programmers direct it so — for social interaction. Recognition also receives a high potential rating for special event programming. Many events are designed to culminate the efforts of participants in regular repetitive class and performance activities. Special events are based in large part on demonstrating mastery of a skill or ability and recognizing it.

The special event helps the programmer accentuate seasons, retrenchment, financial needs, and promoting and changing routine. It allows him to give shape to what he is doing, to start things and to end them without seeming arbitrary and without drifting in and out of programs. Despite a strong desire for non-regimentation and conformity that many earnestly seek in the spontaneous life, the characteristics of order are urgently needed to assure most of us that we are engaged in something that others consider important. It sustains our interest.

The program of an agency is laced together by the special event. Some elements of service to others are found in bringing together activities like music, dance, and drama so that participants can feel the value of their activity as part of a greater whole. People from the various activities feel that they are making possible something rewarding not only to themselves but to others. They see their interest put to use in a larger framework. For example, the stage scenery, the musical background, and the actors performing in front of the dancers illustrate the possibility of bringing together in a stage production what are often separate program activities. The crafts people decorating for a party or the girls' drill team boosting the spirit of spectators at the local football game are further examples of this involvement.

The sound of a special event is loud and clear in the promotional area, too. A programmer knows that getting attention isn't easy. You get it by making things stand out from the rest of the environment, which is the nature of the special event, and the clever programmer uses it as a device for delivering messages to the largest possible cross-section of the public. The result is the stimulation and recruitment of new participants and community approval.

PLANNING PRINCIPLES

One thing that you can probably always say about special events programming is that it's big. Bigness is what causes the specialness in many instances. Big means complexity, great quantities of organizational details, crowds, and problems never before encountered. Special events are the programmer's ultimate challenge in planning.

All the general principles of planning program are appropriately applied in special events production. The following should be stressed as vital:

Plan for the total community It is the nature of the special event to stretch over a multitude of interests and activities because we create specialness by making it very large. To create an event that covers all subgroups in the community the programmer must set up a highly organized plan that delegates authority. Bigness can become a destroyer otherwise. It often cannot be handled by existing machinery.

Plan with the total community This principle is, of course, our basic approach for involving participants in order to gain their support. But, as pointed out, creating a large, complex project beyond normal staffing demands means that the programmer will have to go to all elements of the community and to other sponsoring agencies to develop the original plans and gather physical assistance.

Trying to shoulder the entire event seldom is accepted by others who have a stake in the production, for they feel left out.

Encourage family recreation In a changing society in which traditional family concepts are altering, this classic recreation principle may seem idealistic. But we believe that society retains its nature by means of some sort of primary grouping, for which the term "family" seems quite satisfactory. Family recreation is closely related to planning for and with the total community, but it goes further by emphasizing the cohesive power of recreation activities in drawing relationships closer together by providing mutual involvement. Not many activities outside the special event are capable of opening up such an opportunity.

Be aware of momentary trends or interest fashions of the day in programming Programmers feel comfortable with the tried and true in constructing program in general. Experimental interests are undertaken with great hesitancy. We fear failure and its reflection on other programs. We also are wary of putting out time, money, and energy on something that may disappear overnight. This is especially upsetting if special equipment designed only for the activity has been purchased. Large ceramics kilns sit gathering dust in the corners of many recreation centers, while trampolines have become attic relics from a passing fad.

But try we must, or we can never open up new experiences.

The special event permits the introduction of a fad on a temporary basis to test reactions and to stimulate demand for additional programming if an appeal is evident. The special event has the possibility of leasing or borrowing of special talent or equipment for a one-shot try-out.

Consider public, private, and commercial offerings within a community when planning This is related to a master calendar concept, i.e., making sure that there is no duplication or competition by other service agencies. The best special events have fallen flat because a programmer didn't bother to find out a local shopping center had picked the same day to give away a million dollars.

This principle reemphasizes that all possible units in a community that might benefit by having a stake in a special event should work together. A big May Day festival can accommodate the playground dance troupe, the commercial dance studio, some fumbling about by the Campfire Girls and a lot of other possibilities.

There is a closely allied principle that calls for *augmenting rather than competing with other community activity*. It seems that the two might be easily combined to say the same thing with a little broader dimension.

Plan on the basis of traditional seasonal activity Special events have a close relationship with holidays in most people's minds. Halloween seems to say, "And now here's recreation," as does Christmas, Easter, and the Fourth of July.

Although this principle is primarily designed to give guidance to seasonal sports programming, it serves special event programming as well. The holiday spirit is a strong foundation on which to build.

Use all available resources in a community We seem to be back to planning with and for total community again, but this principle refers to the programmer's awareness of places and materials. For example, if a Huck Finn fishing derby was set up to take place at the swimming pool which can be done — a programmer who didn't give a thought to the new artificial lake at the local golf course would be remiss. The golfers wouldn't be too happy with the idea, but then you can never be sure. They have kids too, and kids grow up to be golfers, which no future-profits-oriented professional can ignore.

Recreation programmers tend to make do with their own existing facilities. Perhaps it's the ego at work again or simply a justification for facilities that already exist. But as meritorious as this stand-alone approach may be, it shouldn't bind special events programming.

Introduce new ideas, organizational patterns, and environments to stimulate lagging spirits and interest The special event is the perfect vehicle for this. Anything new can be easily unveiled or buried, if necessary, in the furor of the special events bigness and excitement.

Excursions have become a large part of special event programming for most recreation service agencies. Nothing makes new experience as easy to predict as physically transplanting participants to another setting. That, of course, is what travel as a recreation is all about.

But before we fire leaders and hire bus drivers and pilots, do not forget that even Paradise can be traumatic if the programmer does not determine participant needs and the possible experiences. Letting things just happen is a Las Vegas way. Trips, as with all special events, don't succeed only because of a change of environment. Good things occasionally happen, but effective programming means they always happen.

LEADERSHIP

Leadership in special events calls for the same approach that is found in business when a one-man pretzel shop becomes a pretzel manufacturing plant or diversifies into a food conglomerate. There is a scramble to decide who does what for whom, why, and when. The natural thing is to set up an organizational pyramid with a good organizer at the top.

202

"Special events are just a lot more details and things to think about. The more special events there are, the more work and jobs there are. That's what makes them so different, so big, so special. There should be a special person in charge, a manager who can think of a dozen involved steps all at once."

The recreation programmer who grumbled this at us had been trying for several years to procure a staff position entirely devoted to special event production. Many large agencies assign a top level staff position to handle special events. A few of the really large organizations have full-time programmers assigned to several or even one giant event. Production of such an event becomes full time, year round.

This seems to be a very important clue. If we look into the one event, year-round effort, we will witness the highly developed inner workings of the special events programmer.

"You could go farther than that. Why not look at the organizer of a World's Fair, Centennial, or America's 200th birthday party? People can spend ten years in planning and preparing for one. That's really big time. But when one aspect is completed the world has turned, a lot of changes have taken place, and the promoter has to start all over."

The possibility of discovering special event leadership opens an endless passageway down which we discover events to which entire lifetimes were devoted, e.g., some coronations of the great leaders in the world. But let's look at the leadership that manages some routine program and perhaps an equal number of special events.

In most recreational environmental service areas, joint responsibility is traditional. Since the specials should relate, enhance, and complement regular program, a leader with familiarity and conscience about both provides the best balance.

"When you have to keep the regular program running and still think about the production of a special event, you'd better be a good juggler. It's not a matter of sacrificing one for the other. A good recreation programmer handles both well, at the same time, by organizing himself. That means he has to have long-range vision so that he can pace himself."

We asked the grizzled recreation professional who said the above what attributes characterize the leader who can handle this dual responsibility.

"Like leading anything, you have to want to lead, dominate people, things, and what's happening. Only with special events you're going big casino, you know, taking on the champion. You assume really big and varied responsibilities. The bad decisions, the mistakes, show up like billboard warts. It's a monumental drive to be in charge of something bigger than the regular, daily activity."

But the old professional was talking about power hunger, almost completely disregarding what happened to the other people taking part in the production. If organizational theory prevails, and the man at the top is to succeed, then he has to manage the event by the skillful manipulation of jobs that he can't possibly do himself. He must make others cooperate in the effort.

Here's a list of special talents that the big event organizer must have to succeed:

1. *Emotional maturity.* He keeps his head while others around him are losing theirs. He's patient, flexible, and has a sense of humor.

People gravitate to the unruffled eye-of-the-hurricane leader in the fury of preparation and the chaos of production. He is vocal, consistent, and confident in command.

2. *Final decision maker.* Special events are new experiences for everyone. They create problems never previously encountered which demand swift processing. Democratic involvement must yield to dynamic, authoritative leadership in many instances. If ever authoritarianism is justified, the unforeseen emergencies of the special event provide the grounds.

3. *Multi-dimension thinker.* Most common garden variety leaders get by very well thinking about one area of responsibility. The leader in charge of the special event has to think continuously on many different thought levels. He has to correlate them into a progressive process leading to a unified success. He serves as the link between the leaders under him to whom he has delegated specific jobs.

4. *Communicator.* The special events programmer must keep in touch to pull everything together and to keep his subordinate leaders cooperative. He has to keep flowing a two-way exchange of ideas and progress-to-date. Communications keep the bigger picture in front of everybody, impress deadlines on them, and reinforce the effort of each individual.

Some of the best communication happens through counseling rather than command. It is probably a matter of timing. If the raft is going over the falls, there is only time for a shouted command. But providing sufficient time for planning may also provide sufficient time for counseling, thereby discovering the falls ahead.

5. *Charmingly impervious to critics.* Programmers don't have rabbit ears

so don't be overly sensitive to criticism, second-guessing, or unsolicited advice. There's a world of experts standing by to tell the special events' leader what he should have done. The effective leader smiles non-committally and replies, "That's interesting."

6. *Knowledge of social customs.* You have to know the territory with special events. They're something new, bigger, and different. Unforeseen developments may occur which violate local social customs. Draw a crowd from outside the local environment and a rat pack of degenerates may come roaring in. The rock concerts of the past decade are examples of this. Acceptable events such as rock concerts were placed in alien environments in which conservative, traditional outlooks were offended.

"Anything goes" may be a beautiful motto for ultimate freedom, but if it interferes with the enjoyment of others because of their customs and beliefs then the programmer who violates these beliefs through ignorance or malice is not a good leader, for otherwise he would have avoided the difficulties before they arise.

Once a programmer has been through special events leadership he has scaled the heights. The general reaction is "Never again," muttered just before saying, "Now next year what we'll do is . . . "

CLASSIFICATION

Special events have been identified in the past emotionally. We know one is happening because it feels differently from what we're used to in regular program. That is, we can plan for it to be different and it might not make it. Just calling a programmed experience "special" and an "event" isn't good enough any more.

Traditionally we've established certain yearly happenings as special events — the Christmas party, the Fourth-o'-July picnic, the Easter egg hunt and Labor Day excursion. We're pretty safe scheduling them and having them turn out to be big and special. But measurable guidelines for determining when an experience has achieved special event status are not part of our professional technology. The following is an attempt to create a technology.

Classification by Size and Uniqueness

First of all, there are a lot of simple one-dimensional experiences that are very unimposing but nevertheless uncommon. Some can almost be classified as stunts. Take, for example, a Big Toe Contest, decorating big toes and giving prizes for biggest, ugliest, etc. Special as it is it is hardly of event proportions. Nor does "special activity," a term used here and there in the field to describe a lesser special event, seem appropriate. A scavenger hunt would seem to be a special experience of enough scope to exist as an entity in itself but more reasonably encountered as a segment of a more complex program activity.

Uncommon programs fall along an ascending scale. A recreation experience is slightly special if it doesn't occur daily. Perhaps once a week is the beginning of the scale, moving to monthly, to seasonally, to yearly, even to centennially. The extent of specialness grows with the ascent. The greater is its infrequency, the greater its specialness.

In terms of size and scope of the experience, an event begins as a simple experience, the first rung on a ladder rising to event status at its zenith. As we mentioned, some of the literature utilizes the term "special activity" to describe the lesser special event that serves a small local group. They give event status to program with a community-wide coverage. Unfortunately the local program may lack territorial size but have great complexity and meaning for the participants — and participants' reactions are what we base our success upon.

Our recommendation is that one-dimensional program elements be called "special experiences," because they involve short term undemanding participant involvement and are more likely to be a fragment of a larger program. Examples of this are the tug-o-war contest which can stand alone but is normally part of a picnic or festival of culture.

Classification by Objective

There is more understanding of the nature of special events if we classify them in terms of objectives. We have examined long lists of traditional program activities that have been so heralded. Referring to our basic needs model we can place special events in the following categories:

1. *Performances* are structured events that permit participants to demonstrate their mastery of skills. Performances, as all special events, provide opportunity for new experiences. Additionally, they have high potential for fulfilling needs related to physical activity, mental activity, creativity, dominance, and recognition.

Performance includes three subcategories:

    a. *Culminations.* "Culminating special event" is a term heard often in recreation. Culminations refer to climaxing events that summarize and recognize achievements of participants in regular program activities. The emphasis is upon participants' interaction.

    b. *Entertainments.* These may occur any time during routine activity, but in a sense they also are events staged to show off participant achievements. They differ from culminations in that they stress the importance of interacting with an audience.

    c. *Skill contests.* These are self-contained special events, complete in themselves and not necessarily related to regular program activities. The contest doesn't culminate an activity but is the activity. It may stimulate some recreational preparations such as exercising to enter a decathlon or building racers for the soapbox derby. The contest stimulates the scheduling of regular activities rather than serving as their climax.

2. *Exhibits.* These are special events that provide an opportunity similar to performances. The difference is that objects are shown off that symbolically represent either regular program activity or self-directed pursuits. The crafts show culminates a crafts class but a doll show only

reflects an individual's accumulation and interest. Of course, either could be structured to serve the other way around. The crafts could have been collections and the dolls dressed and decorated in regular program activity.

Exhibits provide new experience, recognition, and relaxation. Cooperative display takes the place of competition and awards found in performance and skills contests.

3. *Social Occasions.* These special events are designed for high social interaction. They provide new experience, security, belonging, and service to others as well.

There are five sub-categories:

a. *Fund Raisers.* These events are centered around making money through cooperative group play. Rummage sales and auctions are good examples.

b. *Conglomerates.* These are big multi-interest events that use experiences, activities, performances, and contests in a conglomerate form. They are often gigantic events made up of smaller special events. They exist primarily to manufacture large scale social interaction.

c. *Indoor Parties.* These are simply social activities that happen infrequently in a confined space.

d. *Outdoor Parties.* These are big social activities in the wide-open spaces subject to unpredictable weather.

e. *Celebrations.* These are the pearly buttons of special events. There is no mistaking them — fireworks, street banners, street parades, Kleig lights, and all. They are special events that recognize important occasions, holidays, achievements, and significant dates. There is a flamboyant pageantry and ceremonial flare that create the specialness.

4. *Amusements.* These spring forth as special events for their own sake. They don't have to relate to any other programs. People aren't inspired to pursue any interests beyond them, nor are they moved to improve themselves. They require little preparation on the part of the participants, and they allow everyone to participate with whatever skill or knowledge they bring to the event. They pass the time for people in a non-demanding, entertaining way. They provide need fulfillment for new experience, social interaction, relaxation, and some recognition.

There are two sub-categories:

a. *No-skill Contests.* Beauty contests or a baby show are examples. These are very sticky events, the selection of the winner being determined by the subjective judgment.

b. *Stunts.* Goldfish swallowing, flagpole sitting, teeter-tottering for records qualify as stunts.

Spectators usually get as much out of amusements as the participants.

5. *Instructionals.* These are events that teach and inform. New experience and social interaction are involved, as well as self-improvement. Examples are workshops and conferences.

6. *Promotionals.* These are events staged to arouse interest in the agency or programs. They provide new experience, social interaction, and some recognition. The open house is such an event, as are pep rallies and often sports skills days.

7. *Excursions.* These have grown to gigantic proportions in recreation

programming. They are special events emphasizing new experience by way of changing the environment. Our new mobility has allowed trips, travel, and tours to take participants to places with activity and facilities far beyond the local potential. But programmers must be quick to realize that excursions are events based on the total experience, the in-transit happenings as well as what the destination has to offer.

Here are some listings of specific events under the classifications:

Performances
Telegraphic Meet
Sports Tournaments
Drama Tournament
Dog Obedience Trials
Talent/Variety Shows
Dance Revue
Band Concert
Theatre Production Play
Debate
Barbershop Quartet Songfest
Puppet Show
Musical
Rock Concert
Olympics/Decathlon
Sandcastle Sculpturing Contest
Spelling Bee
Car Rally
Baking Contest
Model Boat Regatta
Pinewood Derby
Soap Box Derby
Shingleboat Races
Flower Arranging Contest
Sports Day
Square Dance
Roundup
Rodeo
Film Festival
Recital
Fence Art Contest
Sidewalk Chalk Art Contest

Amusements
Treasure Hunt
Community Sing
White Elephant Exchange
Scavenger Hunt
Hobo Day
Penny Hunt
Dress-Up-Day

Social Occasions
House Parties
Social Dances
Dinner Parties
Tea
Las Vegas Night
Carnival
Circus
Country Fair
Anniversaries
Birthday Parties
Reunions
Easter Egg Hunt
Award Nights
Banquets
Balls
Commencements
Mardi Gras
Family Night
Play Day
Winter Carnival
Christmas Party
Halloween Festival
May Day Festival
Fourth of July Picnic
Arbor Day
Coronations
Graduations
Movie Nights

Exhibits
Doll Show
Doll Fashion Show
Crafts Show
Art Show
Hobby Show
Pet Show
Science Fair
Flower Show
Fashion Show

207

Instructionals	Fund Raisers
Workshops	Rummage Sale
Clinics	Flea Market
Symposia	Swap Meet
Demonstrations	Auction
Lectures	Box Social
Forums	White Elephant Sale
Conventions	Antique Show
Conferences	Trade Show
	Bazaar

Promotionals
Open House
Master Demonstrations
Exhibition Games
Sports Skills Contests
    Basketball Free Throws
    Pass, Punt and Kick Football
    Catch, Throw and Run Baseball
Grand Openings
Pep Rallies

Excursions
Hikes
Trips
Tours
Outings
Trail Rides
Hay Rides
Picnic
Penny Carnival

Special events are the biggest organizational challenge of all. The point has already been made that the special event is both big and complex. All the organizing and planning directions applied elsewhere work here — only this time in quadruple proportion.

Pin down a special events promoter, crowd manager as they call themselves sometimes, and ask him where planning an event begins.

"There has to be a good reason for doing it in the first place. Making a profit or promoting goodwill, in the case of the non-profit people, is only part of it. The event has to be needed. There has to be a market for it. Start with something people are looking for, and you have a rolling start. That's why holidays work for certain events because people are looking for something out of the ordinary to lift their spirits."

Does this mean that if we have a good idea for a special event that it won't work unless there's already a demand for it? Can't we promote a demand?

The promoter takes hold of our question. "Any new product has to be sold to people who didn't know they needed or wanted it before. It's just easier to get a big, complex program in the air if the interest foundation is already there. That's why the traditionals — the annual Christmas party, parade, festival, or picnic — keeps getting bigger and usually better. A producer has a chance to repeat himself on top of what's already accomplished . . . "

Then we proceed to ask him if the organization pattern is different based upon whether it's a first-time event or an old perennial.

"Of course! Veteran events can be turned over to a robot if the discovery work has already been pioneered. Last time's file, the records of who does what, where to go for help, the contracts, old news releases and flyers — it's like a big rubber stamp, ink it, and do it all over again if you were satisfied. Most programmers want to show growth and improvement so they have to extend or alter parts or all of the event. If a new leader is assigned he usually has to do everything all over in his own image so that he really feels it's his event.

"But the new special event, especially if there are no models to follow, means not only mixing all the raw ingredients from scratch but the whole frustrating task of discovering what the raw ingredients are. It's a research job combined with imagination. Fortunately, almost every special event has a precedent somewhere."

From what the promoter is telling us, we see that organizational patterns are either unknown and imaginative with a first-time event or solidified and imitative with the repeat event. The role of the programmer in its best sense is not to caretake past efforts, see them accurately repeated, but to soar to greater heights when repeating or trying something new.

A word of caution from the professional promoter: "When you've got a winning horse, don't try to change it into a cow so you can get milk, too."

With unchanging conditions a good special event could be put back together again and again as you would a jig saw puzzle. But conditions rarely remain rigid. If they do it is a job for a routine clerk, not a dynamic programmer.

The best approach to setting up organizational patterns for a special event is to describe the procedure in the toughest situation, like the first-time event. Everything that is done with any event any time is done with the beginning occasion.

There are major organizational pattern areas to consider:

1. Establishing objectives.
2. Delimiting the participation.
3. Selecting the program segments.
4. Stimulating interest.
5. Producing the event.
6. Managing the crowd.
7. Cleaning up the mess, evaluating what happened, and reinforcing the good things.

1. We won't belabor establishing objectives. It has already been strongly advocated. But since special events are complex there may be a larger variety of them. With a company picnic we may be programming to help hold personnel, to uplift morale, ease tensions, develop *esprit de corp*, give the company a write-off, or introduce workers in a social setting. It is probably best to set up a priority listing of all objectives so that proper emphasis and selection of activities can be planned.

2. Delimiting participation is another basic step in all program. With special events we deal with extraordinarily large mass attendances. Groups that have no relationship outside of the event will often come into contact for the first time. Strangers from afar will be attracted, some desired, some not. A rock concert can encourage a stampede of visitors sufficient to level a

town. A friendly condominium party can burst its seams, inviting the law, when unknowns move in.

The programmer must decide what his attendance will and should be. He directs himself to the quality and quantity of people he desires. He must identify his primary preferred participants and concentrate on attracting and serving them. The company picnic, for example, may be set up for only employees, those at main headquarters, families of employees, friends of employees, or just assembly-line personnel.

3. Key representatives should be secured from the expected public to participate in the plan. Their ideas should be welcomed but not controlling. The programmer must have a tangible but flexible format already in mind before he gives open season to others.

The programmer should involve regular staff, interested lay parties, established volunteers, and, of course, professional specialists in event segments. A steering committee or advisory board can be established so that event is — or appears to be — a team effort.

With the company picnic all recreation personnel can be thrown into committee with a representative from each department in the company. The hope is not just to manufacture support through this tactic but to have an official roster of people who can be delegated responsibility for various fragments of the special event, e.g., a refreshments chairman, awards chairman, and so on. The programmer hopes that his chairmen will work out, but is prepared to back up or step in when failure threatens.

4. We're dealing with a coming new event, which in itself stimulates interest. Since it's new, it's an unknown and the mystery and speculation produce a built-in anticipation. Newness itself drums up interest.

All is not lost, however, with the repeat event even if it previously bombed. A programmer just has to borrow a gimmick from the restaurant world in which after a ptomaine poisoning disaster a sign is posted proclaiming, "Open under new management." The programmer doesn't have to go that far, and of course he still may be that old management, but he can accentuate the new ways or the new look for the event. He can also pick out the things that did go well and underline them, which is exactly the thing he does with a winner he is repeating.

There are common devices for interest stimulation that are used in hustling all program: publicity and broad participant involvement in the planning as we've already discussed. There are additional ones, as follows:

a. There are some unique aspects and efforts available that will pump up participant enthusiasm in advance of the event. One is the scheduled attendance of *celebrities*. In the promotional fraternity, it's called "name insurance." It's like an advance testimonial by someone almost everybody knows, the famous, movie stars, the star athletes are the classic prize catches. Politicians and television personalities also serve to deliver bigger-than-life-images to the scene. The premise is that people want to see the reality of these images, the real flesh, blood, and warts models. They believe that if the event is good enough for celebri ies, who have other exciting things to do, then the event must be something.

A good company picnic for the Hughes Tool Company would do well with Howard himself scheduled to make an appearance — the rarer the personal appearances of celebrities, the more magnetic their draw. The mayor or governor is often used for picnic-highlighting, and home-town-boy-makes-good-people, like astronauts and baseball stars, make good grand marshals for local parades or picnics.

b. *Crowds.* Special events mean unusually large numbers of people, from full club membership at a Christmas party, to the whole plant at the company picnic, to an unexpected third of a million at a rock concert.

The anticipation of a crowd and the chance to have so many targets for interaction are important. The same it-must-be-important attitude we had with celebrity attendance also works because of the crowd.

Program promoters know the impact of predicting, "Expected attendance of 10,000," or the line, "Everybody who is anybody will be there." Sometimes these predictions are made with fingers crossed, for the appearance of the crowd may hang with a lot of individuals believing there will be a crowd and coming — and then of course the prediction is validated.

c. *Atmosphere.* The environment for a special event is often the same place people usually go. So, if transporting them to someplace different isn't feasible, then the imaginative programmer has to import potted foliage, blow up balloons, hang crepe, repaint the walls, erect amusement rides, and mount new illuminations.

Fireworks have been the classic device for taking Podunk, USA, and making it seem like the Riviera with a night sky full of flashing, bursting color explosions. But that's for the actual happening. We're interested in advance awareness.

Altering a place can be done by the professional and lay staff you've gathered for the event. There's a great deal of creative satisfaction in altering the mundane into a bright, shiny wonderland. People respond to platforms and booths being erected, the thump of hammers, the rasp of saws, the general huffing and puffing of people getting ready. It's all part of a new atmosphere emerging, and participant expectations jump in relation to it.

d. *Regular program relationships.* Special events have a natural build-up arena if they are closely tied to existing routine program. Culminating events are benefitted particularly. It is through regular program that the event participants prepare to take part in events that measure their achievement.

There is no event that can't be related to regular program, even if it's only a matter of using the event as an occasion for recognizing people, e.g., awarding sports league trophies at the company picnic.

There are several functions that must be filled to produce an event successfully. Orientation of staff means clearly understood directions on latest developments and a staff feedback to assure the programmer that all responsibilities are understood. A *communications system* must be arranged so that the program director and staff can discuss unexpected problems and make necessary changes. Double-check to make sure that all supplies, awards, equipment, food, and judges are on hand. Advanced preparations must be checked to be sure that everything is present at event time. A check list is obviously needed. Keep your best activities until the full crowd has arrived. This means having some lighter involvements planned for early birds. Keep it simple until everyone warms to the occasion and then build to a climax. Balance is the key.

Make sure *safety consciousness* prevails with staff. Remind them to stay alert. Be flexible by altering any planned activity that becomes hazardous, but don't permit officiousness or unnecessary caution to destroy the natural unexpectedness of the special event. It is the unexpected that creates the need for resourcefulness.

7. Face-to-face program leaders are used to maintain order with individuals and small groups. Crowd management has an altogether different quality.

Crowd management is probably one of the most neglected areas of professional recreation training. We only know how to call the police when an ugly mob begins to gain control. The programmer who attempts to plead or shout down the rebelling crowd is merely using a bucket to stop a tidal wave.

Obviously we need some methods. We need research to discover universal principles that will always work. But special events are infrequent, and the upsets are even less frequent; consequently, we haven't been able to gather enough information about incidents with similar characteristics to discover general rules.

There are a few techniques, however, that might be universally applicable to managing crowds.

Set up *crowd communications*. The public address system is the classic equipment for this, but it works most effectively when the speaker is visible on a platform.

Clear directions — verbal, signs, and printed flyers — avoid misunderstandings and set the rules of participation. Most people tend to comply when rules are carefully planned but rebel when rules appear to be manufactured for the troubles of the moment. Official rules promulgated in advance have the nature of a social contract and allow participants to choose involvement or not.

Identify and coopt your opinion leaders in advance if possible. Never take on the whole crowd but isolate its catalysts and attempt to reason with them — or buy them off if necessary — to influence the crowd positively. Open confrontation with crowd leaders places them in a rat-in-a-corner crisis, and they are pushed to attack to save face. Some event programmers have employed or appointed dissidents to staff policing positions but the results in most cases have been traumatic. It breeds the idea that bad behavior is rewarded with power. That power can be misused in untrained hands. At a rock concert a motorcycle gang acting as a special law and order force killed one of the misbehaving spectators.

Control the mind benders. Booze and drugs are both associated with special events. They are crutches for people and programmers who don't have the ability to create natural high spirits. No doubt they do the job for a lot of people and their use is to be determined by individual conscience.

The company picnic without cold beer is considered a failure by a large segment of mid-America; the rock concert is merely noise without drugs for a large portion of the youth population.

But alcoholic beverages and drugs remain elements to contend with in the future. Other mind benders are inflammatory words, ethnic slurs, swastikas, hand signs, and some types of music. All should be anticipated whenever possible and removed when discovered if they have no relation to the event in process.

Tending the early birds is also important, as we've mentioned. Restless people drum up trouble. Crowd management is easy if the program is a good one.

8. Nothing spoils the aftermath of a special event like a few people getting stuck with the residue. Good planning will insure sanitary facilities and waste receptacles. Disneyland has always maintained an army of custodians who are in constant motion, clearing the litter as it occurs. A sparklingly clean environment is an atmosphere conducive to high cooperative spirits. Don't let clean-up be a nasty surprise to yourself or the few people who stayed behind.

Evaluation has been treated in depth elsewhere in the book. Do not let the zeal for discovering reactions cause you to force people to find fault, spoiling recollections of an essentially satisfying event. The event's success is more important than its isolated flaws.

Ask for suggestions, not criticisms. Take a positive attitude with your staff before you bother the participants. It's best for the event director to float free, listening and observing.

Reinforcement is merely a lot of thank-you-very-much's. Appreciation should be sincere, personal and where possible directed toward the specific contribution of the individual. Praise is always better than gifts or pay. But it has to be honest. Reinforcement is part of getting ready for the next time with a premotivated group with whom to work.

Let the participants know, too, that things were good. Follow up the event in newspapers with a recollection of its positive aspects. Even if the company picnic was rained out point out that everyone had a wild, intimate, different experience feasting on chicken while huddled in people-puzzles under the picnic tables. The programmer could say that it was so good that rain should be planned every year. That's called reversing a negative. But people want to be told that things were joyous and successful to confirm their own hesitant feelings. If positive assistance in recalling the best elements makes people more fulfilled, then it is valid.

213

CURRENT STATUS AND TRENDS

Today's special event is tomorrow's routine. We live in a world of specials, from supermarket sales to television shows.

"What, another special," yawn the people. "Let us know when you've got something really special." The urban public is jaded. They've seen it all before.

That is the current status of special event programming. The programmer has competition everywhere he looks. Consequently he must be alert to rival scheduling and hone his imagination to a fine edge.

The ideas that are the bits and pieces that come together to make up a special event have lost their surprise — effect. Television continuously has revealed all.

Charades used to carry many a party, but television and commercial fun kits over-exposed it. Its specialness has eroded.

The amusement rides that used to come to town for the fair or picnic are permanent fixtures everywhere, daily pumping out diluted thrills like recreation gas stations.

Some things still work with children because they're still discovering everything. Programmers have to work fast before ennui sets in. But overall the mass public has become brutally demanding with its criteria for a special event. While it was once possible to add to the specialness of an event with celebrities or awards, the spectacular, the gaudy, or just plain bigness, their overuse has diluted their effectiveness.

What is left then? Ask an experienced special event programmer why he keeps at it.

"Of course it's tougher today. Seems like there's a World's Fair in process on every corner. The spoilers always figure that something that comes off so great once a year ought to do at least fair on a weekly or daily basis. Of course, that idea immediately blows the whole special feeling born of infrequency. I keep at it because there's always more to a special event than the idea itself, but the exploiters, the amateurs, think they just have to make an announcement."

"What more is there?" we asked, suspecting a secret formula is being withheld.

"Pride and hard work. You're only willing to put the hard work in if you have pride in producing the event. And of course you have to know where to apply the hard work, what has to be done. First, detailed hard work guarantees that the potential of an event is going to happen. Secondly, people are used to superficial experiences, surface decorations, plastic, slipshod craftsmanship. It's the little touches, the details that make a truly fine product. That's why the most overworked special event — a picnic or party — can seem fresh and new when it's put together with sweat and care."

We talked to a lot of special event programmers. They echo this same feeling. The competition is rough, but events are succeeding. The people want quality once they get a taste of it. There will always be a place for the well-wrought event and its specialness will always be better than the participants expected because of hard work and craftsmanship.

The Trends There are a number of indications for the future about special events. Here's what programmers are saying:

"Take Halloween. It used to be the last pure playground special event the commercial boys hadn't touched. The bonfire, the spook house, the costume parade . . . Disneyland has it booked every day. It's part of our affluency again. Somebody is going to market anything that people respond to. The Halloween carnival has taken over and it's usually based on a money-raising stimulus. Money talks loudly today."

"Special events are better than ever because of technology. There's contractual service by experts for anything a programmer could want. Need rides, decorations, or food? A programmer is a contractor pulling the available resources together. If he has to learn everything about an event, build everything from scratch, he'll never make it. He can't compete with a totally homemade effort when the competition uses the specialists and their expert equipment and services. He takes advantage of the fact that people are willing to pay for what they use."

"We're depersonalizing special events more than any other recreation program. If we buy it as a plastic kit, we lose people's involvement in the preparation. I think there'll be a turnabout. Packaging leads to all events looking alike until any small event put together by the hands of the programmer, his staff, and some participants will be an oasis in a gigantic, redundant desert."

"Special events are going to work best when they specialize for a subgroup in society. They always have, but we're going to be more informed about how to identify the thousands of subgroups in every community. We'll zero in on specific needs and structured events for the right target."

"Special events on holidays, not just around them, may become one of recreation's biggest responsibilities. There are large masses of people who suffer their greatest psychological needs because on holidays they feel especially depressed, lonely, and bored. Programmed special events could solve the problem.

"There's been too much reliance on travel to provide people's recreation needs. Cities lose revenue when people leave town on days off. Special events in the inner city could hold the people and cut down on damage to the environment. The city doesn't have to be routinely the same; a special event can bring a whole new flavor to a tired environment."

"We've got too many people atrophying in front of television sets or in bleachers today. We'll see more of it, too, because authorities see it as a great way to monitor the masses, keeping them passively contented. Look what would happen if they all decided they wanted activity. That's what a programmer is obligated to do — get active participation, need fulfillment — not just to contain and subdue people. Look for a big push for active participation events, like sports interest clubs, flea markets, and competitive events for a broader range of age and skill classifications."

215

"We've listened to a lot of feelings about the future. It seems that we have crowded our world to the point that the first concern with a special event in the future is how to limit the crowd and then to make it passive. But professional programmers see their role as more than crowd managers. We will not substitute distracting people for the real challenge of filling their basic needs. We think the responsibility of the recreation programmer is to push forcefully the production of active participation special events."

CAPSULE CLASSICS

A bunch of boys are moping around on the curbing in the main street of a little town. The sun has warmed everything to a lazy limpness. The buzzing of flies is the only sound. Lots of sighs, and no one seems to be going anywhere.

Recognize boredom? The sameness of everyday routine is the most cursed social disease we've inherited.

"Hey mister, what's that sign you're putting up there?" One of the boys notices a derbied man in shirt-sleeves brushing a poster onto the side of a building behind them.

"Can't you read, boy? That's the circus. It'll be here in three weeks."

Pandemonium! The limp forms collapsed on the curbing exploded into motion, jerking erect like bead-string pull toys.

"Yea, the circus . . . When's the parade coming? . . . Hey, let's put on our own, today . . . Mike, you get your sister, Lotta, to be the fat lady . . . "

Nothing beats the circus as an explanation of what a special event can be. The original traveling circus in 19th century America had all the attributes. It came around once a year and brought elephants and clowns and freaks and all those things not part of the normal routine. What the circus was — a rare and flamboyant happening — represents the essence of special events. Even the backyard amateur circus has that flare.

1. A modern day agency successfully borrowed the magic of the circus to structure one of the best capsule classic special event systems of all time. The Los Angeles City Recreation and Parks Department fields a *traveling circus* to cover its playgrounds every summer.

The specialists have put together the circus wagons and other apparatus that create the circus flavor. Each area books the skeleton circus kit on wheels and sets up a preparation program to turn their own local youngsters into performers.

It's been duplicated in part but never excelled.

2. The *rodeo* is very American. The cowboy is our eternal heroic figure, and a rodeo is a kind of a cowboy circus. The professional rodeo still holds its own in county fairs, the rural communities, and even slick, modern cities, where people hunger for a bit of the raw, rugged and real.

We see it as a classic whether imported as a professional entertainment or staged for amateurs with substitute bucking broncos and wild steers. Nobody can resist playing cowboy, and certainly our entertainment media is constantly promoting that interest.

Without the animals, a programmer can still stage lassoing and fast draw contests. Trick riding can be done on bicycles, mini bikes, automobiles, or donkeys. A rodeo is an exhibition for the skills of cowboys in a pure sense or, to be more precise, a roundup of cattle. There are some who feel the adulteration of the rodeo in any form is a sacrilege and we empathize. But life is a process of adaptation, and a programmer uses inspiring concepts as resources to provide experience for people.

The rodeo is adaptable, but we think authentic events should be attempted if feasible. We've all wondered how long we could stay on a bucking bronco and not just a saddled barrel being bucked by two big guys with manipulative ropes.

One last thought on rodeos. They are classic skills contests for cowboys but are part of a family of skills contests involving woodsmen (log rolling and cutting contests), pilots (trick flying), and even cannery workers (sardine-packing championships).

3. The *film festival* is one of the hottest growth items in the special events arena. The growth has a lot to do with the progress of technology. We develop new, cheaper, and better cameras and films. The masses are grinding out miles of amateur and professional films. The same is true to an even greater extent with color slides.

The problem is that most of it sits in shoe boxes on closet shelves. One's own family is only good for one showing. Photography is not a spectator sport while photographs are being taken. The audience has to be manufactured after the act. That's where film festivals come in.

Audiences are not easy to come by, however. People are constantly bombarded with visual images on television and in the movies, so seeing films or slides has become routine fare. The programmer needs a theme for his festival to draw special interests. That means the films exhibited should be on a particular subject, e.g., skiing or underwater exploration, or they should represent the products of special sub-society, e.g., films shot by celebrities, high school students, or the mentally retarded.

The film festival meets a big need for creative people who must have the approval or at least attention of an audience. It can also be staged as a complete event in itself or integrated into an arts festival or conglomerate affair.

4. *Theme overlays.* This probably belongs under organizational patterns somewhere. It's a rather superficial technique used to make routine things seem different.

It's appropriate to place it here because in a sense, the circus, rodeo, and film festival aren't especially different if analyzed in terms of their essential natures. They are cut from the same cloth — skill culminations — but their designs differ.

We have always used themes to give shape to special weeks on playgrounds, e.g., space week, foreign country week, or cowboy-and-Indians week. Themes are used throughout programming as a device for making old ideas appear new by applying different wrappers.

We see the theme concept used more effectively with parties, which tend to lose their specialness if they are not bound to an annual scheduling or to specific holidays. Therefore we have costume parties, come-as-you-are parties, Valentine parties, and hard-times parties, to raise a specific party out of the ordinary.

5. The following are some one-dimensional, hip-pocket special events that we like:

Penny Carnival. No big deal, just another home made carnival with booths manned by local clubs, except everything costs a penny. But it has become a successful and popular event in children's recreation programs no matter what the economic class of the service area. A peanut carnival is the same thing, except you buy a 5¢ bag of peanuts on the way in, pay for things with peanuts, and win peanuts for prizes.

Flea market and auction. This is old but new. Both have become gigantic events for the masses. The flea market brings out the merchant in some of us and the shopper looking for bargains in the rest. It's easy to stage with everyone emptying their garages and laying their junk out on blankets in assigned stall spaces. Haggling over prices, making offers, wheeling and dealing are the fun of it. It's excellent for collectors.

Auctions are a little different. They're very close to the feverish tension of gambling. The air crackles with fast excitement as participants attempt to judge and time bids to "steal" something at the lowest possible price. The essence of the game is here.

The Doll Tea. Dolls are one of the biggest collection hobbies in America for both children and adults. They reign supreme as the number one toy, bigger than trains.

The doll tea is a sharing experience for youngsters, girls maybe, but it seems a shame to let it be so narrow. We say open it up.

The best doll tea doesn't fool around with giving awards to super dolls. The main idea is that a cookies-and-punch-refreshments tea party creates a formal, special event-proportioned fantasy play. Dolls are dressed for the event as are their mistresses. Each young lady gets to tell a story about her doll. A doll buggy or wagon parade can be thrown in.

No one loses with this one. We've even seen big neanderthal program directors enraptured with the success of a doll tea.

Snail race. Lizards and cockroaches are just as good. We've used them all. It's just that snails always seem to be available and although not universally adored seem less repugnant than other crawly things. The big part of the snail race is the preparation, decoratively identifying the personality of each snail with paint, and festooning feathers and sequins on the shell. Ecologists and conservationists, however, may have a rumble about this, which may have to be considered.

Crawling out of a circle is a better setup than a laned track. In the Bahamas, we ran the race with hermit crabs and in the Philippines with coconut crabs.

The Jumping Frog Contest. This is the invention of the 49'ers. It's a big tourist event in Northern California. You need frogs, of course, and be careful if you allow foot stomping to stimulate the jumping . . . they squash easily. Use the circle and measure the farthest point after three jumps. One carnival rents the frogs to people and gives prizes at the end of the day.

Crazy critter hunt is just like any scavenger hunt or treasure hunt but less complicated. Call it an insect rodeo. Everybody captures a crazy critter in the area and builds an exhibit cage to display it in the critter zoo.

Big toe fashion parade. Another one of those decorating time killers but funny. Paint and dress up participants' big toes with faces or whatever. Bulk it up if you want by having them cut a hole in a big potato and slip their toe into it.

Tongue twisters and spelling bees. This is a real skill event, so watch out. Someone wins and a lot lose. But it's a good school-oriented recreation event and gives some of the verbal people a chance to shine over the jocks.

Sand castle sculpting contest. This is a great beach event. Some beach cities get thousands of people participating and some impressive architecture sometimes occurs. It can be run on a small scale in sand boxes at inland recreation centers. There is a lot of creativity in this as well as a sense of the moment, for like ice sculpture the completed project has a short lifespan.

Balloon to moon. This or a space shot is a kind of dum-dum stunt actually but it's been elevated into event proportions. Participants send up hot air or helium balloons with postcards. Awards go to the first one back, the one from the farthest place, and such other non-skill achievements. Unfortunately, the launching is the whole event and the return of the postcards happens days later. It is like putting messages in bottles and tossing them to sea. Better check with ecologists on this one, too.

Beauty and brawn contests. Toss baby shows in here, too. These Miss Shapely and Mr. Muscles displays of personal beauty are considered negative programming in some sectors. The issue seems to be around the non-skill aspects. To remedy this some contests require an aspect of talent to be included in the judging.

218

No matter how it's juggled, there seems to be a certain amount of upset connected with all of them. The events are not noted for gracious losing. We lost in a baby show and were outraged — we were robbed.

But nevertheless these contests have a great spectator appeal and when not standing on their own can dress up any conglomerate special event. Since they serve to inspire body-building classes and charm schools they do present a positive aspect.

One type of beauty contest is a three generations beauty contest. Grandmother, daughter, and granddaughter appear together, one presenting a talent, another beauty, and the third a moving statement about philosophy of life or some such thing.

The Fad contests. There have been many amusement toys developed over the past years. They have a grand flurry then drop out of sight and then are revived. What's interesting is that at one time they were programmed into major special events, virtually guaranteeing a happy full house.

Skate boarding was a recent such phenomenon. Actually it was a carryover from the old 2 x 4 and apple box with broken skates nailed to them. But surfing caused a lot of spin-off ideas and business firms began manufacturing the skate board that required the balance of a surfer. A magazine began which sponsored contests. It boomed and burst, but its remnants are still around. Marbles, yo yos, and tops are historic toys, which don't take much to drum up an event around. Yo yos were programmed into special tournaments rivaling major sports just after WWII because a manufacturer made it easy for agencies by issuing kits.

The hula hoop and the frisbee also made the grade and had their innings. None has ever returned with its original explosive appeal, but they all had some kind of magic.

We suggest putting all the fad fun contests into one big special event as a second chance for them.

9. *Festival of arts* is a cultural conglomerate special event that has picked up recreation programmers' interest in recent years. As a counter-revolution to the sports emphasis the more refined planners have set up festivals that combine art exhibits, concerts, and Shakespeare-on-the-grass, to appeal to those with music, drama, and art interests. The assumption is that the cultural arts draw as a unit, complementing each other.

The main programming concept is that one dramatic or musical event won't stand on its own. Audiences aren't easy to draw, so a package deal allows bigger promotional effort. Central Park in New York and Laguna Beach, California have done a masterful job with such festivals. Small cities realize that such festivals serve as prime tourist attractions, guaranteeing the support of the business community.

10. *Food.* Not all special events depend on food, but the best ones lean rather heavily upon this common denominator between people. Try a picnic or a party without it.

But here we're interested in the special event totally involved with food. Cake and cookie baking contests are widespread favorites. The Navajo Indians at their annual roundup have a huge men-only bread making contest that is nearly their number-one special of a four-day affair. It is not necessary to judge the finished product, although we've used this to get some free food. Watching the cakes being made is fun, especially if done in face-to-face combat.

219

Activity	Dominance	Physical Activity	Creativity	New Experience	Social Interaction	Security and Belonging	Relaxation	Mental Activity	Recognition	Service to Others
Christmas Party	L	L	L	H	H	M	M	L	L	L
4th of July Picnic	L	H	L	H	H	M	M	L	M	L
Easter Egg Hunt	L	M	L	H	M	L	M	L	L	L
Halloween Carnival	M	M	L	H	H	L	M	L	M	M
Weekend Trip	M	M	M	H	M	M	M	M	L	L
Baseball Tournaments	L	H	L	H	M	H	L	L	M	M
Street Parade	L	H	L	H	M	M	L	L	L	M
Social Dance	M	H	L	H	H	L	L	L	H	L
Arts & Crafts Show	L	L	H	H	M	L	M	L	H	M
Bazaar/Rummage Sale	L	L	L	H	M	M	M	L	L	H

H – High Potential
M – Medium
L – Low

SPECIAL EVENTS NEED FULFILLMENT POTENTIAL RATING SCALE

There is the watermelon feed which grew out of the picnic, but it has become a special event of its own on playgrounds. There's more to it than just eating, of course. The seed spitting contest has been a spin-off activity programmed to rival some of the great tobacco spitting contests of the South.

Our all-time favorite is the world champion eating contest, which is really a lot of fun. The pie eating contest or ice cream eating contest are small-time versions. The W.C.E.C. is a big-time event in itself. It's mostly spectator, of course, but everyone can identify with it. Budgeting may require a time limit in which all food is weighed, or you may have to give points for eating style, e.g., no spills, no waste, etc. An economical contest could use a lot of jello, soft drinks, frozen cream pies, or giant poor boy sandwiches made of whole bread loaves.

Better check protocol on this one. Impoverished areas where food is scarce may be resentful.

There are many more events deserving classic status, and we broadly cover them in the top ten list in the next section. The pet show, whether it's the hodge-podge playground variety or the exclusive Russian Wolfhound best-of-the-breed affair, is not found on the list, but it is a winner. Sports tournaments are a classic as well.

Ten Top Special Events Considering all ten recreational service environmental areas, the mass of people served, and the quality of the experience in terms of fulfilling needs, the following ten, ranked in order, deserve super-star status.

1. The Christmas Party—New Year's Party
2. Fourth o' July Picnic
3. Easter Egg Hunt
4. Halloween Carnival
5. The Labor Day Weekend Trip
6. Baseball Tournament
7. The Street Parade
8. The Social Dance
9. The Arts and Crafts Show
10. The Bazaar/Rummage Sale/Flea Market

221

Chapter 10

EVALUATION PROCESS

It's tempting to rush past a discussion of program evaluation to actually do it. The professional literature in recreation tends to speak in reverential tones about evaluation for a few paragraphs but then rushes off to less serious, more manageable topics.

In part, this is because we don't really know how to make an accurate evaluation. We know its philosophy well, that we can only avoid future errors if we know what the past ones were.

It is possible to dodge the issue. Our field typically announces that scientific evaluation is needed badly but impossible because there are neither accurate instruments nor trained personnel to use them; furthermore, it is difficult to identify what is to be measured.

This is true, but there's also complacency derived from the assumption that recreation is a growth service of society. Recreation will survive because leisure is expanding and facilities are being erected which must be attended. There is also a fear, however, that if we measure the quality of recreation program's achievement, we might not only discover mediocrity but traumatize some people. Activity in itself does not guarantee positive results.

A terrible superficiality is bred into the box office concept of show business, the sales index of commercial marketing, and the thinking of our professional programmers. Ask them how they measure the success of program and their criterion turns out to be oriented toward quantity, the old numbers game:

"Do they come back for more . . . ?"

"Measure the success by the number of people that participate."

"By survey. The test of time, if a growth factor ensues. The box office . . . "

"Did attendance hold up if the activity was continued?"

"Maximum use of facilities."

"Numbers . . . attendance figures . . . people come back in numbers . . . amount of community involvement . . . the turnout . . . participation . . . head count . . . demand . . . sheer numbers . . . willingness to participate . . . continuity . . ."

In a survey of 300 recreation programmers we conducted in 1970, attendance figures comprised the entire success evaluation process in 21% of the responses, the major criterion in 48%, and was given equal weight with two or three other criteria in 93%.

Numbers alone indicate something, but what? There are numbers in riots, traffic jams, and stampedes. Obviously we need to use attendance figures in a more sophisticated way. With continuing program, e.g., series of classes and activities, we can count those who return and compare attendance records. But we are still left with only assumptions based on simple measurement, not real evaluations of worth.

Evaluation should cover values, *quality*, not simply bulk involvement. What other criteria do programmers suggest for measuring success besides attendance?

"The enjoyment and enthusiasm observed."

"They ask to have program repeated."

"Visual survey of people to see if they are getting satisfaction in what they are doing . . . "

"Comments of participants about enjoying activity."

"They'll tell you if it's good."

"Interest response, verbal feedback, word of mouth."

"Improvement of individuals . . . "

"If they say they don't want to, you're not reaching them."

"Measure the achievements . . . "

"Absence of complaints."

"Comments that drift back after the event is over."

"Solicited and unsolicited remarks . . . written survey . . . questionnaire."

"Performance before audiences."

"Much later, years, when people come back to tell how much they enjoyed it . . . nostalgic reflection."

The 300 programmers we surveyed mentioned subjective processes in the following frequency:

Verbal Response	55%
Observed Enjoyment — Satisfaction	35%
Lack of Complaints	25%
Measured Achievements	25%
Delayed Reflective Response	5%
Written Response — Questionnaire	5%

What can we make of this information? It should be noted that while a random sampling was taken of all recreational environmental service areas, from playgrounds to hospitals, almost 90% of the responses referred to voluntary situations. The other 10% covered captive audiences in detention facilities and hospital wards. Attendance figures aren't very helpful in measuring success if the participants are obliged to be on hand. Even in a voluntary situation, if nothing else is competing, there is no other choice, the mere presence of people doesn't justify any assumption of an activity's qualitative success.

The alternatives to counting are the subjective processes of watching and listening or scientifically measuring achievement.

Today programmers tend to operate by the feel of things, vaguely identifying mysterious visual emotions like joy, pleasure, fun, and satisfaction. "See? People are laughing, smiling, attentive, excited . . . that's how we know." There's no doubt that we've made some accurate interpretations of these intangibles. If no one is curled up in a corner sucking his thumb or getting ready to jump off the top of the building we may have a good activity in progress. But we've probably misguessed a lot of times, too, seeing the obvious surface responses and missing the underlying emotions. We never know how accurate we've been with our visual readings.

The therapeutically-oriented areas of recreation program go beyond attendance and visual reaction — they do measure achievements. Measurable goals are prescribed. This is still a counting process, not a true evaluation of an activity's worth because definitive concrete values have not been assigned to the measurements. It is difficult to develop comprehensive, clearly defined values to assign to measurements in volunteer program services which are a form of therapy. Assigned values are fairly easy with skills and knowledge but our real challenge for measuring participation is in the area of attitudes and emotions. These values which are the most meaningful, are difficult to determine.

For example, we can pace off how far a boy can throw a softball or find out if he knows how to mix paint colors, but what he feels as a result of it escapes us. We need to know how perennial right fielders feel. We need an easy, accurate system that tells us what is happening inside a participant with each program experience.

For example, a group laughing at the expense of another reinforces destructive behavior with all the guilt and false sense of security that go along with it; or nervous tense reactions may be misinterpreted as enthusiasm.

The need fulfillment framework which is the focus of this book is one possible means of evaluating these responses.

225

OBJECTIVES RESTUDIED

In the beginning there is a reason for doing anything. As we have indicated in our analysis of planning, the programmer sets idealistic goals to strive toward and objectives to attain. The objectives are more concrete since they are achieved periodically on the way toward final goals, providing a map against which we can overlay achievements.

We should clearly delineate goals from objectives to avoid confusion. Goals are always there. They might be, for example, the wholly satisfied person, which is like dreaming the impossible dream. Trying to reach the goal is what makes programming a continuously exciting challenge. But we need points along the way through which we achieve part of the ultimate goal — concrete, measurable achievements and these are objectives.

After the objectives are determined, we schedule the activities according to principles or guidelines, produce the activities, and then wonder if they worked. The activities worked if the participants completed the objectives or at least enough of them to justify the effort. For example, let's say that we're going to stop certain people from feeling lonely and give them good health. Then we help them participate in a recreation experience and see if they're not lonely any more and if they're healthy.

That means the objectives have to be rather explicit, such as "to provide mentally stimulating activity that will exercise the mind so that there is no boredom and the participant develops a feeling of worth and identity because of his mental achievements." That objective may be met for a specific individual in a particular activity in a given moment. We fill a gap with recreation, but it eventually opens again, perhaps as soon as the activity is over. But we know how to fill the gap if we know where it is and when it exists.

At this point our set of basic needs comes in. It's a good framework for setting specific objectives. If you are willing to subscribe to the concept that our main priority is serving individual participants, complimenting each life style to make it more desirable and rewarding, then the objectives of any program or its supporting functions can be molded around need fulfillment.

Evaluation is looking back at those objectives. They are the backboard against which we bounce the measured achievements. They are the targets at which we aim our efforts and upon which we determine our success.

There are, of course, objectives for evaluation itself. Evaluation should be used to contribute to staff growth and morals, gauge program response, eliminate safety hazards, detriments to personality development, update activities, impress politicians, and control costs.

AREAS FOR EVALUATION

Our interest is what happens to people. We want to find out if the activities we program for them are making life better in terms of how they feel physically, mentally, emotionally and socially.

Even when agencies establish elaborate efforts to evaluate space, facilities, equipment, personnel, administrative procedures, or public relations functions, they are indirectly concerned with their effectiveness in serving people. These are support functions.

Our direct areas of program concern, the product that justifies the existence of a recreation profession, are basically the activities, the participants, and the leadership. All three of these elements are vital for quality program.

But it is with the participants that we find our greatest difficulties in establishing areas for evaluation. Where crowds and large groupings are revered as success symbols, programmers react with sarcasm to the idea that individual participant evaluation is the ultimate determination of whether program is succeeding:

"We have hundreds of people involved at one time, big leagues in operation, and you're expecting us to be psychologists with a couch, find out what each one is feeling. There isn't the time, money, or competence. Look, we're organizers, keeping lots of people actively involved, which takes no small effort. They've got places for people who need counseling."

We can't argue with the logic or the realism of these feelings about programming for the public. But the idea is not to lessen organizational effort but to add a dimension that will refine the understanding of its results, reinforce the position of the organizer/producer, and bring him more financial and specialized personnel support. There's no reason why people must be counseled and their need fulfillment measured outside of recreation program.

Our problem really lies in the size of the participant load that is carried. The public area man is pressured to produce numbers, a priority forced upon him by the forces above him who hold the purse strings. But with the extension of fee programs or government subsidized programs small group activity is becoming a more widespread form of programming in all the environmental service areas. It is by no means the kind of ideal one-to-one, leader-to-participant relationship that is found to some degree in group work and therapeutic/rehabilitation recreation services. But small group activity can combine the best of both — mass activity and individual attention.

What constitutes the small group is open to much speculation at this time. There seems to be some ideal numbers for different specific situations but we cannot verify them. Experience suggests a range of six to twenty participants allows maximum opportunity for interaction yet maintains optimum intimacy for contact between members.

The areas for evaluation in recreation, despite what is being measured, must relate to the effect on the participant. In our direct dealings with participants certain environmental service areas are structured to deal with the individual and his needs. The other areas, even the mass-oriented public with its continuing emphasis on numbers, have the opportunity to move into this kind of evaluation through small group programming.

Activity itself can be assigned values according to its potential. We have suggested possible values in our chapters on activities and, primitive though they may be, they are one step toward understanding and documenting even the bulkiest participation.

PRINCIPLES OF EVALUATION

There's a problem with giving too many directions. It conjures up the frustrated father on Christmas Eve trying to assemble complex toys from the enclosed instructions. There's no doubt that the list of principles you are about to read are very good guides, but they're too much for anyone to commit to memory.

They're also a bother to read when consumed in the matter of trying to find out how you're doing. Let us suggest you pick out a couple that please your style and build an evaluation approach of your own around them. But don't stop there, keep looking. There are more principles that will arise in the future as we become less primitive in our understanding of just what the recreation experience does to people.

EVALUATION SHOULD BE A CONTINUOUS PROCESS INTEGRATED INTO THE PROGRAM BY RECREATION LEADERS THROUGH ACCEPTED TECHNIQUES CAPABLE OF MEASURING THE FIELD WITH RESULTS THAT CAN BE COMPREHENSIVELY INTERPRETED.

Evaluation in recreation should:

A. Guide analysis of activity in light of overall recreation objectives as well as those of the specific activity.

B. Be carried out as a continuous process as if it were an integral part of the program.

   1. Employed during the planning stage.

   2. Employed during the program activity.

   3. Employed most thoroughly and intensely following a program activity after all relevant information is available.

C. Lead to improvement rather than criticism.

D. Recognize individual differences.

E. Be based upon a commonly accepted terminology of the field.

F. Employ evaluation techniques time-tested in other fields and applied where appropriate.

G. Utilize various approaches but strive for a practical, productive uniform system.

H. Be the subject of periodic in-service training sessions or staff meetings.

I. Note the difference between spectator and participant response in activity.

J. Document its findings for future use.

Measurement

Evaluation in recreation should:

A. Analyze attendance in terms of the following factors: weather, other environmental conditions, available leadership, competing community activity, extent of specific interest in community, public relations and promotion, and response of participants.

B. Measure the number of persons involved in a given activity.

C. Correlate the actual number involved in an activity with the number anticipated.

D. Encourage objectivity in measurement.

E. Use registration to predetermine attendance in various activities.

Evaluation in recreation should:

    A. Encourage self-analysis and improvement on the part of the leader, supervisor, or administrator.

    B. Be sensitive to informal evaluative expressions of participants.

        1. Recognize the spirit of enthusiasm.

        2. Identify reflections of personal satisfaction.

        3. Recognize personality growth.

    C. Measure and interpret individual participation separately from group participation within a given activity.

    D. Assign guiding criteria to trained evaluators where subjective judgment is required.

    E. Utilize sampling techniques to determine the social, physical, mental, and emotional growth of the individual and then relate the interpretation to the proper source activity.

RATING SYSTEMS

We will confess that the system we're proposing is a crude beginning. **229** Unfortunately existing systems are even cruder.

We may begin the discussion with the prevailing attendance records of the open-to-the-public, volunteer participation agencies. There are two methods now in vogue for counting participants. One is slapdash, requiring periodical *sampling*. It originated from mass activities in which complex happenings over a period of time did not permit accurate counting. The sample count takes place at a peak period. Some agencies have devised formula whereby counts are multiplied to account for the comings and goings of participants. The public summer playground is a prime example with its organized and free play activity and open door policy. The NRA created a system in 1938 that continues today. Flow periods on playgrounds are recorded by taking a headcount in the morning and multiplying by 2, in the afternoon and multiplying by 2.5, and in the evening by 1.5. This roughly accounted for "visits" — as they called their unit of measurement — but nothing indicated the purpose, result, or length of the visit.

A more revealing method is the *registration record*. Technology has given us electronic eyes to count and register people breaking a light beam through an entrance. The sale of tickets has been the box office approach. Along with the small group activity based upon special interests, recreation agencies have been able to sign up participants in this controlled format. The registration system gives a much more refined understanding of the spread of participation over program activities.

Expressed reactions are the next plateau in rating systems, in which a number of programmers place great stock. Being aware of more than the physical presence of the participants is a start toward sophisticated evaluation.

There are several types of expressed reactions based on the degree to which the reaction is structured or allowed to be spontaneous. The in-progress activity remarks and comments are raw, honest expressions, pure emotional reactions, but they can be hard to understand. The programmer who hears the equivalent of a shouted "Whoopee!" or a "Eureka, I did it" or a "Hey, this is fun" may feel there is nothing ambiguous about the message — people are enjoying themselves, being satisfied. One experienced programmer had this to say:

"Recreation is supposed to be consummatory . . . "

"Consummatory?"

"Yeah, it's a new word I picked up. Recreation is an end in itself, and when people are all consumed by the participation and not aware of themselves or future uses of an experience, then you have a real recreation reaction occurring. So it seems logical that if the greatest value is in the happening, not the carryover benefits, then spontaneous response is the best index of success."

But does the spontaneous expressed reaction, the grunt, the sigh, the chuckle, signify the feeling of the participant or what the programmer wants it to mean? If the spontaneous response serves any purpose, shouldn't it be identified both with the element of the activity that evokes it as well as the specific need being satisfied?

Some programmers say, "Of course it is a subjective judgment on our part, based on experience, and it takes time to learn. Maybe the new leader or supervisor will need some measuring scale, but isn't that what the new ones are learning in school? I don't know if there is any way to isolate the elements and specific needs while putting on a good activity. The reaction is probably based on the whole experience, whom they're with, the time of day, how they like the leader. I don't want to ruin a good thing by poking around, looking around for the exact feather that tickled somebody."

God bless those rough and ready wood choppers who have produced piles of activities out of which have come many benefits to people. But society demands that we become more accurate if we are to obtain material support. We need precision carvers to meet modern sophisticated demands, not wood choppers.

Accuracy lies with finding a system that identifies the elements that cause specific responses. And play for play's sake doesn't seem to serve the general needs of society. Exact causal relationships between isolated program experiences and both immediate and delayed benefits to the individual participant have to be identified through an analytical system. That system should be designed for recreation and be part of every programmer's professional technology.

How else are expressed reactions obtained? Beyond spontaneous expression, following an event there is immediate review of participant suggestions and comments, such as "Let's do this again," or "Next time we'll play on the other field, it's safer," or "Can we split up into smaller groups if we do this again," or "What a bore." Still fairly honest but beginning to be more analytical with later uses of experience. Then there is the *recall reaction*, when old customers return to comment favorably — rarely unfavorably — on the good old days.

But these inputs are manufactured haphazardly by amateurs. The professional programmer is professional because he has some training in the area of survey, measurement, and evaluation. That training should lead him to ask the right questions. The questions can be in interview form or by written questionnaire. The questions should be based on some predictable expectations as well as open ended to allow unforeseen discoveries. They could serve as a guide for the observing supervisor who prefers not to be in direct contact with the participants.

Great care must be taken in soliciting a reaction. Ugly cans of worms lie open all over the place because overeager researchers forced participants to look too closely at activities. The rosy glow from an activity is easily dispelled by clinical analysis that lays bare the elements, each by itself often seeming foolish and trivial.

Another danger is that insecure participants when questioned may feel the need to show a higher standard of taste than they really have. The result is negative criticism, often uncovering aspects that can be seen as flaws only by the greatest stretch of the imagination.

Many of these hazards can be avoided by properly structured questions to direct a positive outlook. For example:

"What was the most enjoyable aspect of the activity," not what was least enjoyable.

"How would you add to this experience to make it even better in the future," rather than what was wrong with it.

"How could the leader be of more help to you," rather than "In what ways did the leader fail you."

"This craft project was:

     a. exciting b. interesting c. acceptable d. other"

We recognize that we are suggesting a loaded approach, one structured to give the program an advantage. But in the case of participants, untrained evaluators, the responses may be emotionally honest but not necessarily accurate analysis of what happened. Much harm is done to activity by solicited critiques that are not arranged with public relations in mind.

One of the worst developments in unstructured expressed reactions is the informal *post mortem*. Because recreation is personal and subjective to a great extent everyone believes he knows the score. A lot of experts — tacticians as we have classified them in our personality types — who participate in activities get together or pull together participants in a deadly autopsy of the activity. In many cases the effort is damaging and carried out with either malice or irresponsibility. The shrewd programmer heads this off by following up on planning with people. He organizes his own appraisal group for the activity to operate under fair ground rules and positive principles of evaluation.

Professional observations have already been touched upon, but it is important that we differentiate between general staff appraisal and measurement by specialists. Most general staff people are capable of gathering information and making measurements if given uncomplicated instruments. The trouble lies in how and if they are to assign values to the gathered data. If we permit them to make simple judgments we are dealing with evaluation at a primitive and basically unscientific level.

But any system that makes us pause to consider an event has at least some merit. For this reason we recommend using some of the crude self-appraisal and inventory check sheets that proliferate in workshops and field manuals.

The following sheet suggests clues if not tangible facts about any program activity:

Activity Appraisal by Leader

	High	Medium	Low
1. Everyone was actively involved			
2. Utilized all available resources			
3. Participants felt sense of achievement			
4. Participants interacted comfortably			
5. Program ran smoothly as planned			
6. Activity met legal and safety rules			
7. Activity reflected philosophy of agency			
8. Entire population considered			
9. Activity had carry over values spontaneously repeated in free play			
10. Basic needs of participants met			
11. Activity had flow and balance			
12. Attention and interest were sustained throughout			
13. Flexibility existed for emergencies			
14. Equal opportunity provided for all			

A high rating would mean that this activity was in the top third of all comparable activities built into his model. A medium would constitute the middle third and a low the bottom third.

This kind of comparative values rating is certainly some boost to either morale or effort to improve. Similar checklists can be made from our listings of principles to cover the comparative measurements of facilities, promotion, or leadership.

All professional observations have some good in them. They prove that at least an effort is being made to consider changes. Recreation as a field has not been subjected to any official auditing system except on rare, isolated instances. Its hunger for professional status may eventually force the issue. It is strange that a field that gives so much support to the accreditation of college curriculas hasn't applied the same self-study concept and official program certification to itself. We do need some overall evaluation plan to be used for all recreation services every five years, even with a crude instrument.

Need Profiles

The only way we can be sure that program is a positive force is by scientifically measuring psycho-physiological-spiritual *need deficiencies* in people. This book offers a set of ten identified needs as a starting point as well as ways of recognizing clusters of needs in the form of personality types. A test is provided as an identifying instrument. Additionally, the needs have been assessed against specifid program activities, and they are rated as to their potential to fulfill in each need area.

For example, this book's "Need Indicator Word Reaction Test" was designed to produce a working profile of the need structure of an individual. It might read as follows:

	Demand Profile	Need Type
1.	High	Dominance
2.	High	Recognition
3.	High	Physical activity
4.	Medium	New experience
5.	Medium	Service to others
6.	Medium	Creativity
7.	Medium	Mental activity
8.	Low	Security & Belonging
9.	Low	Social interaction
10.	Low	Relaxation

The demand profile roughly establishes the nature of the need hierarchy. It suggests a somewhat stable index of the personality to be programmed. The need established may or may not be in the process of being fulfilled. The occupational experience and existing recreation involvements must also be calculated in order to make a final adjusted demand profile which allows existing experiences to meet needs. For example, the U. S. Government's Occupational Index provides a good guideline in that area. The following analysis demonstrates how we arrived at some of the rough ratings shown for various program activities in other sections of this book.

Let's take the basic league bowling experience for men. It would rate the numbered needs according to the chart above, as follows: 1—low; 2—medium; 3—medium; 4—low; 5—low; 6—low; 7—low; 8—medium; 9—medium; 10—medium.

Compare these against the demand profile and we see by adjustment that demand for dominance remains high, recognition becomes medium, physical activity is medium, new experience remains medium, service to others remains medium, creativity is medium, and mental activity remains medium.

Let us assume that job provides for the remaining areas as follows: 1—low, 2—low, 3—high, 4—medium, 5—medium, 6—medium, 7—medium. Balanced against the original demand profile, we are left with high adjusted demands in dominance and recognition.

With this information we need to know which activities have the potential for fulfilling these demands. The index of activities might reveal that taking over the leadership of a boys' football team would aid the dominance demand. Recognition needs require deeper analysis, but a drama activity with extensive audience performances in which the individual shows possibilities for success could do the job. Obviously, a great deal of refinement is necessary for our process of evaluating and rating activities if what is now a rough frame of reference is to become a system.

233

It is a primitive beginning but a good foundation for a rating system that can be activated instantly and continuously by programmers.

The methods exist for getting at participants' own interpretation of needs and the effect of activities on them. Some have already been covered. Additionally there are anecdotal records, case studies obtained by observation, personal interviews, and the encounter group.

For example, following a basketball game, the team could huddle in a corner and spend five minutes letting their feelings out instead of giving a grudging cheer for the other team or jumping up and down. The benefits of playing the game might be solidified by those few moments as well as dispel a need trauma before it becomes malignant. The session might go like this:

"Well, we won, and that's what counts."

"Yeah, but we played badly, and I really don't feel we deserved it . . . like I didn't achieve anything."

"If we played badly you can take the blame, you weren't passing off. I'd like to have shot more."

"Look, nobody was passing the ball around, there wasn't any sense of being part of a team. I didn't feel any special cooperative spirit, so . . . "

"I didn't even get in the game but I was feeling good about being on the team . . . now you guys are spoiling it . . . "

It is possible to see the encounter group method taking over in program evaluation with our emphasis on participant involvement, immediate response, and a play atmosphere. This method can be built into the end of every activity to get a playback of feelings. If it gets out of hand it can ruin the glow, so the moderating hand of the professional leader must be there. That leader must have the advance need profiles on his participants so that a meaningful job of interpretation is possible.

234

Sociometrics

One of the best socio-psychological rating systems for recreation purposes has been a workable small group method for discovering the popular people, the isolates, the lonely, the disliked, and the cliques, and, consequently the social interaction problem.

It works by asking each member questions like "Whom do you prefer to play with," or "Which member of the group would you select for a leader," or "Who is least liked by you?" On the playground choosing teams was a crude and hurtful way of getting the same results. Even sociometrics with carefully managed, confidentially classified information still can produce hurts in inexpert hands.

To work, the questions should be about a real situation, be desirable for the participant to answer, and allow a number of choices. There should be time allowed for participants to get a feel for each other in an interacting situation before the method is tried.

Its great value is in enabling the programmer to restructure groups for the best opportunities to fulfill needs for each individual. An imperfect interaction can block fulfillments not only with response needs, but with dominance, security, new experience, and, to some degree, all the others as well.

There is a lot of work ahead in developing rating systems that really work for recreation. We have just begun.

MPLEMENTATION OF FINDINGS

"What do you do with all this information you get from measuring things and rating them?"

"We store it for future use."

"Is that what all these files are for?"

"Right. Great information. Tells us a lot of things."

"But does anybody ever use it for anything. I mean, don't you use it to change the things you're doing?"

"Well, most people don't understand it, and most of it just tells us what we already know from experience. It's like the hydrogen bomb, gives us a warm, confident feeling just knowing it's there."

We don't suppose any conversation ever took place in just this way — but it should have. Then someone should have become upset.

It always seems that there are revolutionary studies in process and then by the time the results show up they've been written in a language that only a research librarian could understand. Program people are pretty basic, action people. They're ready for more than comic books but not academic monographs.

235

But that's not all. In order to be accurate and valid, on any rating results, the evaluation has become so narrow in scope that it has become trivial, hardly worth reproducing.

We're talking about scholarly research that often shows up without any potential for application. But rating systems are subject to the same considerations.

We can't wait for perfect, infallible devices with incontestable results. We have to get started, even if we're doing the equivalent of pacing off rather than measuring with a ruler. We've done some of that pacing already, and it seems to work. We need to do more and develop the precise rulers as we operate.

Let's talk in very practical terms about implementing findings — that means using them. Don't print them up and pass out waste basket reading matter. Get everyone involved, being careful of public relations and personal hurts. Bring them together to talk about what it all means and how it can be used immediately.

For example, if leadership appraisal reports indicated a strong resistance to enforcing behavior rules sent out as a blanket policy to all recreation centers from a remote headquarters, a gathering of local leaders might reveal to master programmers that a new young breed was on the scene who were effective in meeting program objectives with permissiveness and situational adaptation. Someone would learn something by that gathering and a change would probably come of it. The old-style treatment of such a situation would be an impersonal written directive to personnel "to get on the ball."

Evaluations are terrible when they are used to find fault, place blame, or condemn. The people they relate to deserve to have those results presented to them in a gracious and orderly way, in understandable and basic terminology, which will encourage change and improvement.

It's that obvious concept that bears repeating: Evaluation is part of the great circular process of planning, promoting, production, measuring, and back to planning. It's done best *with* people rather than for them.

Index

237